Cognition and the Visual Arts

MIT Press/Bradford Books Series in Cognitive Psychology
Stephen E. Palmer, editor

A Dynamic Systems Approach to Development: Applications, edited by Linda B. Smith and Esther Thelen, 1993

A Dynamic Systems Approach to the Development of Cognition and Action, edited by Esther Thelen and Linda B. Smith, 1994

Cognition and the Visual Arts, by Robert L. Solso, 1994

Cognition and the Visual Arts

Robert L. Solso

A Bradford Book
The MIT Press
Cambridge, Massachusetts
London, England

Second printing, 1997
First MIT Press paperback edition, 1996

© 1994 Massachusetts Institute of Technology

This book was set in Bembo by DEKR Corporation and was printed and bound in the United States of America.

Library of Congress Cataloging-in-Publication Data

Solso, Robert L., 1933–
    Cognition and the visual arts / Robert L. Solso.
       p. cm. — (MIT Press/Bradford Books series in cognitive psychology)
    Includes bibliographical references and index.
    ISBN 0-262-19346-9 (Hb), 0-262-69186-8 (Pb)
    1. Visual perception. 2. Art—Psychology. 3. Cognition.
  I. Title. II. Series.
  BF241.S63 1994
  701′.15—dc20   93-48658
                                                                    CIP

This book is dedicated to those professors who influenced me most:

Gordon H. Bower
Donald H. Kausler
Roger N. Shepard

Contents

Series Foreword

This series presents definitive works on cognition viewed from a psychological perspective, including undergraduate and graduate textbooks, reference works, research monographs, and edited volumes. Among the wide variety of topics addressed are perception, attention, imagery, memory, learning, categorization, language, problem solving, thinking, and cognitive development. Although the primary emphasis is on presenting psychological theories and findings, most volumes in the series are interdisciplinary, attempting to develop important connections between cognitive psychology and the related fields of anthropology, computer science, education, linguistics, neuroscience, and philosophy.

Stephen E. Palmer

Preface

Non ha l'ottima artista alcun concetto
Ch'un marmo solo in sé non circonscriva
Col suo soverchio, e solo a quello arriva
La man che ubbidisce all'intelletto.

Even the finest artist has no idea that the block
Does not itself constrain beneath its surface;
To release that form is all the hand can achieve,
The hand that is obedient to the intellect.

—*Michelangelo*

Art and cognition have always stood as two convex mirrors each reflecting and amplifying the other. Yet, surprisingly, in spite of monumental recent developments in both aesthetics and cognition, the connection between the two disciplines has not been studied systematically. This book is a reflection of what is currently known about the nature of the perceptual/cognitive system and visual art.

For most of my life I have been intrigued by two features of the human animal. The first is the thinking side, which is generally called cognition. This fascination has occupied my professional career for the past 25 years. The second side is art, which has captivated my attention for even longer. About five years ago I considered combining these two interests and, with the encouragement of Frank Hartigan, developed a series of lectures to be delivered at the University of Nevada's University of London campus during the spring of 1990. The opportunity to offer a course on "Cognition and the Visual Arts" was exhilarating. I was familiar with the cognitive literature, having written several books on that topic and dozens of research articles. I was less conversant with the world of art (although I thought I knew a lot!). The literature on psychology and art was disappointing. On one hand there was the piquant interpretation of art—much of it inspired by the writings of Freud and other psychoanalysts—that focused on the "darker" side of human nature; on the other hand there were psychophysical studies of vision and art that concentrated on laboratory studies of the relationship between visual signals and perception. Also, some sources attempted to integrate findings in experimental psychology with "fine" art. Although some of these efforts were both informative and scientifically reliable, they did not cover the new cognitive psychology and its importance to art. These matters remained unexplored.

For the course at London I read everything I could on psychology/perception/vision/cognition and art. Of course, living in a city that holds the finest art in the world made the task of illustrating my lectures easy. On more than one occasion, in the middle of a lecture, I would announce that a perfect example of linear perspective in Egyptian art, for example, could be seen in the British Museum, which was about five minutes from the classroom, and I would bolt out the door followed by a dozen giddy students and dash down Malet Street to see the real McCoy. The following year I offered a course at the University of Nevada and the following summer offered a course on the theme of cognition and the visual arts at Stanford University. By the time I lectured at Stanford my once sparse lecture notes had grown to an enormous lot of documents that were organized in a working manuscript. This photocopied behemoth was read and criticized by dozens of students, to whom I owe a great debt. These extensive lecture notes were organized into nine chapters that became the book you now hold.

The reason for this book became increasingly clear during these past five years of teaching and lecturing on the topic of cognition and art. There is, after all, a palpable interest in both topics. The cognitive revolution that swept through psychology during the second half of this century captured the interest of a new generation of scientists who were disenchanted with traditional behaviorism and psychoanalysis and drawn to a more comprehensive view of the internal structures and processes of the mental life of people. Throughout this period, cognitive psychologists produced an impressive collection of data about how we humans perceive, process, and store information. It was time to apply this knowledge to the perception and understanding of art.

While the science of the mind has made spectacular discoveries during the past 50 years, art is one of the most glorious achievements of humankind. Long before psychologists contemplated the basic nature of the mental life of people, or philosophers reflected on the meaning of life, prehistoric man drew unsophisticated (but not uncomplicated) images on the walls of caves and fashioned human likenesses in stone sculptures. All sorts of decorative arts have graced the lives of all sorts of people through all periods of history. Art is part of us and we are part of art. Mind and art are one. When we create or experience art, in a very real sense we have the clearest view of the mind. We do not "see" art, we see the mind. This reverse view of art and cognition is evident in every chapter in this book.

A few caveats are required. The first is that the art selected to illustrate cognitive ideas is limited in scope, and the second is that the number of cognitive principles selected to illustrate art is also limited. I tried to illustrate the book with a wide range of examples, from African to Asian to prehistoric art, but nevertheless have focused on Western (mostly European) art and have not discussed photography, cinema, or video. Likewise, the number of cognitive themes, while broad, is not comprehensive. For example, the topics of social cognition and color perception are only briefly addressed, although these topics and many more are interesting and important.

Another qualification is that I have minimized the use of technical jargon whenever possible, while not abandoning complex scientific concepts. The choice of a more informal style, bordering on the whimsical at times, was not intended to create an impression of intellectual ambiguity, but to tell a good story that would be a delight to read, fascinating in facts, and intellectually stimulating. Sometimes, so unbridled is my enthusiasm for both art and cognition, the prose has a purple hue. Please understand. Similarly I have minimized the use of references cited in the text. I have tried to give credit to my more substantial sources; if I have slighted any author or artist, I apologize in advance.

A final caveat concerns the use of "inclusive" language and examples. While I am an avowed egalitarian and am sensitive to the frustrations of disenfranchised people, I believe that conspicuously flaunting those beliefs on every page detracts from the main message. I am reminded of Patricia Churchland and Terrence Sejnowski's quotation to the effect that "ideological shoehorning frustrates readability."

Many people have supported my effort to write about cognition and art. My foremost acknowledgment goes to the legions of psychologists and artists who throughout centuries have created the basic material from which this book was fabricated. Richard Bisset read the entire manuscript and made important suggestions on the grammar and style. Paul Horn did many of the original illustrations for the book and has won my thanks. Calvin Nodine of the University of Pennsylvania and Lawrence Wright of the University of California, Berkeley, were generous in their support as well as gentle in their criticism and provided original figures that are used in this book. Jerry and Doris Ginsburg, Glenn Wilson, and Maria Arakie were wonderfully encouraging throughout these long years of writing and editing. Betty and Harry Stanton of the MIT Press proved to be the most gracious of book people and Matthew Abbate the most skillful of editors. Alan Rees and Cristy Collier carefully read proofs and made cogent suggestions. Finally, I have received support and affection as well as intellectual stimulation from members of my family, who in many ways are all coauthors.

Robert L. Solso
Lake Tahoe

The world and I have a common origin
and all creatures and I together are one.
Being one, our oneness can be expressed . . . or unexpressed.
The one, with the expression, makes two,
and the two, with one (what is unexpressed), make three.

Chuang Tzu

Cognition and the Visual Arts

1   The Big Window: The Science of Vision

If the Creator were to bestow a new set of senses upon us, or slightly remodel the present ones, leaving all the rest of nature unchanged, we should never doubt we were in another world, and so in strict reality we should be, just as if all the world besides our senses were changed.

—*John Muir*

This book is about the way the eye and the mind see and understand visual art. In many important ways, however, it is also about us, as, in the course of unraveling the many strands of the cognition of art, we will ultimately learn more about human psychology. It is likely that you will learn more about how the eye works, how the brain interprets visual art, and how each of us brings to the viewing of art his or her unique perspective. Many topics will be considered, including the evolution of the sensory systems, the relation of brain and vision, eye movements and art, perspective and art, and the perceptual/cognitive aspects of art: all topics that touch the human mind.

During the past few years remarkable progress has been made in the science of human cognition, the branch of psychology that studies perception, memory, and thinking. Among the most exciting developments—especially for those of us interested in the visual arts—are discoveries made by cognitive scientists regarding human vision that tell us how we "see" and "understand." Of the five senses with which we behold the physical world—vision, audition, taste, touch, smell—vision is the faculty that is most directly related to the perception of art: it truly is "the big window."

Vision is also the sense that has most fascinated and perplexed thinking men and women. Because of vision's exceptional importance to art, it is fitting that a book on cognition and art include an overview of the physiology

1.1 Mary Cassatt, *The Bath* (1891). Photograph © 1993 The Art Institute of Chicago; all rights reserved.

and psychology of vision as a basis for understanding a major component of the subject.

Seeing with Brain and Eye: The Dynamic Properties of Vision

When we see an object—it could be a painting, such as the gentle scene of a mother and her child depicted in Mary Cassatt's *The Bath* (figure 1.1), or the turbulence of the heavens shown in Vincent van Gogh's *The Starry Night* (figure 1.2)—our knowledge about it is based on a stream of neural activity

1.2   Vincent van Gogh, *The Starry Night* **(1889).**

initiated by light reflected from a surface. This light, which is purely physical in nature, reaches the retina of the eye, where it is converted (or *transduced*) into neural activity and passed along to the brain. The physical characteristics of light follow regular and lawful rules. So, too, the laws of neurotransmission are regular and lawful, with few structural differences among people.

Visual impressions, however, are not limited to sensory experiences that excite receptor neurons of the peripheral nervous system. They also involve the observer's cognitive background, which gives such experiences meaning. Thus, the emotional/intellectual reactions you might experience when seeing the Cassatt painting might be far different from my experience; and your reaction to van Gogh's *Starry Night* is likely to be entirely different from your reaction to *The Bath*. Each of us "sees" the world in profoundly different ways because of the vast diversity in the way we humans develop individual mental structures of the world. Lest this claim become too exaggerated, it should be noted that there are broad areas of common experience among people that ensure a degree of intellectual equivalence. In addition, since we share a common physiology with other members of our species, the initial processing of basic visual stimuli is the same for all of us. An important conclusion we can draw from this simple example is a dual concept of seeing: *seeing is accomplished through* both *the visual stimulation of eye and the interpretation of sensory signals by the brain.*

Light reflected off objects does not fall on the eyes of mindless creatures; each of us is endowed with a thinking brain that we use more or less effectively to comprehend what the eye senses. We are endowed with an immense capacity for thought and cognition, applied so routinely to the world around us that much of our everyday behavior may seem a simple matter of stimulus and response. We now know that the sensory/cerebral machinery involved in the execution of "simple" tasks, such as stopping an automobile when we see a red light, is the most complex entity known in the universe.

Our common ability to "see and understand" allows us to read and comprehend the great literature of the world, to formulate elaborate botanical taxonomies, to classify types of artists, to perceive and understand the motion of planets, to enjoy and grasp the inner meaning of baseball, Beethoven, ballet, or bungee jumping, to make sense out of everyday conversation, and to otherwise move around in a three-dimensional world without getting killed. We will have much more to say about the dual nature of seeing, but for now it is valuable to recognize that seeing is initiated by sensory objects—in our example, a painting—and the interpretation of sensory stimuli by the brain.

In this chapter we will concentrate on the physical nature of visual objects and then consider the physiology of the eye and brain involved in processing this information. These topics are related to the sensory part of the dual theory of visual perception. Later we will consider the interpretive/cognitive aspects of the problem.

The Physical Side of Vision

To "see" the world, and hence to see art, requires first of all physical energy: without the swing of electromagnetic energy there is nothing to sense, nothing to see, nothing to understand.

Seeing is an enormously complex phenomenon that is difficult to grasp in its entirety. However, by considering the individual components of seeing—the physical properties of light, the structure and function of the eye, the neurotransmission of visual signals to the brain—we can begin to sort out and understand the steps of this very complicated process.

INFORMATION PROCESSING THEORY

The analytic operation of "divide and conquer" is particularly suitable to the study of vision because the process seems to follow a logical flow of information, from the presence of light energy, to the detection of that energy by the eye, to the transmission of the signal to the visual cortex in the brain, to the cognitive interpretation of signals throughout the brain. This flow of information (physical energy → eye → visual cortex → associative cortex) is compatible with a major theoretical paradigm in cognitive psychology called the *information processing paradigm*. The information processing (INFOPRO) paradigm (or model) proposes that information is processed through a series of stages, each of which performs unique operations. Each stage registers information from a preceding stage, processes it, and then passes it along to another stage. This is sometimes casually called a "conveyer belt" model.

The perception of visual art seems to follow the orderly sequence of processing stages expressed by the INFOPRO model. In the first stage, reflected light energy (emanating from a painting, for example) passes through the pupil in the eye and falls on the retina, permeated with photosensitive neurons that line the interior of the eyeball, where initial optical processing occurs. These retinal receptors work with other neurons—some processes are activated and others inhibited; lines, edges, contours, contrasts, and colors are initially processed, and so on—in an intriguing amalgamation of neurochemical actions (to be discussed in detail in chapter 2). These initial processes operate automatically and without conscious control. Light energy is transformed to neural energy and passed along to the visual cortex in the brain for further processing.

To many, the activities performed by the brain are even more fascinating than the optical processes. Here, basic information is received from the eye and organized into meaningful patterns. It is in the brain that multitudinous connections are made between incoming signals and numerous neural units that give meaning to the visual object that initiated the process. It is during this stage that vast knowledge about the world in general, and art in specific, is applied to the sensory information; the object is interpreted.

Using the INFOPRO model, we will begin with an analysis of the first part of the process, the characteristics of light.

Nighthawks: An Example of Information Processing

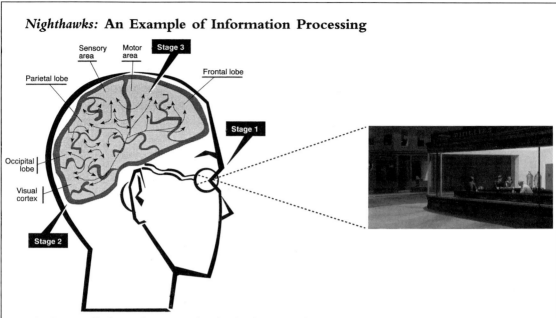

1.3   Stages of information processing in viewing art. Edward Hopper, *Nighthawks* (1942). Photograph © 1993 The Art Institute of Chicago; all rights reserved.

The forlorn figures in Edward Hopper's *Nighthawks* instantly evoke a feeling of loneliness and desolation in many observers. Perhaps the scene created by this American artist even reminds you of a melancholy episode in your life. Certainly, children of the American Depression view this scene in light of their experience, while people reared in happier times might see a cozy refuge from the bleak street. (Not all reactions to this painting are the same. An artistic parody called *Boulevard of Broken Dreams* by Helnwein hangs in my study; close inspection shows that the people in this scene are James Dean, Humphrey Bogart, Marilyn Monroe, and Elvis Presley as the cook.) These impressions are the consequence of a series of processing stages in each of which information is processed, or in some way transformed, and passed on to a subsequent stage for further processing.

In the first stage, reflected light from the painting passes through the lens of the eye, is inverted, and is focused on the retina. Several electrochemical functions take place in the first stage, in which light energy (photons) is converted (transduced) to neural impulses. These impulses are routed to the visual cortex by means of the optic nerve. There the second stage of processing takes place, in which visual stimuli are "analyzed" according to primitive features, such as vertical and horizontal elements, angles, and curves. These primitive features are "recognized" and "classified" and dispatched to other parts of the brain by means of a massively parallel network for processing. It is during this final stage, in which signals are scattered to distant parts of the brain, that associations are made between this painting and the vast personal knowledge of self and the world. Consideration of these three stages will guide the discussion of art throughout this book.

LIGHT

Vision is impossible without light.[1] Yet reliable information about this topic has been available for only a relatively short period, in spite of centuries of speculation. To understand vision, which is the way the external world (including art) is largely represented to humans, it is important to understand at least the rudiments of light. Electromagnetic waves, of which visual light is but one form, have bombarded the earth from space since its beginning. Only relatively recently have people lighted their dwelling places with fire and other artificial means of light. Two seemingly contradictory theories of light have been debated since the seventeenth century. One, advanced by Isaac Newton (1642–1727), argues that light is a string of particles. Another, suggested by Christiaan Huygens (1629–1695), reasons that light is pulses traveling along a wave. Contemporary scientists accept both theories and believe light manifests itself as both a particle and a wave.

PHYSICAL PROPERTIES

The physical properties of light have been a puzzle to scientists throughout the ages. In addition to the obvious question, "Of what is light made?," there is the question of the speed of light. One view posited that light arrives instantaneously from its source, another that it travels at some finite speed. We all know that the chaps who argued for the finite speed hypothesis won. But an important lesson for the history of science, and more specifically the science of psychology, is embedded in this controversy. Scientific knowledge is based on observation. In the case of measuring the speed of light, the observation of early seventeenth-century scientists, unaided by telescopes and other devices, was that light traveled instantaneously. When one snuffed out a bedroom candle, its illuminating rays to the far corners of the room ceased immediately, even before the swiftest being could jump into bed. Furthermore, light from the most distant of hills appeared to arrive instantaneously, unlike sound which was observed to have a time delay that could be measured.

Convincing evidence for the finite speed of light was presented by Ole Roemer (1644–1710), a Danish astronomer who, using the telescopes of his day, estimated the speed of light by observing the time that light took to reach the Earth from the satellites of Jupiter. With greater knowledge of the size of the solar system and more accurate measuring systems, we know that the speed of light is about 300,000 km per second, or 3×10^{10} cm/sec; this speed is regarded as one of the basic constants of the universe.

As far as the human eye can discern, however, light arrives from terrestrial sources instantly. Thus, when conventional two-dimensional art is perceived (as well as most terrestrial phenomena) the psychological effect is one of "instantaneousness of percept," because the human sensory system is incapable of discriminating the infinitesimal temporal differences of arrival of visual signals from different locations. When you look up from a book and see a distant mountain, the perception is that the visual signals from the book and mountain both arrive at the same time. Technically they do not.

One implication of the finite speed of light is that we always see the past: the light striking our eyes brings us information from some finite time ago when it was reflected from or generated by some object at a distance from us. While the terrestrial past is very short, the cosmic past is very long indeed. Look at the stars tonight and think how long it took the light to reach your retina, which is effectively how far into the past you are viewing. To give some scale of the time involved, light from the sun takes about eight minutes to arrive, while light arriving tonight from the Andromeda nebula was already one million years old before humans appeared on Earth (Gregory, 1978).

VISUALIZED LIGHT

The light we can see with our human eyes is but one form of the electromagnetic radiation that surrounds us. Electromagnetic radiation consists of waves produced by electrically charged particles. They have definite physical characteristics, a type of physical signature, which can be described in wavelengths, defined as the length of one complete cycle of a wave. Figure 1.4 depicts two waves, one with a long wavelength and the other with a short wavelength. The length of an electromagnetic wave within the range of normal human vision determines its color, with long wavelengths corresponding to red and orange and short wavelengths seen as violet and blue. Green and yellow fall in between. Wavelengths also vary in terms of their amplitude. Wavelengths within the visual spectrum that have large amplitudes produce a bright light, while smaller-amplitude signals produce a dim light (figure 1.5).

We humans can see electromagnetic wavelengths that fall between approximately 380 nanometers (nm) (deep violet) and 780 nm (red). (A nanometer is one billionth of a meter.) There are individual differences in

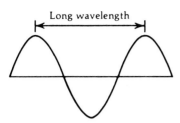

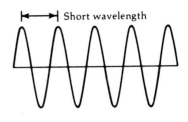

1.4   Examples of light waves of varying wavelength.

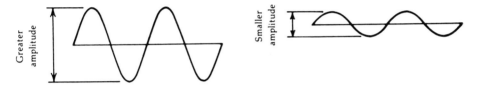

1.5   Examples of light waves of varying amplitude.

these parameters; some people can perceive wavelengths as low as 360 nm and others as high as 800 nm (De Grandis, 1986). Other creatures can detect shorter or longer wavelengths, although no animal can detect the full range of light. Some insects, bees for example, can perceive ultraviolet rays that are invisible to humans. Pit vipers have sensory organs that allow them to detect long-wavelength signals and stealthily track their unsuspecting prey. Undoubtedly, these infrared signals are of far greater importance to a pit viper than to humans and figure more in its survival scheme. Figure 1.6 shows the portion of the electromagnetic spectrum that is visible to humans. The human eye is sensitive to only a slender band of all the electromagnetic waves. Other waves are distributed throughout the spectrum and range from gamma rays and X rays, which are tiny, to AM radio waves and the waves of AC circuits, which are very broad. It is within the narrow band of the visible spectrum that all

Art imitates nature. By virtue of creative action, a work of art takes on a living quality. Thus, the work will appear fruitful and endowed with that same internal energy and vibrant beauty that can be seen in works of nature.

—*Henri Matisse*

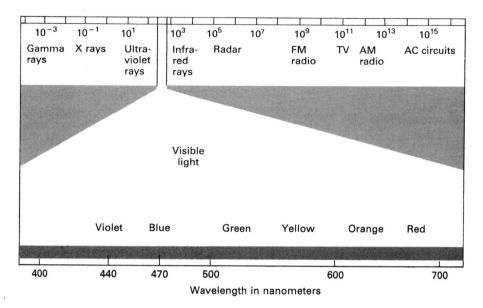

1.6 The wavelengths in the electromagnetic spectrum, with the visual spectrum enlarged and labeled. From Solso (1991).

visual experiences are compressed: from the image of your mother's face, to the sight of Tahiti's blue-green waters, to the words on this page, to the subtle use of reds, browns, and golds by Rembrandt to create an air of deep emotion, to the yellow signpost on the interstate highway. They are all there, between 380 and 780 nm. This is all we can sense; it is all we can see.

Electromagnetic waves in the visible range enter the eye through its lens, are absorbed by the photoreceptive rods and cones in the retina, are transduced (converted) to electrochemical charges, and are passed on through the nervous system to the brain. The waves are rarely "pure"; they are usually altered by the atmosphere. Moisture in the atmosphere, for example, diffuses or disperses light and causes a hazy image. Clear daylight scatters the short (blue) wavelengths, creating the sensation of a blue sky, while during early morning and evening the long (red) wavelengths are emphasized, inducing a sense of dramatic sunrises and sunsets. This distortion of light is recognized by photographers who capture the "feeling" associated with different visual spectacles, and by artists who skillfully incorporate "mood colors" in their palette to evoke certain emotions in their audiences.

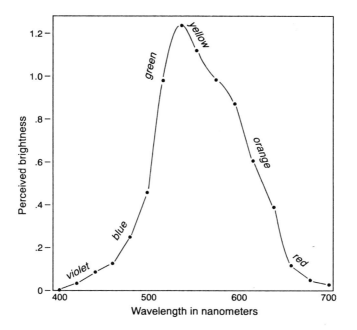

1.7 Perceived luminosity of different colors with the same amplitude (intensity).

There is an interaction between perceived brightness and color. "Deeper" colors, for example saturated blues, violets, and reds, appear less bright than greens and yellows, even though their physical intensity may be equal (figure 1.7). Thus, the human sensation of brightness depends on the reflected luminosity (the physical brightness) of a color, not only its intensity. For centuries, artists have explored the subtleties of color effects, using colors of different luminosities to produce different psychological effects.

COLORS

In addition to their different sensations of brightness, different colors have different psychological effects on us: bright colors tend to cheer; dark to depress. Even our mood (and the attitude of people who see us) may be affected by the color of clothing we wear. No less important is the impact colors have on the mood of a painting, which reflects the larger influence of colors in our everyday life.

1.8   Newton breaks sunlight into spectral colors.

The scientific study of the physical characteristics of colors can be traced to Newton, who analyzed the composition of light. In a darkened room he allowed a thin ray of sunlight to fall on a triangular glass prism and found that the white ray instantly separated into the familiar colors of the rainbow. This finding was not new, as humans had observed the rainbow since the beginning of time. But then Newton placed a second prism in the path of the spectrum and discovered that the composite colors produced a white beam. Thus he concluded that white light can be produced by combining the spectral colors. The history of science does not give a reliable account of Newton's reaction, but we can speculate that he must have been delighted in the spectacular little light show he had created. Newton named the colors of the spectrum red, orange, yellow, green, blue, indigo, and violet. We now usually do not use "indigo" as one of the basic colors, and it is thought that Newton added the seventh color because of his strong mystical belief in the importance of the number seven.

The Eye

Without light there would be no art, but without an eye to register the light there would still be no art. So the next strand in the puzzle is the structure and function of the eye.

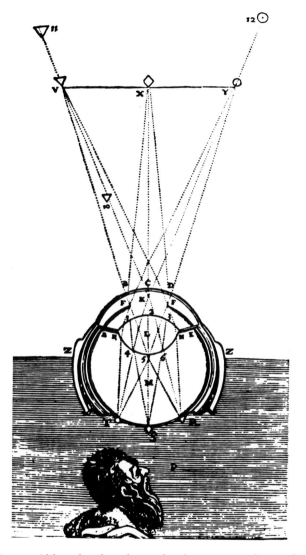

1.9 Descartes's eye. Although others knew that images were inverted on the retina, Descartes's description in *La Dioptrique* (1637) was the most complete to that time. This figure shows the result of his experiment with an ox eye from which the outer back surface had been removed and replaced with paper, allowing Descartes to see tiny inverted images.

It may come as a surprise to learn that our human eyes are not the most complex optical systems in the world. They are complex and sophisticated, but other beings have more complex optical structures. The eyes of simple arthropods (such as insects), for example, contain many lenses and receptors, while we have but one lens with numerous receptors. In general, more simple-brained creatures have more complex optical sensors while more complex-brained creatures have simpler optical sensors. Offsetting the relatively simple lens of the human eye is a fantastically complicated brain that permits us to "see" far more than we sense. The earliest known visual sensing device has been remarkably preserved in the fossil remains of trilobites, which in-

> *Painting is, first of all, optical. That's where the material of our art is: in what our eyes think. Nature, when we respect her, always tells us what she means.*
>
> —*Paul Cézanne*

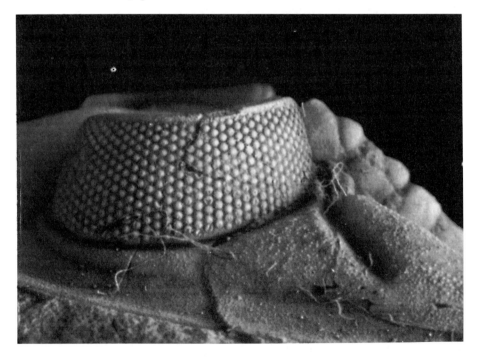

1.10 The fossil eye of a species of trilobite. This is the earliest known fossil remains of an eye. Each of the circular facets is a corneal lens similar to the structure of modern insect eyes. Some trilobites could see 360 degrees. From Gregory (1978).

habited this Earth over 500 million years ago. These marine arthropods, ancient relatives of crabs and shrimp, lived mostly in the murky waters of ocean bottoms. Figure 1.10 shows an example of this early eye.

Basic Anatomy

The basic anatomy of the human eye is shown in figure 1.12. Light enters the eye through the pupil, the opening in the eye that is surrounded by the colored iris. On the surface of the eye is the cornea and behind the iris is the lens. Contrary to the popular view, the lens does not bend the light, at least very much; it is the fluid (aqueous humor) in the cornea that bends incoming light. The lens does serve an important role in accommodation, the process that allows us to focus on near things and far things as we choose. Through the action of the ciliary muscle, the malleable lens can change its shape. In viewing near objects the ciliary muscle is relaxed and the radius and curvature of the lens are reduced. For far objects the muscle is tightened, changing the lens to a more convex configuration. The mass of the eye is filled with a dense fluid called the vitreous humor, a jellylike matter that helps maintain the shape of the eyeball. The vitreous humor is mostly transparent except for floaters, which most people observe as they grow older. Floaters are thought to be caused by residual parts of red blood cells that seep into the humor and clump together in strings. To see an example of these floaters, gaze at a light surface for a few seconds. If you don't see any floaters you must be very fortunate or very young.

Retina

The retina is the most interesting part of the eye for students of the psychology of art. The word *retina* is derived from the Latin *rete* or "net"; it is so named because if you look at the back of the eye, or the retina, a network of blood vessels is visible. Behind these blood vessels is the part of the retina that, because of its importance in perception, some scholars call an outgrowth of the brain. The retina is a thin sheet of nerve cells no thicker than a page of this book. The basic purpose of the retina is to absorb light rays and transform them to the electrochemical signals that comprise the language of the brain.

Three different types of cells found in the retina are important in passing visual sensations to the brain (see figure 1.13): (1) receptor cells (rods and

The Evolution of the "Big Window"

The human eye is the most important sensory instrument for detecting information. The "big window" is open to a wide range of visual information, from the sight of a setting sun to the words on this page. Human eyes are also prominent social instruments, signaling interest, as is well known among amorous couples. The evolution of this most remarkable sensory channel did not occur overnight, or even during the period of prehistoric man, but required hundreds of millions of years before reaching its present stage of development. Long before the first humans scratched out an existence on the African plains, their distant forebears had highly developed eyes and brains that saw and comprehended the sights of the world.

The very earliest "eyes" were scarcely more than a cluster of photosensitive cells that were connected to locomotive devices. Thus, the detection of light (or heat) might activate an appendage that would move the creature toward (or away from) the stimulus. Eventually these photosensitive cells became more densely clustered and situated in an indentation on the body surface. The opening to the indentation was closed with a transparent membrane. These components later developed into what we now know as the retina and the lens. Figure 1.11 shows the eye pit in the limpet, a shellfish similar

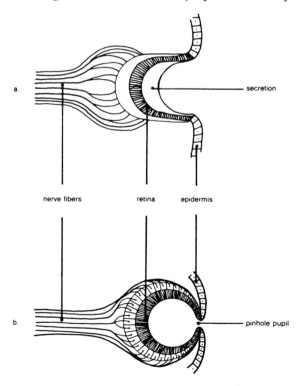

1.11 The eye pit of the limpet (above) and the pinhole eye of the nautilus (below). From Holland and Quinn (1987).

January 2000

Sunday	Monday	Tuesday	Wednesday	Thursday	Friday	Saturday
					1	2 Amphibians
3	4 Reptiles - Insects	5	6	7	8	9
10	11 Dinosaurs - Mammals	12	13	14	15	16
17	18 Prosimians	19	20	21	22	23
24	25 Monkeys emerge	26	27 Apes emerge	28	29	30 Australo-pithecus
31						

9:00 p.m. Humanoids, 11:59 p.m. Recorded history

to a scallop, and the "pinhole" eye of the nautilus, a shelled mollusk related to the octopus and squid.

The first multicelled organisms with their rudimentary "eyes" emerged during the Proterozoic Era (1.5 billion to 600 million years ago). Sometime during the Paleozoic Era (600 million to 220 million years ago) something like a "real" eye (and its important sidekick, the brain) materialized. Only within the past three million years have a humanoid eye and brain graced the earth; an eye and brain not unlike the ones reading these words and understanding the message.

All too often we act as if our eyes and brains were invented during the twentieth century, or perhaps during the Renaissance, to see and understand art. Wrong! Eyes, primitive and unknowing instruments that they were, emerged hundreds of millions of years ago, and their purpose was not to see Rembrandt, van Gogh, or Picasso paintings, but to see and comprehend light, movement, and contours. It is that old-fashioned eye and brain that we use to see and understand the universe.

To place the evolution of the eye (and brain) in context, consider only the past 248 million years of organic evolution. This spans the Mesozoic and Cenozoic eras and includes the period in which complex eyes appeared. During this period, insects, dinosaurs, giant reptiles, sabertoothed cats, grazing mammals, and primates (including your mother and father) emerged. Each had eyes and a brain of some sort. Now, depict this period as one 31-day month (we will use January 2000). Each day in this immensely long month is equal to eight million years.

During the first week of this month amphibians, reptiles, and insects were abundant, all of which had well-developed eyes. (Primitive eyes had emerged during the previous month.) On about January 10 mammals evolved, during the Triassic period. During the next period (Jurassic), which ended after the second week, huge dinosaurs walked the earth and birds evolved. Only on the last day, January 31 in the early afternoon, did a humanlike form appear; within the last 10 minutes of the month falls the entire history of visual arts, and about 4 minutes before midnight humans recorded their impressions on the caves in Lascaux, France. At the beginning of the last minute of the last day the pyramids of ancient Egypt were still 1,000 years away, and the entire history of Western art is crammed into the last 30 seconds. Most of the twentieth century, with its revolutionary scientific and artistic change, is allocated only one second in this scheme.

The human eye, the instrument we call the "big window" that gives us so much information about our world and is the source of our knowledge about art, emerged relatively recently.

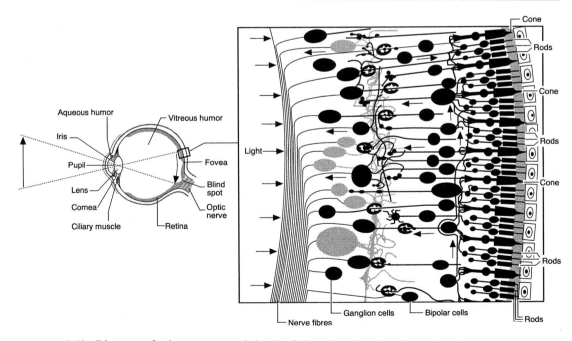

1.12 Diagram of a human eye and detail of the retina showing the rods and cones.

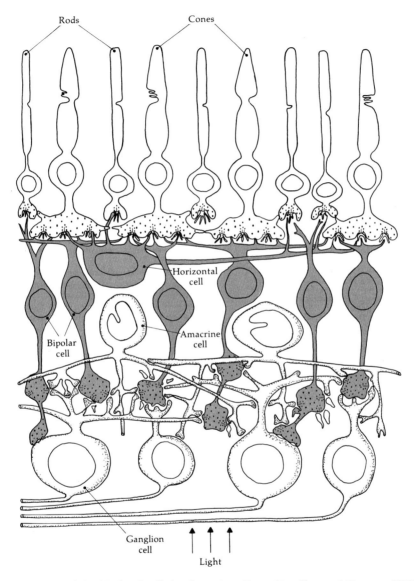

1.13 Diagram of the kinds of cells in the retina. From Dowling and Boycott (1966).

cones), which are sensitive to electromagnetic energy; (2) bipolar cells, which receive information from the receptor cells and pass it along to the next level; (3) ganglion cells, which collect information from the bipolar cells and pass it along to the optic cortex in the brain. In addition to the "vertical" processing of signals from the eye to brain, visual information is also processed in a "horizontal" fashion across the retina through two other types of cells: horizontal cells and amacrine cells. Horizontal cells allow sensations from receptor cells (rods and cones) to be passed along to other receptor cells. Horizontal cells are also connected to bipolar cells; thus, a limited network of communication is possible among the receptor cells in the retina and the bipolar cells. Amacrine cells connect ganglion cells with each other and thus allow communication among ganglia. Amacrine cells are also connected to each other.

RODS AND CONES

When viewed through a microscope, two distinct types of light receptor cells can be seen in the retina. They are the rods (so named for their polelike appearance) and the cones (so named because they are broader than rods and bear a slightly conical appearance).[2] A schematic cross section of the retina is shown at right in figure 1.12. Light enters the eye from the outside, passes through the pupil, and then must penetrate several layers of tiny blood vessels and supporting nerve cells (ganglion and bipolar cells) before reaching the rods and cones. It is almost as if we "see" inside-out, with the receptors located on the rear periphery of the eyeball and supporting cells, blood vessels, and nerve fibers on the inside.

Rods work under conditions of low light intensity, such as at dusk or at night when you try to make your way to the bathroom without turning on the light. They specialize in producing vision in varying shades of gray. Cones specialize in producing the full range of color vision and are active under well-illuminated conditions, such as in broad daylight. The fovea (see below) contains numerous cones; rods are mostly absent from the fovea but are plentiful in the periphery of the retina. For this reason, visual acuity under dim illumination, such as dusk, is actually better a few degrees off center than directly on center. (The next time you are in a dimly lit environment, try to view an object by looking a few degrees to one side.) Astronomers, sailors, hunters, and boy scouts have known this for a long time.

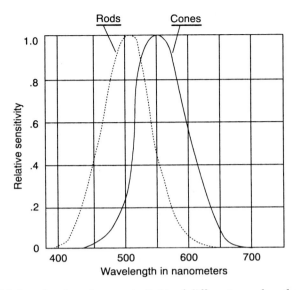

1.14 The sensitivity of rods and cones to light of different wavelengths.

The relative sensitivity of the rods and cones to different wavelengths is shown in figure 1.14. The sensitivity of rods is greatest at about 500 nm and drops off sharply from there. The visual information detected by rods is not of color but of the intensity of black/gray/white stimuli. Cones are most sensitive to colors in the 550 nm range, colors seen as yellow-green. Colors away from the maximum sensitivity of rods and cones require greater intensity to be detected—an important consideration for the artist who wishes to create a certain atmosphere through the use of colors and intensities.

FOVEA

Opposite the pupil (close to the optic nerve) is a small indented area about 2mm in diameter called the fovea or *macula lutea* (yellow spot). Rods and cones are distributed throughout the retina but they are unevenly concentrated. Rods are generally distributed throughout the retina except for the fovea, which is densely packed with cones. Overall, there are far more rods than cones. Each eye has about 125 million rods and 6–7 million cones. Together, there are about as many rods and cones in your eyes as there are

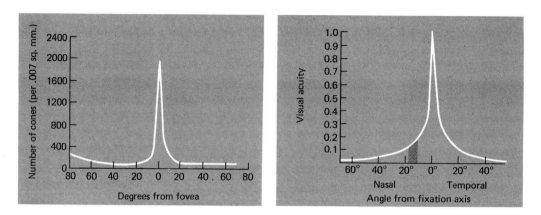

1.15 **Distribution of cones and of visual acuity in the retina. The shaded area is the "blind spot" (point of attachment of the optic nerve). From Solso (1991).**

people living in the United States, and they are bunched together in an area about the size of an American silver dollar. Of course, they are very small.

Figure 1.15 shows the distribution of cones in the retina and its relation to visual acuity. Foveal vision, in which an image is focused on the very sensitive fovea, encompasses a visual angle of only about 1 or 2 degrees. It is within that very limited range that vision is sharpest. Indeed, visual acuity for images that fall even a few degrees outside of foveal vision is very poor. The human fovea is minuscule in size but immense in importance. It occupies a space about the size of a pinhead, and yet, because of the vast number of cones crowded in this space, it more than any other structure is what we see the outer world with. (Medieval theologians who contemplated "How many angels can dance on the head of a pin?" had no idea that the principal visual mechanism was that size.)

The limits of our visual field are shown in figure 1.16. Humans can detect some visual cues from a field of more than 180° horizontally (about 90° to the right and 90° to the left)

It might be said that by moving from the center of the human retina to its periphery we travel back in evolutionary time; from the most highly organized structure to a primitive eye, which does little more than detect movements of shadows. The very edge of the human retina . . . gives primitive unconscious vision; and directs the highly developed foveal region to where it is likely to be needed for its high acuity.

—*Richard L. Gregory*

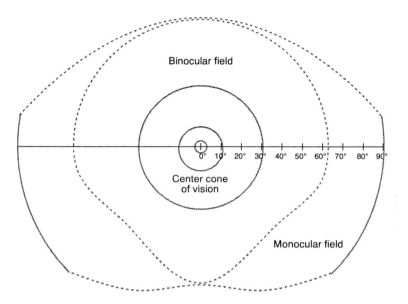

1.16 **Visual field showing the limits of monocular and binocular vision. (Vertical and horizontal axes in the diagram correspond to vertical and horizontal angles of vision; the angle is measured from the perpendicular straight ahead of the eye.) The lack of symmetry in the binocular field is due to occlusions by the nose.**

and 130° vertically (about 65° up and 65° down). However, sharp vision is restricted to a much smaller region. As mentioned, foveal vision subtends a very small angle of view, while impressions in the parafovea (the region surrounding the fovea) are somewhat less distinct. Even impressions up to 30° from the center are discernible, but are much less clear than central impressions. Stimuli in peripheral vision are poorly resolved; however, some type of information is still available. For example, movement of objects in the periphery significantly enhances our ability to detect them—likely a hangover from our evolutionary past in which the detection of moving objects was important for survival.

The parameters of the visual field can be conceptualized as a "cone" of vision, as illustrated in figure 1.17, which shows a three-dimensional view of the confines of vision. The uneven clarity within the visual field is illustrated in figure 1.18, in which central items are sharp and clear and peripheral objects less clear. Because sharp vision is restricted to a narrow band of available stimuli, we view objects, such as paintings, with eyes that are

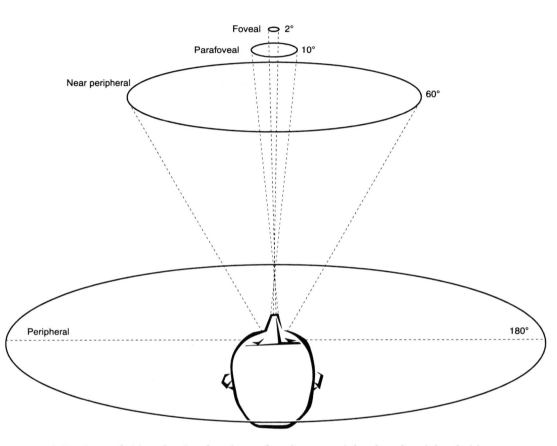

1.17 Cone of vision showing foveal, parafoveal, near peripheral, and peripheral vision. (Here the angles measure the field of vision from one side to the other.) These are discussed further in chapter 6.

constantly refocusing on different regions (see chapter 6). A consequence of this eye movement is that we do not see a painting all at once, as is commonly thought, but by forming an impression based on a large number of individual eye fixations that examine details falling within foveal vision.

To better appreciate how narrow foveal vision is, try this simple experiment. Close one eye and extend your arm with the thumb pointed upward. Now look at some object across the room. The area covered by the thumb is roughly equal to the angle subtended by foveal vision. It is within that small slice of the entire visual field that visual perception is sharpest. While doing

1.18   What the eyes see. Notice that the face and nearby objects are clearly perceived, while peripheral objects are fuzzy.

this, contemplate how fuzzy are the impressions only a few degrees from foveal vision.

Dynamic Vision

Finally, visual perception is not a static operation in which one fixes one's gaze on a single feature, but is dynamic, with the muscles located on both sides of the eyes tirelessly contracting and relaxing. This muscle activity, which may be brought under conscious control, moves the eyeball so that it is directed first at one feature and then at another and on to another and so on. Most eye movements are automatic, as in reading, but can be controlled, as in looking at a person who enters the room.

These eye movements are called saccades and were initially studied in relation to reading by Emile Javal during the last century. We now know that during reading there are about two or three saccades per second. Between saccades, the eye focuses on an object or scene for about 200 or 250 milliseconds (msec), although the duration of specific fixations may be several times this long. (Patterns of saccadic activity can vary widely for different people and for one person at different times.) In general, we gaze longer at interesting or puzzling things and shorter at mundane or simple things. It is during this fixation period that we "see" a feature before moving on to another feature. During the actual movement of the eyes, which occupies only about 10 percent of the viewing time, vision for features is sharply reduced, a condition felicitously called "visual smear."

When we look at an object (such as Cassatt's *The Bath,* figure 1.1), we do not see it "all at once," as common wisdom suggests, but go through a series of scans in which the eye momentarily stops on one feature, such as the child's foot, then darts on to another part, such as the mother's eyes, and then on to another, such as the pitcher, and so on. Each feature is seen in a brief glimpse, then our eyes focus on another point for additional processing. The span of material clearly seen at each fixation point is sharply limited due to the narrow field of foveal vision. Since this scanning/stop maneuver takes place over very short time periods, the subjective experience is that we are seeing the picture all at once, when, in fact, our visual perception of it is built up from a series of discrete "snapshots."

It should be emphasized that the above discussion applies to optical detection by the eyes, the initial stage of information processing. These visual sensations are collected and passed on to the brain for further processing, which takes a different form. Whereas the eye processes information sequentially, the brain is thought to do so in massively parallel operations. But that most intriguing part of the story must wait until the next chapter.

2   The Brain and Vision

The brain is an enchanted loom, where millions of flashing shuttles weave a dissolving pattern, always a meaningful pattern though never an abiding one.

—Sir Charles Sherrington

There is much more to the understanding of art than light and eye, and to many the next part of the puzzle is the most fascinating. It is the human brain, without which there would certainly be no art.[1]

While artists have perfected their skill over centuries, scientists have investigated the anatomy and functioning of the brain for just over a hundred years. However, scientific progress during this period has been astonishing, and the latest discoveries have led to thoughts of a unified theory of the brain encompassing all of its functions, including the appreciation of art. While the neurosciences were making real progress in understanding the brain and sensory systems, art critics, philosophers, and historians paid little attention to these discoveries. Neuroscientists were equally uninterested in the topic of art. Art and science were conceptualized so differently that not enough common ground was available for a good squabble. Slowly, we are beginning to understand that ideas from each discipline may help to explain the other.

The Brain

The human brain is the most complex system we know. Our brain, whose workings baffled our forefathers, is now yielding its secrets under the steadfast investigation of a group of dedicated scientists armed with dazzling new instruments. The brain is the nucleus of the emotions, giving life feeling; it is the center of thinking, providing associations for rational thought; and it is

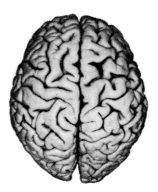

the locus of visual perception, endowing us with the ability to see, feel, and understand art. Without a brain we would be simpler than the Straw Man thought he was in the *Wizard of Oz.*

Sometimes the meaning of the words "brain" and "mind" become muddled. The brain is the part of the central nervous system enclosed in the skull, consisting of billions of neurons. The mind is what the brain does.

The outer layer of the brain is called the cerebral cortex, which contains the associative regions and optic cortex, essential for vision. Without the cerebral cortex humans would be senseless, speechless, thoughtless, and sightless.

Although the brain and its functions are not completely understood, much is known about its physical characteristics and processing functions. What we do know about the brain has not yet been applied to the understanding of art. This is a sad deficiency, as the appreciation of art provides a wonderfully comprehensive laboratory in which technical information from the scientific study of the brain can be integrated with the psychological aspects of art perception.

Mind, n.—A mysterious form of matter secreted by the brain. Its chief activity consists in the endeavor to ascertain its own nature, the futility of the attempt being due to the fact that it has nothing but itself to know itself with.

—*Ambrose Bierce,* The Devil's Dictionary.

VISUAL PROCESSING, THE BRAIN, AND EDGAR DEGAS

We begin our discussion of visual processing and the brain with the example of Edgar Degas's *Ballet Rehearsal* (figure 2.1). This painting was done in pastel

2.1   Edgar Degas, *Ballet Rehearsal.*

and gouache, a kind of poster paint that gives a chalky appearance. Although technically speaking Degas was not an impressionist, his work captures much of the dreamy softness of artists of that period. His *Ballet Rehearsal* is filled with interesting light effects that create an unmistakable mood of the theater. Notice that the light source is from below the figures—the location of gaslights used in the 1880s in the opera houses of Paris. The eye and brain immediately detect forms, colors, shapes, and meaning (e.g., the possible relationship between the dance master and the ingénue). The eye and brain, working together, perform all of these functions effortlessly, swiftly, and accurately. Of the many success stories of the evolution of organic systems, none is more spectacular than that of the human eye and brain.

What eye and brain functions are activated when one sees this picture? The moment reflected light from it reaches the retina, a series of irrepressible sensory/cognitive functions are activated that define the experience. As soon as the eye has focused on a part of the artwork it darts off to another region and then to another (see chapter 6 for details). Almost immediately, colors, contours, and figures are organized into sensory signals that are swiftly dispatched to the region of the brain called the visual cortex, located in the very back of the head. There, further featural analysis takes place that activates many other regions throughout the cerebral cortex. One of the many regions activated is the motor cortex, a center for muscle actions located in the center of the brain. There impulses are sent out that mobilize the muscles controlling the eyes, causing the eye to move to another section of the painting. The entire process of focusing the eyes on one part and then moving on to another is repeated hundreds of times in the time required to read this discussion. Each of these impressions is transmitted to an ever-branching network of cerebral neurons and combined with previously stored information to give thoughtful interpretation of the painting. Figure 2.2 presents the basic sequence of stages through which information is processed.

Visual processing of information from the receptors is hierarchical, moving from the eye to the neurons of the primary visual cortex and then to the associative cortex, in which numerous connections are made with other neurons. At each level the processing becomes more entangled with higher-order functions, so that in a very brief time we interpret the visual signals into meaningful thoughts.

Physical Characteristics

Physically, the brain is unimpressive; a gray-pink substance about the size of two clenched fists, weighing about one and a half kilograms, deeply furrowed, and divided into two seemingly identical halves. Contained within the brain are billions of neurons, each with the potential of passing on and receiving messages from numerous other neurons. The brain is alive with electrochemical messages, which dart through millions of intricate connections—choosing some pathways while rejecting others. Through the most elaborate system known to man, original percepts are combined with other impressions, encoded for future use, and stored in electrochemical archives. After the basic perceptual elements of Degas's romanticized impression are recorded by the eye and optical cortex, the multitude of neural units in the cerebral cortex are compelled to search for "deeper" meaning.

The anatomy of one side of the human brain is shown in figure 2.3. The brain is divided into two hemispheres called the right and left cerebral hemispheres. The hemispheres are covered with the cerebral cortex, a thin,

Stages of Visual Information Processing

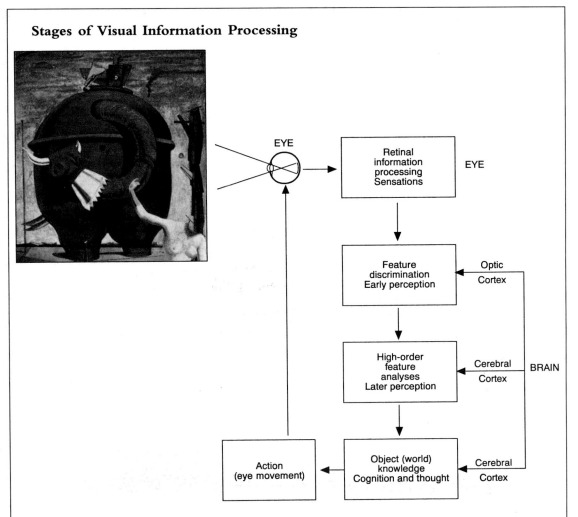

2.2 Max Ernst, *The Elephant Celebes* (Tate Gallery, London), and a model of information processing.

Here we see the INFOPRO stages involved in viewing *The Elephant Celebes* by Max Ernst (1921). The painting shows a grotesque mechanical object that combines human and animal forms. The work is surrealist and suggests (to some) how fragile people are, especially in relation to machines and animals. To arrive at this conclusion, or any other, involves a series of stages beginning with reflected light energy falling on the retina. These basic sensations are sent on to the optic cortex for feature discrimination, in which lines, edges, contrasts, and the like are processed. Neural impulses are sent on, in a massively parallel fashion, to other parts of the cortex for higher-order processing, including cognition and thought, which redirects attention to featural processing and activates eye movements. The eye then focuses on another part of the painting and the sequence is repeated.

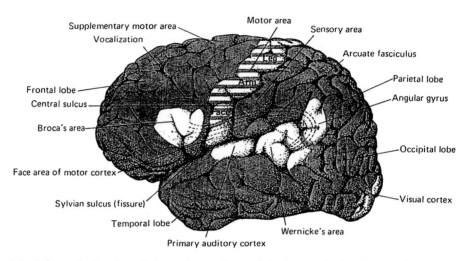

Supplementary motor area
Vocalization
Motor area
Sensory area
Arcuate fasciculus
Frontal lobe
Central sulcus
Parietal lobe
Angular gyrus
Broca's area
Occipital lobe
Face area of motor cortex
Sylvian sulcus (fissure)
Temporal lobe
Visual cortex
Primary auditory cortex
Wernicke's area

2.3   Schematic drawing of the major sections of the human brain. From Solso (1991).

gray, moist matter richly equipped with the tiny neurons that carry vital information. A diagram of the network of cortical neurons is shown in figure 2.4. The human brain has more than 100 billion (that is, 100,000,000,000) neurons, each capable of receiving messages from and passing on messages to sometimes thousands of other neurons through its many branched-end fibers. Even "simple" cognitive acts, such as viewing a painting, involve billions and billions of neurons.

PARALLEL PROCESSING

For years the brain was thought to be sharply compartmentalized, with specific functions localized in precise regions. For example, motor processes were thought to be confined to the motor cortex. Recent studies, however, suggest that though there are centers associated with specific functions, the working of the brain is accomplished through the simultaneous activation of many areas, a process that has been labeled "massive parallelism." The concept is central to revolutionary new ideas in neurocognition called parallel distributed processing (PDP).

This theory posits that the brain functions by distributing impulses throughout large portions of itself in a parallel fashion rather than in a series of steps in which one neuron passes information on to another. Neurons pass

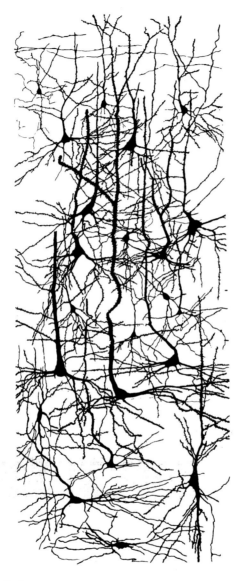

2.4 Diagram of cortical neurons.

messages on to numerous other neurons, which pass messages on to other neurons. This ever-branching network grows more complex within a very brief time. The most important aspect of neural processing is that these multiplicative functions occur in parallel—thus creating a system of analysis that engages countless millions of processing units simultaneously.

PDP research helps explain one of the most fundamental questions about visual perception, including the perception of art: How is it that we are able to recognize and classify visual events in such a brief time? If the brain were "wired" serially, with one neuron passing information on to only one other, then the amount of time required to make sense out of an object would be many minutes—if such an operation were even possible. But if information were distributed over many neurons operating in parallel, the number of processing units would increase geometrically over time.

This concept can be placed in perspective by looking at some recent experimental work in cognitive psychology. In a typical experiment, a person might be asked to discriminate between two visual objects, say the painting by Degas just mentioned and a painting by Picasso. Recognition might be measured by having the person press one or another reaction time key. Experiments of this sort tell us that recognition time for an object is about 300 msec, or less than one-third of a second. Because such experiments typically involve motor responses, which require additional time to execute, it is safe to infer that "pure" cerebral processing of visual recognition takes considerably less time. The time required for impulses to pass from one neuron to another is, in terms of electrical circuitry, ponderous—many millions of times slower than the time required for a computer impulse to spin through its program. Yet the human brain with its sluggish machinery is able to make complex judgments far faster and more intelligently than the quickest computers, because brain processing engages a huge number of units that operate simultaneously. For some time, computer scientists have attempted to fabricate parallel computers that simulate human processing. They have met with mixed results.

From the Eye to the Brain

After a visual signal passes through the pupil and is absorbed by the rods and cones, it is collected and passed along the large optic nerve on its way to the brain. However, its routing to the brain is complicated. As shown in figure 2.5, the optic nerves come together at a center called the optic chiasm. Here

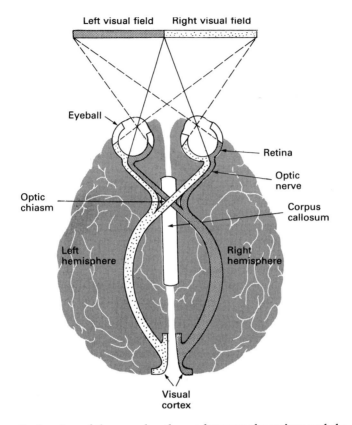

2.5 Schematic drawing of the neural pathways between the retinas and the right and left cerebral hemispheres. Note that some of the nerve fibers from each eye cross over to the opposite hemisphere at the optic chiasm and some do not. From Solso (1991).

a complicated distribution takes place. Half of the fibers from each eye cross over at the optic chiasm are passed on to the visual cortex on the side of the brain opposite their source, and half of the fibers terminate in the visual cortex on the same side. This crossover effect is consistent with other brain-body functions and is called contralaterality. Motor functions, for example, are processed contralaterally. A patient with a stroke affecting the left hemisphere may have paralysis on the right side of his or her body. Even though visual contralaterality is not so simple, it is important for art students to be familiar with its basic aspects.

Refer to figure 2.5 and trace the pathway of the dotted image presented in the right visual field. Reflected light from this object, which is placed to the right of the observer, enters each pupil and is absorbed by retinal cells situated on the left side of each eye. Messages detected in that area of the eye are passed on to the optic chiasma, then to the lateral geniculate nucleus (for our purposes, a relay station located in each hemisphere) of the *left* visual cortex, even though they were shown on the *right* side of the field of vision. Similar routing is shown for the gray object in the diagram, which is presented in the left visual field and processed in the right hemisphere of the brain.

Visual Cortex

It is possible to monitor neural activity in the visual cortex of experimental animals as they view simple stimuli (e.g., vertical or horizontal bars) and thus further identify the locus of this type of visual processing in the brain. The procedure in these experiments is straightforward. A tiny insulated wire is carefully inserted through the skull of an animal. This probe is capable of detecting electrical activities in, say, the visual cortex. Then visual stimuli (bars or gratings, for example) are shown to the animal. Recordings of electrical potentials of selected parts of the brain are then related to the visual stimuli that caused them to fire.

Fundamental research in this area has been conducted by David Hubel and Torstin Wiesel (1965, 1979), for which they shared the 1981 Nobel prize for physiology or medicine with Roger Sperry, whose split brain research is described below. Hubel and Wiesel's basic findings were that different parts of the brain's visual cortex react to different types of visual stimuli. In figure 2.6 we can see the responses made to specific bar shapes and movements in the form of electrical activity in the visual cortex of young and visually inexperienced cats. In Hubel's (1963) words, "Each cell seems to have its own specific duties; it takes care of one restricted part of the retina, responds best to one particular shape of stimulus and to one particular orientation." For each stimulus, such as a type of line (the edge of a line, a slit, or a bar), there is a specific set of brain cells that will respond. If the arrangement of stimuli is altered, then a whole new set of neurons will be activated.

These experiments have shown that specific parts of the visual cortex are responsive to specific visual stimuli (vertical bars and horizontal bars, for example). Such findings have led to powerful techniques of visual perception

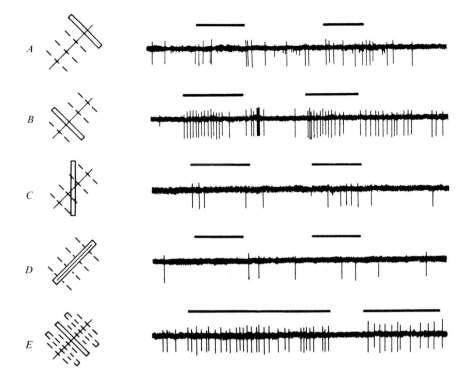

2.6 Responses of a cell in the cortex of a cat to stimulation of the eye with a light slit. The horizontal axis represents time; vertical lines indicate activity of neurons. The diagrams at left indicate the orientation of the light slit (heavy bar) relative to the receptive field axis (dashed lines). In E the slit was oriented as in A and B but moved rapidly from side to side. From Hubel and Wiesel (1963).

called spatial frequency analysis, which suggests that the visual system analyzes visual information by separating light patterns into sine wave components.

The implications of these studies for students of art are striking, as they establish how visual information is represented in the brain. Until these experiments, serious art critics and some scientists believed that visual phenomena were represented in the brain in terms of a holistic image, in much the same way as a visual image appears on the retina. This idea, which was much in vogue among Greek philosophers, is sometimes called isomorphism ("same shape"). The idea is that when we see a tree, for example, our eye records it isomorphically and passes on to the brain (or some other organ) the whole image for further processing and derivation of meaning. Artistic appreciation follows the same logic, assuming the isomorphic image of a painting being forwarded to the brain for analysis. Yet, when the skull was cracked open and surgeons fished around in the brain, no little pictures were found, any more than if we cracked open a television set we would find a whole cast of players doing their acts. We now know that the visual cortex of the brain (that area that initially processes visual stimuli) processes simple forms and shapes, and that only after these primitive forms are processed in other parts of the cortex are the semantic properties of a painting revealed.

NEUROPHYSIOLOGICAL SENSING TECHNIQUES

The most recent studies of brain functioning and vision use modern neurophysiological sensing techniques. Among the most promising of these are the CAT (or CT) scan and PET (or PETT) scan, which stand for computerized axial tomography and positron emission transaxial tomography, respectively. The CAT scanner is based on X-ray technology—in which rays penetrate the brain from different angles, giving an impression of structures—and is particularly valuable in medical diagnosis. PET scans use radioactive particles injected into the bloodstream to measure cerebral blood flow by means of external peripheral sensors.

The logic behind many of these technologies is that cortical activity in specific areas of the brain requires greater volumes of blood. Therefore, if one traces the regions that show increased blood flow, one can identify precise areas of the brain that are currently active. These measurements are then correlated with external events, such as looking at a picture, listening to an auditory signal, thinking, remembering, and so on, to gain a detailed impression of the relationship between environmental stimuli and corresponding cortical activity. In effect, a type of cortical map of external events can be drawn. The implications of these research technologies for the scientific study of cognition and human memory are enormous; for further information, the reader is directed to specialized sources (see Solso 1991 and Tulving 1989a, 1989b).

In one experiment done in Sweden by Lassen, Ingvar, and Skinhøj (1978), normal subjects underwent a procedure in which a tracer was ingested and then various tasks performed while PET scan images were recorded. Of particular interest to students of visual phenomena are the results shown in figure 2.7. In 2.7A the subject was asked to listen to a series of spoken words,

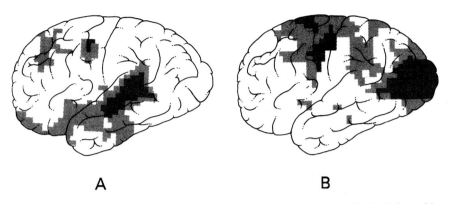

2.7 Brain imaging technique. In *A* a subject listened to spoken words. In *B* the subject followed a moving object with his eyes. From Lassen, Ingvar, and Skinhøj (1978).

while in 2.7B the same subject was asked to follow a moving object with his eyes. Under the latter conditions there is a palpable increase in the activity of the visual cortex and frontal eye fields. These data suggest that visual processing is localized *and* generalized, in that initial processing takes place in the visual cortex (which is no surprise as the optic nerves terminate there) but also that other regions of the brain are activated.

A Tale of Two Hemispheres

In the past, much of what people knew of brain functioning came by way of clinical studies in which either traumatized or pathological patients exhibited symptoms that were associated with specific brain aberrations. Surgeons during the nineteenth century noticed that a brain tumor in the left hemisphere affected the right side of the body and vice versa. So regular were these observations that it was deduced that brain functions were contralateral with body functions. Within the past few years we have learned much more about the specific nature of brain functions vis-à-vis hemispheric specialization.

One of the most dramatic demonstrations of hemispheric specialization was shown in the split brain research pioneered by Roger Sperry, whose observations were based on patients (and experimental animals) who had had the connective tissue (the corpus callosum) between the two hemispheres severed surgically. Remarkably, the patients and animals behaved almost as if they had two brains—with no communication between them. Experiences and learning by one hemisphere did not transfer to the other. In a seminal study by Levy, Trevarthen, and Sperry (1972) a commissurotomized patient (one whose corpus callosum had been cut) was shown a chimeric face, half-man and half-woman. As shown in figure 2.8, the woman's face was on the viewer's left side, which would favor right hemisphere processing, and the man's face on the right, which would favor left hemisphere processing. Interestingly, the patient did not notice anything unusual about this split face. When asked to tell about the face, the patient described a man's face, which was based on information processed in the left hemisphere. Thus it appears that language functions, such as those skills necessary for giving a verbal description, are lodged in the left hemisphere (since the patient's two hemispheres could not communicate with each other). However, if the same patient was asked to pick the face from an array of faces, he selected the woman's face. It would therefore appear that the right hemisphere is more generally involved in the processing of pictorial information. Generalizing from this observation (and many others that yield similar results), it is likely that basic processing of visual information, including art, is generally carried out by the right hemisphere.

The functional asymmetries between the hemispheres have been extended to a number of different cognitive functions, which are summarized in table 2.1. It seems that many forms of sensory stimuli that generally support artistic expression—for example, complex geometric patterns, movements in spatial patterns, nonverbal memory, and geometry, as well as faces—are principally located in the right hemisphere, while other abstract processes are located in the left hemisphere. Some have even argued that cognitive differences among individuals may be attributed to how their hemispheres are organized and how dominant one or the other is; for example Harris (1978, p. 463):

> The left hemisphere operates in a more logical, analytic, computer-like fashion, analyzing stimulus information input sequentially, abstracting out the relevant details to which it attaches verbal labels: the right hemisphere is primarily a synthesizer, more concerned with the overall stimulus configuration, and organizes and processes information in terms of gestalts or wholes.

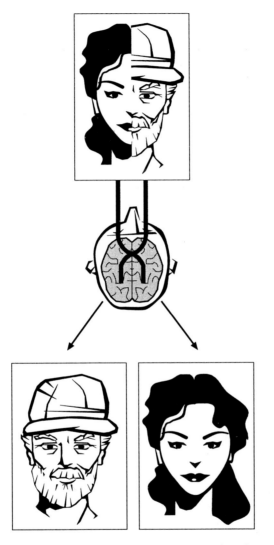

2.8 Display of a chimeric face used with commissurotomized patients. Each hemisphere appears to register separate images: the left records a man's face, the right a woman's. When asked to describe the face, the subject verbally labels it as a man's; but when asked to point out the face among a display of faces, the subject selects the woman's.

Table 2.1
Summary of Research on Cerebral Functions

Function	Left Hemisphere	Right Hemisphere
Auditory system	Sounds related to language	Music "Environmental" sounds
Spatial processes	Unknown	Geometry Direction sense Mental rotation of geometric forms
Somatosensory system	Unknown	Tactile recognition Braille detection
Memory	Verbal memory	Nonverbal memory
Language processing	Speech Reading Writing Arithmetic	Metered prosody (?)
Visual system	Letters, words Surrealist art	Geometric patterns Faces Realistic art
Movement	Complex voluntary movement	Spatial pattern movements

These findings and conclusions have attracted widespread attention among scientists and laypeople alike. Although some such observations have been backed by carefully designed experiments, it is still too early to conclude that artists, or people who enjoy art, are so inclined because of a dominant right hemisphere. However, we can say that a substantial number of highly respected research articles indicate that the right hemisphere is more deeply involved in this type of processing than is the left hemisphere.

A Model of Visual Cognition and the Brain

The biological "hardware" that allows us to see and process the signals of the world is more or less determined by nature and invariant. The structure of your eye and brain are about the same as that of my eye and brain. However, what we make of artistic impressions vary widely. You may prefer Lichtenstein; I, Klimt.

2.9 Which do you prefer? Roy Lichtenstein, *WHAAM!*; Gustav Klimt, *The Kiss*.

The interactive model of artistic perception and cognition

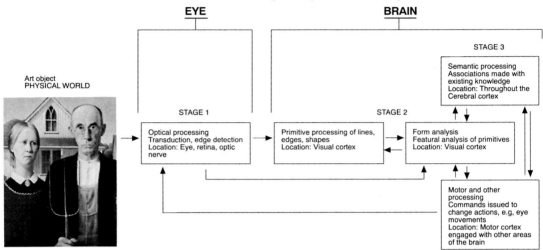

2.10   **The interactive model of artistic perception and cognition; Grant Wood,** *American Gothic.*

   The way the eye and brain process art and other visual stimuli—generally the same for all humans—follows a well-described series of stages that we will call the interactive model of artistic perception and cognition. Each of the stages is associated with specific areas of the brain. However, there is an ongoing interaction between systems, which engage several areas of the brain simultaneously. The essence of the model is shown in figure 2.10. Visual information from the physical world is detected by the eye (Stage 1) and is transduced to neural energy and passed along to the visual cortex (Stage 2), where it is initially processed in terms of primitive shapes and forms. Visual signals are analyzed in terms of simple contours, such as vertical and horizontal lines, curved lines, and angles. These elementary forms are combined into larger units, such as basic components of an entire scene. Information is further processed by other parts of the cerebral cortex (Stage 3) that are activated in a massively parallel fashion in which neural impulses are sent to widely distributed regions of the brain and processed simultaneously. The composite effect of these processes leads to an interpretation of the visual signals in light of previously stored information. For example, commands may redirect the eye to focus on certain regions of the visual display. Semantic processing also happens during this third stage, in which the interpretation of visual signals is undertaken. Your preference for Lichtenstein and mine for Klimt may also surface during this stage, based on our respective intellectual backgrounds and taste.

Look at either one of these works and try to trace the progress of information processing as visual signals wind their way through the sensory/cognitive labyrinth. Keep in mind that all visual processing, from viewing Lichtenstein or Klimt to looking at snow-capped mountains to reading the dial of a watch to reading the words on this page, follow very similar neurological routines. It's how we know the external world.

Perception and Knowledge

If our brain knows the external world—the world that exists outside of human cognition and imagination—through sensory experiences (among which vision is very important), then our impressions are funneled through the narrow band of electromagnetic energy to which the eye is sensitive. This idea is not new; it can be found in the writings of Leibniz, Berkeley, and even Descartes in the seventeenth century. Nonetheless our cognitive life—the life that exists within the mind—is largely a composite of sensory experiences and the unique way those experiences are combined through the exchange of neurological signals by the brain. We understand the paintings of Mondrian and Grandma Moses not only because the reflected light from these paintings is somewhere between 400 and 700 nanometers, to which the human eye is sensitive, but because the brain that "sees" what the eye detects has stored knowledge about forms, colors, shapes, juxtapositions, and the meaning of life.

Had the range of sensitivities of the sensory system experienced even a slightly different evolution, the brain and the entire intellectual history of humankind would be radically different. Think for a moment of the consequences of a subtle shift in the range of electromagnetic energy the eyes might detect. If we humans could see between 475 and 875 nm, the impact on our cognitive world would be tremendous. We would lose our awareness of very dark purples, but would gain sensitivity to infrared rays (see figure 2.11). We would be able to see some forms of heat, much like the pit viper mentioned earlier, but be blind to some deep violets. How would our view of the world be changed? How would the brain and body evolve to capitalize on this

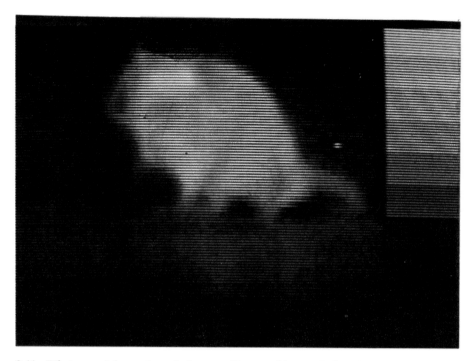

2.11 What we might see in a dark room if we could sense infrared rays. From Sinclair (1985).

altered range of vision? What colors would we use to represent royalty? And what fashions would be inspired by our ability to see infrared rays?

The Evolution of Eye and Brain

Why is the perception of light so important to the human observer? Consider the purpose of visual perception among members of our species and other animals.

It is likely that primitive sense organs capable of perceiving light energy evolved very early in the history of earthly creatures for the purpose of finding food, heat (or cold), and light, and for avoiding harm. The 500-million-year-old eye of the trilobite was mentioned in chapter 1, and it is likely that some forms of photosensitive devices are much older than that. Primitive invertebrates, for example jellyfish, have photosensitive cells. Even echinoderms (e.g., starfish and sea urchins) have eyespots at the end of a tentacle. More elegant seeing instruments developed when photosensitive regions became indented and were protected by a transparent layer of cells, which later developed into what we now know as the lens. This enclosed photoreceptive instrument became more complex, and a profusion of cells within it evolved into the areas of the retina. Over millions of years the highly refined eyes of various insects and vertebrates, among others, have evolved.

According to classic Darwinian theory, the selective evolution of physical attributes enhanced the likelihood that a particular creature would survive and procreate within a given ecological niche. Thus, a being whose sensory system was capable of differentiating light from dark, blues from greens, straight lines from curved lines, and moving objects from stationary ones might measurably increase its chances for survival over other creatures that were deficient in these capabilities.

The evolutionary advantages of the eye, however, could not exist without corresponding developments in the brain. If modern cognitive and perceptual psychology has taught us one lesson, it is that raw sensory signals are as meaningless as random cosmic static. But when these signals fall on a decoding organ, such as eye and brain together, they are woven into a richly patterned fabric in which meaningful relationships are immediately perceived and understood. The most intriguing part of the evolution of perception is in the mutual development of the sensory system (which "sees" reality) and the corresponding neural network (which "interprets" reality). The sensory system (i.e., the eye) and the central nervous system (i.e., the brain) evolved concurrently and complementarily. Furthermore, not only the structure of the brain but also its processing characteristics evolved as a vital part of the system.

Mind and world . . . have evolved together, and in consequence are something of a mutual fit.

—William James

Of central importance for the seeing of art is that the human sensory system and brain, which evolved over millions and millions of years, have remained structurally unchanged for hundreds of thousands. We see and interpret our modern world, including the world of art, with the same old Pleistocene sensory system and brain whose primordial functions included seeing moving prey, avoiding branches, keeping warm and dry, finding and eating food, understanding spatial relations, procreating and loving children, making tools, surviving, and generally eating a few sweet berries in the brief interval between birth and death. This same eye and brain also continue to

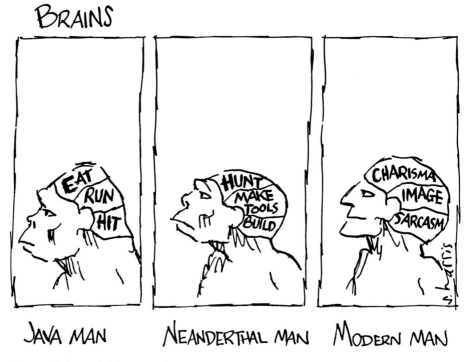

By permission of Sidney Harris.

be useful in the twentieth century as we move effortlessly through a multi-dimensional world, avoiding harm and seeking gratification. The original purpose of these biological systems is clear; less clear is how such systems are used in the fabrication of aesthetics.

Only recently have we begun to understand the vast psychological implications of operating in the twentieth century with a brain born and bred over a million years ago. Within the very recent past (say the past 25,000–35,000 years) the eye has been turned toward an appreciation of artificial images—such things as sketches of wild animals drawn on rudely finished cave walls. Surely the human eye and brain did not evolve to see *these* things, any more than the auditory canal evolved to hear Mozart, or the gustatory sense evolved for the pleasure of gourmets. But it is splendidly serendipitous for those of us who love art (as well as Mozart and chocolate mousse) that the sensory systems that evolved in the service of biological survival found pleasure in things of beauty. Art is the fortuitous by-product of the evolution of the eye and brain. And, from the moment man[2] first saw an image of himself, his lover, his game, his enemy, his god, his imagination, and other wondrous things of the world and of the mind, he has not been the same.

In the context of our discussion of the survival properties of vision, there are three important questions to which vision provides answers:

- What is an object?
- Where is it?
- What is it doing?

Conveniently, those topics are central to our analysis of art. Art is a reflection of the inner structures and perceptions of the mind of the artist and art viewer. This book proposes that through art we might be able to see into the human eye and beyond. For in art—especially art that appeals to universal principles of perception and cognitive organization, and resonates sympathetically to the inner neurological structures of the brain—we can discover the salient facts necessary to formulate general laws of the mind and the often elusive relationship of the mind with the external (electromagnetic) world. So, when I suggested that this book was about art but also about human psychology, I meant that it was about the basic way the brain evolved and how its network of neurons was evolutionarily "wired together." We now turn our attention to what cognitive psychology has taught us about the way we organize and interpret the things we see.

3   Figure and Form Perception

We are so familiar with seeing that it takes a leap of imagination to realize that there are problems to be solved. Consider it. We are given tiny distorted upside-down images in the eyes, and we see separate solid objects in surrounding space. From the patterns of stimulation on the retinas we perceive the world of objects, and this is nothing short of a miracle.

—*Richard L. Gregory*

During the early stages of perceiving real objects, such as scenes of nature and art, the brain classifies the neural messages from the eye into simple patterns: lines, figure/ground, edges, contrasts, and the like. These basic patterns, or "primitives," are then placed in their context and further identified (or tagged) by their orientation and color. When we view Hokusai's *Mount Fuji* (figure 3.1), it is only after the first stage of processing light and analyzing primitive features that an identification of objects, forms, and meaning can take place.

This chapter is mainly about the fundamental elements of visual perception. Complex visual forms, such as make up the great art of the world, are fabricated from simpler forms; the larger understanding of art is based on an awareness of the fundamental principles of vision. Seeing *Mount Fuji,* for example, is dependent on the eye's ability to separate regions from other regions. We "see" the mountain as an entity separate from the sky because an edge is created by a line. The contours, or separations, in this painting (and in most other visual art forms) segregate objects from each other. This separation of objects by contours is an essential elementary stage in the visual processing of painting. To see how they work, first consider the absence of contours—a phenomenon called the *Ganzfeld*.

3.1 Hokusai, *Thirty-six Views of Mount Fuji: Southerly Wind and Fine Weather.*

The *Ganzfeld*

Most contours in art are formed by lines, which separate one area from another. Contours are everywhere the eye searches. They are essential to art, to vision, and to life. A *Ganzfeld* is the conceptual antonym of a contour. *Ganzfelds* (from the German meaning "whole field") are visual fields that have no contours; something like what you might experience if you were lost in a boat in very dense fog. You would not see anything except a uniform gray field.

You can experience a *Ganzfeld,* without rowing a boat into a fog bank, by cutting a Ping-Pong ball in half and covering each eye with one of the halves. (If you don't have a Ping-Pong ball handy, you can use a pair of white translucent spoons of the kind often given with fast food rations.) Stare into these homemade contraptions for a few minutes (or until someone notices you) and you will experience the *Ganzfeld*. Be forewarned, you may experience a sense of blindness. In actual experimental work in this area of perceptual psychology, subjects report a complete (temporary) loss of vision after 15 minutes and may not know if their eyes are open or closed. Others report motor disturbances including the loss of the sense of balance and/or

coordination. Continued deprivation of visual contours may result in hallu-
cinations.

Clearly our visual system and brain are so accustomed to viewing
contours that when they are withdrawn from our sight we become disori-
ented. Contours are among the most powerful environmental cues for human
survival, and it seems that the eye and brain have evolved elegant systems
specifically designed to encode and understand differentiating signals. The eye
and brain are excellent edge and line detectors and process that type of
information in a deceptively casual manner, so much so that our common
impression is that edges and lines are simple components of the "real world."
Conversely, we believe that other processes, such as understanding mathematics or reading, are complex because they require years of training to do
well.

It may be that "simple" and "complex" cognitive operations are more
a function of the constitutional makeup of the central nervous system—what
we might casually describe as "the way the CNS is wired"—than of any
objective attributes of one class of phenomena or another. We see lines easily,
not necessarily because they are simple but because we have eyes and a brain
thoroughly prepared to process these signals. So powerful is the inclination
to see lines that the brain "sees" them where they do not exist. As an example,
look carefully at the drawing of the two zebras on the first page of this chapter.
The two are easily separated because of a contour that separates them, but
upon close inspection you will find that there is not really a line, just one
that is inferred. In a real sense, when we study the perception of simple
contours and gratings we are looking into the eye and brain of the beholder
and seeing clearly how these work.

Gratings

One of the simplest patterns known is that of gratings, or stripes. For this
reason, experimental psychophysicists have chosen to study gratings as a
means of knowing the fundamental process of visual perception, especially
visual acuity. An overview of these studies is presented here, followed by a
discussion of Mach bands. As we shall see, these topics relate directly to the
perception of art. They are central to our understanding of the way the eye
sees simple forms. Furthermore, the use of grating patterns has become
fashionable among many modern artists.

As we saw in the previous chapters, the human eye and brain are amazingly complex structures capable of fine perception and discrimination of form. One means of testing the limits of the human eye is the use of contrasting forms, and among the simplest forms is a black line against varying backgrounds, usually white or a shade of gray. Our common knowledge tells us that we humans are very good at this task. We easily see black, hair-thin lines against a white background—on a dial, for example. However, if the background is changed to a dark gray, not only is it more difficult to detect the line but also *what* we see is altered in unexpected ways (see below on Mach bands).

A slightly more complex task is the perception of gratings, or alternating black and white lines of varying widths and light intensities. A similar perceptual test is used by opthalmologists in eye examinations as a test of visual acuity. In the experimental laboratory, a person being tested for visual acuity is presented with a simple square wave grating, as shown in figure 3.2, and asked to tell which way the lines are pointing. In figure 3.2 the illumination of the black and white bars is sharply delineated and the "shape" of the light intensity is said to be square, as shown in the right side of the figure. In order to do this task successfully, the person must be able to distinguish between the black and white bars. The task is made more difficult if the width of the bars is very small or the background is more obtrusive or degraded in some other way. Signals of this sort are said to have more "noise"; an example is shown in figure 3.3, in which the light intensities of the black and white portions are graphed at right. Here the pattern of light intensity takes the shape of a sine wave, rather than a square wave as in the previous figure.

Very similar patterns have been used by artists, although their purpose was to create a psychological effect in the viewer. An example is found in Claude Monet's *Four Poplars* (figure 3.4). Monet was fond of painting scenes from nature; during his later life spent at his estate at Giverny, few natural

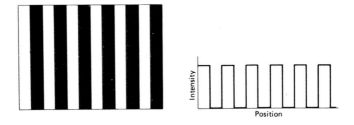
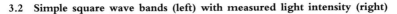

3.2 **Simple square wave bands (left) with measured light intensity (right)**

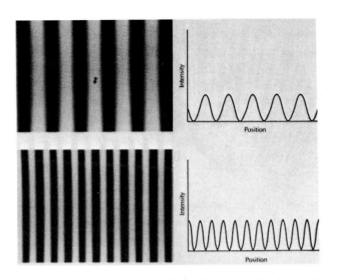

3.3 Sine wave gratings. The sine wave of the lower grating has twice the spatial frequency of the upper. From Cornsweet (1970).

scenes escaped his brush. In *Four Poplars* Monet creates an almost dreamlike landscape. However, in spite of the misty feelings we associate with this work, the scene is divided into sections by the compelling vertical lines. It is likely that these familiar visual signals "bring us back to reality" and give visual strength to an otherwise ambiguous scene. We are drawn to the painting by its combination of ambiguity and clarity of structure, of fuzzy impressions and strong vertical bars. In this painting Monet takes advantage of our propensity to analyze a scene in terms of figure (the salient feature of a scene) and ground (or background, the less salient parts of a scene). The figure is defined by the four trees, the ground, the sky, and the surroundings. Because of basic eye and brain functions, we spontaneously "see" the scene as being composed of two distinct elements, much as we might view a grating in the experimental laboratory or a zebra on the Serengeti plains.

An even more direct application of gratings in art is shown in a painting by Wassily Kandinsky, the Russian modernist (figure 3.5). Kandinsky was a great innovator in art, and is known not only for his abstract geometric style and sensitive use of colors but also for his proclivity to intellectualize art. He attempted to produce a "pure painting" derived from the primary values of color, a position also taken by Henri Matisse and the school of art called

3.4 Claude Monet, *Four Poplars*.

fauvism. His aim in art was to energize geometric forms and colors with a "spiritual meaning" by disposing of all likeness to the physical world. (Was he also seeking Plato's idealized forms?) Kandinsky was committed to separating the real (physical) world from the abstract (artistic) world and to finding common elements in visual art and music. (See the discussion of Kandinsky's work and cognitive psychology in chapter 9.) In a sense his *Pictures at an Exhibition,* based on Mussorgsky's musical tone poem by the same name, is an inventive scheme for visualizing music, but not at all in the conventional way. (The original music is based on a series of representational paintings.)

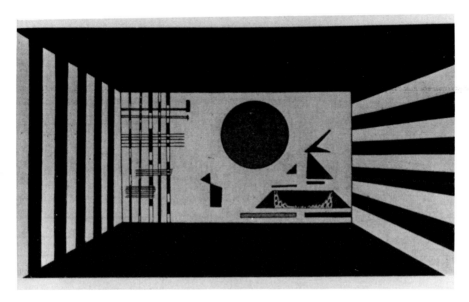

3.5   Wassily Kandinsky, *Decor for Mussorgsky's Pictures at an Exhibition.*

Of particular interest to those interested in the psychophysical properties of art is the use of both vertical and horizontal grating in *Pictures*.[1] The disciplined, square wave stripes on either side of Kandinsky's painting confront the viewer's eye and establish a tone of uncompromising rigidity, only to be attenuated immediately by the whimsical temperament of the center panel. Kandinsky, like Monet several years before, set up a dynamic tension in which the modern viewer experiences, within the same painting, a thing that is both hard and soft. The "hard" part is based on grating patterns that the eye and brain are particularly adept at processing and that require very little time or effort to apprehend. Indeed, they are quite boring. An explanation of the effortless processing of these stimuli is found in psychophysical theories of line processing mentioned above (that the eye and visual cortex are structurally attuned to perceive and process

The true work of art is born from the "artist": a mysterious, enigmatic, and mystical creation. It detaches itself from him, it acquires an autonomous life, becomes a personality, an independent subject, animated with a spiritual breath, the living subject of a real existence of being.

—Wassily Kandinsky

vertical and horizontal bars).[2] The grating on the right part of the display is reminiscent of a musical score (sans notes), but this may be coincidental. It is more probable (and consistent with Kandinsky's overall approach to art) that he was interested in stark (square wave) horizontal bars for their compelling visual impact.

The "soft" part of the picture is more difficult to process, but much more interesting than the bars. This part of the scene requires more time to process and we allocate much more of our attention to it. In the center portion of the painting Kandinsky shows us a novel juxtaposition of geometric forms and, in so doing, creates almost a comic relief from the "prison bars" to the right and left. Look at it. These sights are a delight to the eye, a flower inside a cage.

It was not until the twentieth century that gratings were systematically used as art, in a form that is called op art (optical art) or kinetic art—art that got emancipated from hushed galleries and is popularly displayed on T-shirts, fashionable magazines, and college dorms. Some respected art critics (and many people found standing around the sunny side of a barber shop) politely propose that op art, kinetic art, or geometric art is not "art" at all but merely the use of optical illusions or visual tricks. Despite these objections, op art addresses several fundamental topics that underlie all visual perception—even the perception of classical art.

Notable among recent artists is Bridget Riley, a British painter who composes mathematically precise scale models of dark and light lines. From these small models, full-sized paintings are produced (usually by Riley's assistants). One example of her work, titled *Current,* is shown in figure 3.6. Hold on to something sturdy and stare at this figure for about 20 seconds or more. What do you see? Incredibly, this static piece comes alive. So compelling is the illusion that some people report feeling vertigo. Artists in Riley's studio work on only a small exposed area at a time, with larger portions covered to avoid the compelling illusion.

People report several reactions to paintings of this sort:

• The contrast between dark and light (black and white lines in *Current*) becomes less intense over time; the sharp black and white contrast seems to fade to gray.

• An illusion of motion is created, but it is uneven: some parts "move" faster than others, which is disconcerting to the emotionally unstable viewer.

3.6 Bridget Riley, *Current* (1964). If you look at this painting for a few seconds you will experience a feeling of movement.

• Some parts do not seem to move at all.

• Some parts seem to scintillate or shimmer. The narrow connecting bars between the small semicircles in the center of the object seem to disintegrate into an oscillating beehive of activity, in my perception of this figure.

• Some viewers report the formation of mental images that are bizarre, emotional, and sometimes frightening. One person may report "seeing" a line of cobras gently rocking back and forth, while others may see the rapids of a river (and Riley's title of *Current* suggests that this latter interpretation is common).

Many of these effects can be understood in straightforward neurological and psychological terms. From studies of the perception of gratings (and other phenomena), it is known that the human visual system fatigues rather rapidly. If an ensemble of sensory (visual) neurons are stimulated by strong stimuli, such as the contrasting lines in the black and white field of a grating, the resulting fatigue renders them less sensitive to continuing stimulation. Experimental studies show that after only a few seconds, subjects report a "fading" of the apparent contrast in a black and white grating, a process that is called *adaptation*. This diminution of contrast effect (the graying of gratings, one might say) continues for about a minute and a half, after which the effect becomes reasonably stable, i.e., the graying doesn't get grayer. With exposure to harsh black and white lines, the neurons become less able to sense sharply defined visual signals (square waves). This neural fatigue accounts for the first noticeable effect—the fading of sharp black and white contours into a more muted, or gray, field.

The sensation of motion—scintillation, or shimmering—may also be the result of neural fatigue, although the exact mechanisms in this illusion are still not completely known. This effect is particularly strong in patterns that have little concrete reference and are highly redundant, as happens in many forms of op art. By the use of curved lines (see figure 3.6), the fatigue process is distributed unevenly over the art piece, which heightens the subjective sense of movement. Also, because the lines in Riley's painting are of uneven size, the rate of neural fatigue is uneven. Some ensembles of cells fatigue rapidly, others more slowly, and still others hardly at all. Thus, some features seem to "gray out" to such a degree that they shimmer, others move, and others remain still.

It may be that the visual system is distressed when viewing highly redundant figures. The basic logic of this analysis is that when we see a portion of a highly redundant scene, such as Riley's work and the work of other kinetic artists, we can infer the rest of the figure. The visual system normally uses redundancy to save itself effort in the processing of repetitive information. With overwhelming redundancy, however, the visual system is confused and distressed.

Still other theorists suggest that the disturbing effects of op art are due to a type of "flicker effect," something akin to old-time movies. This idea is based on the action of the eye in viewing. In addition to the conscious movements of the eye, there are also minute movements that are autonomic. When viewing highly redundant figures, these small eye movements, some argue, create a continuous aftereffect—which "flickers."

Finally, what the eye and brain sense is interpreted by higher-order cognitive processes, the sensory messages becoming associated with a person's previous experience with similar objects (cobras waving in the wind, for example).

It is likely that all of these explanations are valid and that all principles are working simultaneously. We do know that the effect can be dazzling to some and disturbing to others. Certainly, it is the purpose of many op artists to activate the viewer's eye and thinking brain and thereby stimulate him or her to provide a great portion of the "meaning" of the art.

Within the past few years the use of parallel lines in geometric art forms has become increasingly popular. Among the best known artists to use them is Frank Stella, whose *Itata* is shown in figure 3.7. These patterns are generally less distressing to the eye than op art forms and, in a sense, demand less of the viewer. In contrast to some forms of op art, these paintings are frequently relaxing and soothing, while giving the impression of modernism and synthetic intellectualism. Because they are devoid of tangible meaning, they seem ideally suited for the outer offices of executive vice-presidents—a place they are commonly seen.

Mach Bands and Lateral Inhibition

Another arrangement of monochromatic bars, in which a series of gray stripes is arranged in ascending order of brightness (see figure 3.9), is called "Mach bands." These curious visual stimuli have attracted the attention of psychophysicists and artists for over a century, as they help answer a thorny question

3.7 Frank Stella, *Itata*.

in the perception of contrasts and contours: How does the mind see distinctive edges in art (and other visual stimuli), given an imprecise retinal image of these stimuli? Humans are excellent edge detectors: we can read finely calibrated instruments, thread a needle, and detect minute differences in shades of gray, for example. Yet because of the structure of the human eye, the image that falls on the retina, with its millions of receptor cells, is far from crystal clear. Light is distorted and blurred as it passes through the lens and cornea, and further distorted as it passes through the liquid medium of the eye; the impression that falls on the retina does not have clear-cut lines or contours. How is it, then, that we are able to perform as if we could see such fine contours? Part of the solution is given by Gleitman (1981, p. 197): "The answer is that brightness contrast accentuates intensity differences between adjacent retinal areas, so much so that it sometimes creates perceived boundaries where physically there are none."

Mach's View of the World

Mach held that all fields of study, including physics and psychology, have the same subject matter: sensations. In *Contribution to the Analysis of Sensations* (1897) he illustrated the power of sensations with the sketch reproduced here. The accompanying text (trans. C. M. Williams; Chicago: Open Court, 1984) reads:

> Thus, I lie upon my sofa. If I close my right eye, the picture represented in the accompanying cut is presented to my left eye. In a frame formed by the ridge of my eyebrow, by my nose, and by my moustache, appears a part of my body, so far as visible, with its environment. My body differs from other human bodies . . . by the circumstance, that it is only partly seen, and, especially, is seen without a head. If I observe an element A within my field of vision, and investigate its connection with another element B within the same field, I step out of the domain of physics into that of physiology or psychology, provided B, to use the apposite expression of a friend of mine made upon seeing this drawing, passes through my skin.

3.8 Mach's view of the world.

3.9 Mach bands. Notice how the gray becomes lighter within each panel as viewed from right to left.

Mach bands provide one way for experimental psychologists (and others) to study the eye's ability to detect clear-cut lines. (They are named after the nineteenth-century Austrian physicist-philosopher Ernst Mach, who is better known for his measurement of the speed of sound.) Mach bands create a visual effect so convincingly that most people do not know they are an illusion, let alone understand the basis of the illusion. Yet the illusion is useful in making fine contour judgments, especially when viewing art. An example of Mach bands is shown in figure 3.9. Before reading the next paragraph, take a moment to look at these bars of varying degrees of gray. What do you see, especially at the place one bar touches another?

Look carefully at the edges (the lines between the rectangular bars). Notice that they are lighter when placed next to a darker panel (as you view the panels from right to left) and are darker when they are placed next to a light panel (as you view the panels from left to right). What you are experiencing is an illusion; the intensity of the gray is consistent within each panel. Place your hands over the other panels (or use two pieces of paper to cover up the other panels) and look only at one panel at a time. What do you see? How is it that our eyes can be tricked so spectacularly?

The actual (physical) intensities and the apparent intensities of the Mach bands are graphed in figure 3.10. In this figure the position of the band is

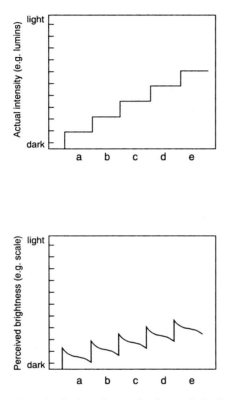

3.10 Actual light intensity (physical) and perceived (psychological) intensity for panels of Mach bands.

shown along the horizontal axis and light intensity along the vertical axis. The actual intensity is measured by physical means, for example with a photometer or light meter, which records light intensity (lumens). The apparent intensity is roughly equivalent to what we "see," not what is physically present. Adjacent gray bars are more discernible because the eye exaggerates the contrast between them.

This effect may seem puzzling, but the underlying neurological process is well documented if somewhat complicated. The curious change of perceived intensity is due to a neurological process called *lateral inhibition* (or lateral antagonism), in which neural activity in surrounding retinal cells is suppressed or inhibited when light reaches a given point on the retina. The more intense the light, the greater the lateral inhibition.

From Mach Bands to Neoimpressionist Art

In the left rectangle of figure 3.11 people see a white vertical line, while a black vertical line can be seen in the right rectangle. Yet, physically, the intensity of light from each of the figures does not indicate light or dark vertical lines. The illusionary effect is so strong that many people doubt it, but covering the right- and left-hand portions of the rectangles makes the illusory vertical white and black lines disappear. The effect is due to the excitation and lateral inhibition of receptor cells in the retina, which are involved in the organization of visual stimuli emanating from contrasting areas or contours. This curious neurological phenomenon allows us to see edges and boundaries more clearly than might be otherwise possible. Only recently have the effects of contrasting contours been studied scientifically, although artists have used the technique for centuries. At the end of the tenth century, artists in China used an outline-contrast form of painting whose

3.11   Mach bands.

Lateral inhibition helps account for many of our sensations as visual information begins its passage from the eye to the brain. The neurological process can be explained by reference to some original work in this field. In 1969 two American research physiologists, Frank Werblin and John Dowling, described the basic neural pathways and structures involved in lateral inhibition.[3] They did so by studying the optic neurons in what might seem the most unlikely of creatures for such an investigation: the mud puppy, a peculiar aquatic salamander whose habitat is the murky bottoms of muddy rivers. The mud puppy cannot see very much but its retinal nerve cells are relatively

3.12 Georges Seurat, *Invitation to the Side Show.*

effect was based on heightened impressions actuated by linear contrast. Also, ceramicists have used this technique for a very long time. Some of the French neoimpressionist painters, such as Georges Seurat and Paul Signac, deftly applied shade, half-light, subtle use of tint, and other visual illusions to enhance luminous contrasts between various shapes and the outlines of these shapes. If you look closely at Seurat's *Invitation to the Side Show* (figure 3.12), you will see that no actual lines are used to differentiate objects and people. The artist creates an impression of edges by using contrasting contours. See the next chapter for other examples, and the detail of the painting in figure 5.11.

huge, which makes it an ideal animal for visual research. Because of the size of the cells, it is possible to insert tiny probes (microelectrodes, whose tips are sometimes less than .01 mm in diameter) into them and thus record electrical activity in each cell. These experiments, which have been conducted on several species, are aptly called "single-cell" experiments. The research methodology involves stimulating the eye with flashes of light and recording the activities of various types of retinal cells.

Lateral inhibition is accomplished through the interaction of the different types of retinal cells described in chapter 1. Some receptor cells are initially stimulated, passing the signals along to the bipolar cells and then on to the ganglion cells. Some ganglion cells are excited by the light that falls on the center of the field—normally the spot where the eye is focused. When the horizontal cells then detect signals from the surrounding receptors (through the bipolar cells), they reduce (or inhibit) the processing of off-center signals. The effect is a heightened sense of edge detection in an otherwise ambiguous field.

Virtually all visual art (except monochromatic modern art) has contours and edges, some of which are very subtle. We "see" these edges even though the contrast between the dark and light portions are minute. Among the best examples of subtle contours are the beautiful porcelains from the Song (Sung) dynasty (960–1279) of China. The surface of these bowls and saucers consist of a creamy white glaze upon which designs (frequently of lotus) have been incised (see figure 3.13). (The porcelain bowls from the Ding factory in Hebei provide some of the most famous examples.) The contours of the design can be seen thanks to lateral inhibition, even though the physical contrast between the lighter and darker areas is very slight.

3.13 Ding bowl, twelfth century (Song Dynasty), white on white with contours visible because of lateral inhibition.

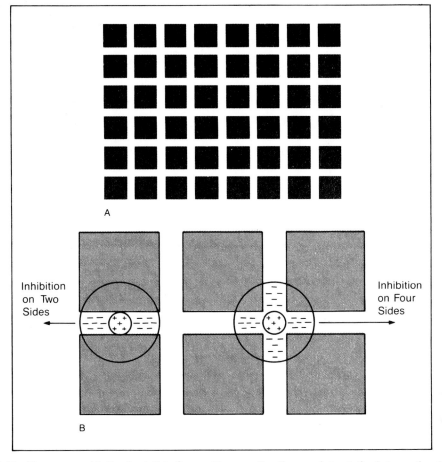

A

B

Inhibition on Two Sides

Inhibition on Four Sides

3.14 Hermann grid. Look at this figure. Do you "see" gray dots at the intersections? Do they disappear when you look at them?

The illusion of brightness contrast so effectively used by artists such as Rembrandt, Leyster, La Tour, Caravaggio, and many others is possible because of neuromechanisms, including lateral inhibition, located in the eye. These mechanisms operate independently of meaning and the larger perspective brought to these paintings by a person's rich intellectual history.

Another type of visual illusion attributed to lateral inhibition is seen in the Hermann grid, shown in figure 3.14A. Take a moment to look at this figure held a few feet away. Most people report "seeing" faint gray circles in the intersections; however, if you look at an intersection directly, the dots

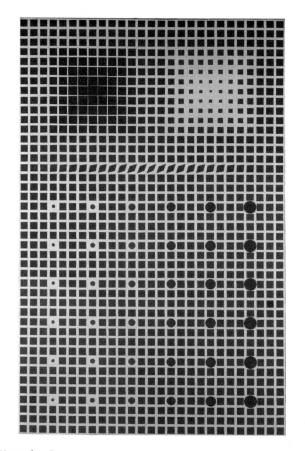

3.15 Victor Vasarely, _Supernovae_.

disappear. The impression of gray dots is purely illusory; the effect is easy to understand in terms of lateral inhibition.

From our previous discussion you know that the processing of signals from neighboring cells is inhibited. In the present case, the white "corridors" are surrounded by dark stimuli (boxes) on two sides and white stimuli on two sides, whereas the intersections are surrounded by four white fields (see figure 3.14B). White regions inhibit neighboring neural cells from firing. Thus, because the cells in the center of the intersection are surrounded by more white cells than other areas, the inhibition is greater than for other regions.

3.16   Victor Vasarely's *Vonal*, which employs a type of Mach bands and other illusionary techniques.

With the processing of the "whiteness" in that area inhibited, the impression passed on to the brain is that of faint gray dots.

The Hermann grid phenomenon has been used by some op artists to create a dynamic tension in their works. Consider the piece by Victor Vasarely called *Supernovae* (figure 3.15). The impression one gets from this work is one of uneasy mobility. Just as you get a handle on one part of it, it slips away and something else appears. Part of this transient impression is due to the appearance and disappearance of small gray dots at the intersections caused by lateral inhibition.

By now, the thought may have occurred to you that our real world is not made up of Mach bands and gratings; with the exception of a few isolated examples, these visual forms are more important to scientists interested in perception than to people interested in art. Yet it is difficult to find an example of visual perception that does *not* involve the structures and processes described above. In virtually all kinds of visual art, discrete forms are juxtaposed with boundaries or lines between them. These borders are clearly sensed by our eye and brain because of continuously working processes, such as lateral inhibition, that allow us to see the world more clearly than we might otherwise.

In your everyday viewing, try to find examples of edge detection that is enhanced by lateral inhibition. I have found an example of a type of Mach band (with the uneven brightness within the bars) in another painting by Vasarely (figure 3.16). As you view this picture, notice how the perceived intensity of the light within the strips is brighter (or darker) depending on the intensity of adjacent strips. Mach band effects and enhanced line detection effects occur all around us in nature and in two-dimensional art, not only in the highly stylized paintings of op artists (although these more closely approximate laboratory stimuli than do traditional art forms). Consider these effects as you study the art illustrated throughout this book.

4   Visual Cognition

> *One may be tempted to suppose that we, who experience the world through vision, experience a very different world from the worlds experienced by bats or dolphins, who rely more on hearing, dogs or rats, who make greater use of smell, . . . or spiders or scorpions who are attuned to mechanical vibrations. But at a sufficiently abstract level, our worlds are all the same three-dimensional Euclidean world.*
>
> —*Roger Shepard*

At the close of the last chapter we saw some examples of op art that are alive with movement. Those effects are largely due to differential inhibition of retinal cells. A much different sense of movement was created by Théodore Géricault, the early nineteenth-century French artist, in his *Derby at Epsom* (figure 4.1). (Ironically, Géricault died at the age of 33 after falling from his horse.) The painting is realistic in that we "feel" the movement, "hear" the thundering hoofbeats, and grasp the excitement of the moment. These sensations are based on a careful attention to reproducing the exact details of the derby. Stop reading the text and reexamine the horses and riders in this example. Do you "see" and "feel" the things mentioned above?

If we examine the anatomy of these horses, however, we find that they resemble no creature that inhabits this planet. Furthermore, the juxtaposition of horses is so pictorially planned that it is really awkward and unnatural. Indeed, the horses in this picture look more like the wooden steeds ceremoniously mounted on a merry-go-round, whose terrible expressions remain unchanged through a circular track. The entire scene might be repeated, with the same impossible horses, juxtapositions, and undulations, as the carousal makes another turn. I can almost hear the organ music. Now, look back at the *Derby at Epsom*. What do you "see"?

4.1 Théodore Gericault, *Derby at Epsom* (Musée du Louvre).

This exercise was intended to show how the same scene can be viewed from at least two different perspectives. In each case, what we "see" is, to a large degree, determined by our knowledge of what we "should" see, which is based on our previous experiences.

A much simplified sketch of Géricault's scene still captures many of the essential features of the painting. With only a few lines, it shows us familiar objects in well-known poses, which we recognize as running horses. In order for this illusion of movement to work, the observer must apply an extensive knowledge of the world to the interpretation of these few lines. The observer processes the information in what is called a top-down fashion. Consider how difficult it would be to design a computer program that would "view" the few lines in this sketch and arrive at the same conclusion as we humans do. Even very young children see immediately that this is a picture of horses being ridden by hard-driving jockeys (or wooden ponies with happy youngsters on top). Fishermen, old women, simple boys, college students, art critics, plumbers, chief executive officers, and all sorts of people accomplish this seemingly elementary task without effort. And yet all the king's horses and all the king's men can't yet design a computer program that "sees" and comprehends simple line drawings, a task we humans do every day with

lighting speed, stunning alacrity, and remarkable precision. Human vision and comprehension are among the most difficult challenges for those working in the field of artificial intelligence.

Visual Cognition

To better understand human visual cognition, we need to consider three stages of the problem.

• First, visual cognition ("seeing and understanding") involves the basic analysis of shapes, forms, colors, contours, contrasts, and movements. These primitives are sensed by the peripheral nervous system located in the eye. Electromagnetic signals in the form of physical energy are transduced to electrochemical signals and passed along the visual cortex for further processing. It is during this latter stage that visual recognition and higher-order processing takes place. (See chapters 1 and 2 for further exposition of these topics.)

• Second, primitive information is organized into fundamental forms. These fundamental forms are the basis for higher-order processing (such as the interpretation of what a form means) and are perceived mostly without prior learning or experience. An example of a fundamental form is the figure-ground pattern, in which an object (figure) stands out from the background (ground). The letters on this page (figure) stand out from the paper (ground). Psychologists who subscribe to the Gestalt (configuration) theory of cognition have studied fundamental forms in detail.

• Third, fundamental forms are given meaning through association with previous knowledge of the world stored in long-term memory (LTM). This final stage of the information processing model is sometimes called higher-order cognition, not because it is more elegant but because it occurs as the consequence of previous, "lower" stages. Furthermore, the thinking brain directs our attention to specific parts of a visual scene, giving greater notice

Seeing—More Than the Eye Beholds

Our mind "sees" things that the eye alone never could. Take the figure of an ice skater that was used as a symbol at a recent Olympiad. Most people recognize immediately these few lines—16 of them—as an ice skater in full stride. In the context of the Winter Olympics, the facility for correctly identifying this figure would be even faster and more accurate.

The next figure illustrates a striking example of "information" and perception. What do *you* see? If you have difficulty seeing any meaningful form, try to squint your eyes, place the figure five or six feet away, or, if you are nearsighted, remove your glasses. Do you see the brunette woman? The form was created by "information" in the form of shadings distributed over a screen, which in the present example is 22 dots high by 26 dots wide, or 572 total dots. In effect, this is a kind of "information palette" from which a meaningful image is constructed, similar to the display on a television screen, which is composed of a raster with pixels (individual light cells).

The third figure is an effort by Victor Vasarely to fashion a portrait of Georges Pompidou (for whom a modern art museum in Paris is named) out of 37 lines of varying density. As in the previous two examples, a type of paradox exists in this picture: the more it is degraded, the clearer it becomes. If you squint your eyes or look at this picture at a distance, the perceived image is actually seen more clearly. The individual contours, lines, and dots, which are sharply delineated at close range, become less clearly defined at a distance. As our perception of these separate elements is distorted, cognitive mechanisms are activated. In the present examples these mechanisms now tell us we are viewing a skater, a brunette, and a famous person.

Two perceptual/cognitive processes are at work here. (1) If the image is further degraded, the impression is more easily recognizable. The visual explanation of this effect is that information from specific contours is reduced if the contours are degraded. These specific contours are irrelevant, or even distracting, in decoding this image; therefore, their diminution enhances the perception of the object. Contours blend and the image is perceived as a whole. (2) The image is given meaning. We see people's faces and forms. These images are long familiar to each individual, and those impressions are important parts of the LTM. We are able to classify these impressions as belonging to a "class" of stored information (e.g., faces, skaters, and so on). Furthermore, we expect to see these objects because of context. We use top-down processing to assist in their recognition. Thus, someone visiting the Olympic village during the Winter Olympic games would *expect* to see an emblem of an ice skater.

4.2 **Three figures, including Victor Vasarely's** *Portrait of Georges Pompidou.*

to salient features or things that are of personal interest. Finally, the brain adds information to the raw visual impressions, which gives a richness of meaning far beyond the simple stimuli it receives.

In modern cognitive terms, the first two stages initiate the process of visual cognition and are sometimes called bottom-up processing, in which the stimuli drive the workings of visual awareness. The third stage is called top-down processing because cognitive operations drive visual awareness, although at both stages elements of top-down and bottom-up processing are operating.

Both top-down and bottom-up can be illustrated in the droodle shown in figure 4.3. Try to guess what these few lines "mean." (For the "answer" see the end of this chapter.) Each of the three stages through which visual processing takes place can be identified for this figure. During the first, information from the simple line drawing is received by the photoreceptors in the eye and begins its voyage to the brain.

Painting must not be exclu-sively visual or retinal.

—Marcel Duchamp

Fundamental distinctions are made between basic contours, and specific neurons are stimulated in the visual cortex. In the second stage certain features of the figure are perceived as belonging together and others as belonging to other groupings. One might perceive the three features on the left side of the figure as belonging to one grouping and the two features on the right to another. Finally, all of the features are integrated into a meaningful whole—a process called *redintegration*. At this stage we "see" the object as it was intended to be seen. This stage is dependent on our vast world knowledge, and possibly on additional information provided (see answer). Without knowledge, the meaning (at least the "intended" meaning) is lost. Let us examine in some detail the second and third stages as they apply to the perception of art.

4.3 What do you see?

Direct or Indirect Perception?

A central question in the science of sensory/perceptual psychology that pertains to the perception of art is whether visual forms are perceived "directly" or "indirectly." Those who subscribe to the "direct" theory hold that sensory information in and of itself is sufficient for a person to perceive the world accurately. This notion, most closely associated with the late James Gibson of Cornell University, is sometimes called an "ecologically valid" theory (see Gibson 1979), as it holds that the study of perception ought to be conducted under real world conditions. Under these conditions, real objects are perceived accurately by people; it is only under artificial or "ecologically invalid" conditions, such as might be experienced under laboratory conditions of illusions and other unnatural stimuli, that indirect perception occurs.

The original theory of indirect perception was suggested by Helmholtz (and others) during the last century. It proposes that most of our perceptions are constructed from inferences about the real world. If we know what to look for in a figure, then we are likely to see it. The indirect perception is related to top-down processing of visual stimuli, in which perception is driven by our expectations of how the world should look.

Rather than choosing one theory and discarding the other, we might do better to consider both theories as valid but as dealing with different parts of the sensory process. It is certainly believable that complex objects are sensed as primitive figures—detected by the eye and initially processed by the visual cortex. It is also true that the brain is an enormously complex thinking device, rich in memory associations and adept at solving problems requiring insight and imagination. We see things through the eyes, but we understand things with the mind.

The perception of art has struggled with similar questions, and the same answer seems relevant. When we study a piece of art, the complex object is initially sensed as a series of primitive light signals. These signals are integrated into a composite picture, in which the mind adds interpretation. The final perception is the result of these two factors working together.

4.4 Carracci trick drawing. As early as 1600 artists drew sketches similar to what we now call droodles but were then known as "trick figures." This is a modern redrawing of a trick figure by one of the Carracci. It shows "a Capuchin preacher asleep in his pulpit," but we are only likely to see it if we already know what to look for.

Fundamental Forms

Stimuli that are commonly organized into a pattern or basic configuration are called fundamental forms. As mentioned, our eye and brain naturally divide visual patterns into figure and ground. In this section we encounter several types of fundamental forms that serve as the building blocks for more complex images, including art.

Why is the perception of fundamental forms so important to the human observer? To cast this discussion in a broader context, consider the purpose of visual perception among members of our species and other animals. It is likely that primitive sense organs capable of perceiving light energy evolved very early in the history of multicellular creatures for the purpose of finding food, heat (or cold), and light (or dark) and avoiding harm. As mentioned in chapter 1, fossilized remains indicate that the Paleozoic trilobites had primitive eyes capable of seeing. Some fossil eyes date back to 500 million years ago, and it is likely that some forms of photosensitive devices are older than that. Primitive invertebrates, jellyfish for example, have photosensitive cells. Even echinoderms (e.g., starfish and sea urchins) have eyespots found at the end of a tentacle. More elegant seeing instruments developed when photosensitive regions became indented and were protected by a transparent layer of cells that later developed into what we now know as the lens. This enclosed photoreceptive instrument became more complex and a profusion of cells within it evolved into the areas of the retina. Other refinements of the visual sensing apparatus developed over millions of years until the eye, as we presently know it, emerged.

From our discussion of the survival properties of vision (chapter 2), recall the three important things that vision tells us:

4.5 Figure and ground illustration. Even though we cannot tell what it is, this figure is seen as standing out from its background. We naturally separate figure from ground— an important step in form perception.

- What is an object?
- Where is it?
- What is it doing?

It is hardly coincidental that the topics of *form perception, depth perception,* and the *perception of movement* are three major areas of visual research and theory. All three of these topics are important for the perception of art. The first will be considered here and the others later.

What is an object? First of all, an object must be a thing distinguishable from other things. A rowboat made invisible by a dense fog is not an object, at least not an object we can see. Something must differentiate an object from its context, and a commonly perceived demarcation is achieved through figure-ground separation, as shown in figure 4.5. This seemingly meaningless white blob is clearly seen as separate from its background: everyone with normal vision sees it this way. This process is one of the most elementary in object perception. (Keep in mind that complex forms, as expressed in two-dimensional art, are composed of elementary forms.) Look again at the blob. Notice that the contour, the transition between one level of reflected light and another, is more a part of the figure than it is of the ground. We see the figure as resting on top of the black ground and infer that the black background continues beneath the white form. (We can reverse this illusion by imagining the white portion to be a hole cut out of a black card.) A further

4.6 Do you recognize this famous couple? (See figure 8.14.)

aspect of visual perception is illustrated in this figure: the role played by orientation and top-down processing. Rotate the figure 90 degrees counter-clockwise. Now what do you see?

Our ability to distinguish figure from ground is, in part, due to the intensities of light reflected from an object. In figures 4.5 and 4.6 the amount of light reflected from the white surfaces is about 80 percent of the light falling on them, while the black surfaces reflect only about 4 or 5 percent of the light falling on them. The ratio of reflected light from the white (figure) and black (ground) is approximately 20 to 1! That gets our attention. To put this concept in a slightly different context, consider the printed type on this page and the background of the paper upon which it is printed. Here the ratio of the light reflected from the white paper and from the black type is about 16 to 1. That is, about 16 times

The first painting was just a line that surrounded the shadow of a man projected by the light of the sun on the ground.

—Robert Delaunay

4.7   A reversible figure-ground form in which either two profiles or a white chalice can be seen. From Gleitman (1981).

as many quanta per second of electromagnetic energy are being absorbed by the neurons in your retina from the white background as from the black type. However, the *ratio* of light reflected from figure and from ground remains reasonably stable over a wide range of ambient light conditions—a phenomenon aptly called brightness constancy. Brightness constancy is one of several important cues that allow us to recognize a black cat regardless of whether it is seen in a darkened room or lighted room. A cat in a dark room reflects less light, but then so do the other objects in the dark room. Our ability to recognize a cat under a wide range of viewing conditions is one of the most spectacular of visual wonders, one we routinely take for granted. This important principle of perception is crucial in the viewing of art: within a fairly wide range of illumination, the balance between figure and ground remains constant.

Another type of figure-ground illustration, interesting to perceptual psychologists, is one in which the figure can be seen as the ground and the ground can be seen as the figure (so-called reversible figures). A well-known example is shown in figure 4.7, in which the viewer may exercise some control over which part of the illustration is the ground and which is the figure. Note that the contour "belongs" to the figure. It can belong to the white vase or to the two profiles, but when part of one figure it is not part of the other. A reversible figure in which figure-ground difference is not based on large black and white regions is shown in figure 4.9. This figure has

4.8   Queen Elizabeth and Prince Philip can be seen in this commemorative vase in a figure and ground representation.

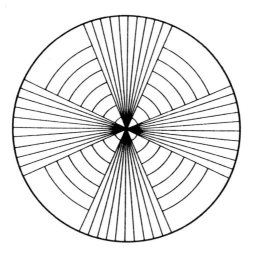

4.9 A figure-ground illusion in which the figures are of nearly equal light intensity.

two equally intense features (circular lines and radiating straight lines), each of which can be seen as figure or ground. Sometimes it is difficult to alternate between the figure and ground (as illustrated in figure 4.9), but, if you have difficulty, continue to look at the object. Sometimes if you squint your eyes, the figure will suddenly switch. Some people get better at switching with practice, while others never seem to get the knack of it. I am mystified by these individual differences and suspect it may have something to do with right hemisphere brain functioning. This illustration is interesting in another regard; when the figure is the straight lines, the ground (the curved lines) appears to continue behind the figure. However, when the figure and ground are reversed, no illusion is experienced of additional straight lines emanating from the center and falling behind the curved lines.

Some artists have incorporated reversible figure-ground illusions in their paintings, with engaging results. Among the most intriguing is the inventive M. C. Escher, whose *Sky and Water I* is shown in figure 4.10.

In the following two figures, two well-known modern artists have used figure-ground motifs in strikingly different ways, one in stark black and white, the other rich in detail. Victor Vasarely uses figure-ground interplay in an illustration of two lovers embracing each other (figure 4.11). This figure is confusing to many people because, if one object is the figure (say the white form), then the other (the black part) is seen as the background. However,

4.10 M. C. Escher, *Sky and Water I* **(© 1938 M. C. Escher Foundation). The figure-ground separation process changes from top to bottom, as birds change to fish.**

in order for this painting to work (to be seen as two lovers), both figures must be conceptualized as "figures" simultaneously—a difficult perceptual task. But then, perhaps this was exactly what the artist intended: to create an ambiguous painting that requires some effort on the part of the viewer. Or perhaps the artist intended that the two figures be seen to alternate rapidly—with first one and then the other appearing as the featured figure, much as happens to our ears when we hear a musical fugue. Or (alas) we might see

4.11 Figure-ground reversal by Victor Vasarely. Two lovers are shown embracing; either can be seen as figure or ground.

an attraction/aversion "fugue," such as we often experience in the capricious nature of amorous relationships. Even if such an elaborate stratagem was not planned, the piece invites critical cognitive analysis and serves to illustrate some interesting principles of perception.

In Salvador Dalí's *Slave Market with Disappearing Bust of Voltaire* (figure 4.12), the bust of Voltaire predominates in most people's interpretation, especially when the painting is reproduced at small scale. However, when viewed at close range (or when this detail is enlarged), the two nuns predominate. As with Vasarely's lovers, it is nearly impossible to see both Voltaire and the nuns at the same time, but one can see each clearly if it is taken as the figure.

Perceptual Organization and Gestalt Psychology

A very interesting episode in the history of psychology was the proposal by a group of German scholars—notably Max Wertheimer, Kurt Koffka, and Wolfgang Köhler—that *form* is the primitive unit of perception.[1] The Gestalt psychologists, as they were called (taking their name from the German word that is close to the English word "configuration"), believed that the key to understanding perception—and thereby the larger domain of all

4.12 Salvador Dalí, *The Slave Market with Disappearing Bust of Voltaire,* with detail below. The two nuns standing in the archway at left-center reverse to form a bust of Voltaire.

psychology—was to be found by studying the way the brain organizes basic stimuli. Furthermore, they postulated that the organization of patterns is an inherent property of humans; knowledge of these organizing phenomena would elucidate the way the brain functions. From the Gestaltists' laboratory dazzling geometric patterns were created, some of which produced visual illusions and others of which showed how the brain naturally organizes visual stimuli—all under the rubric of perceptual organization.

Because perceptual organization is so common to the human observer, we tend to think of the process as being uninteresting, uncomplicated, or routine. Yet, many believe, the way the brain organizes incoming visual patters is fundamental to our understanding of both psychology and art. Several principles of perceptual organization are discussed below.

PROXIMITY

If like objects are located near each other in the physical world, we tend to group them together perceptually. Similar features are grouped together as shown in figure 4.13, in which six vertical lines are perceived not as six independent, unorganized lines but as three sets of two. The six small circles are likewise seen as two sets of three circles. We tend to organize proximal stimuli, if they are similar in shape, color, form, or lines, into patterns. Think of any art piece you have seen, either in this book or in a gallery, and analyze it in terms of proximity (see figure 4.16). It is likely that many images rely

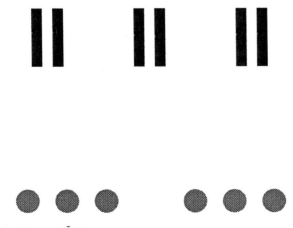

4.13 **Grouping by proximity.**

on proximity, which compels the viewer to "see" the world in a certain predetermined way.

Interestingly, the same principle seems to apply to other sensory stimuli, notably sound and music. When we hear music we naturally organize it into rhythms or beats, so that "six toots on a trumpet" may be heard as three sets of two toots (or two sets of three toots, or one toot and five toots, and so on). What the mind's ear hears is a pattern of information, *just as the mind's eye sees a pattern of information* in the visual display presented in figure 4.13. And what *we* hear and see is basically very much what people have experienced for millennia.

This universal mode of seeing (and hearing, tasting, smelling, and feeling) seems to be an integral, evolved component of the human nervous system—its main purpose being to usefully represent the physical world to a thinking creature. The creatures that performed these operations successfully were presumably more adaptive and more likely to procreate than those that didn't.

Perhaps you have now made the connection between the way the brain organizes visual and auditory stimuli and the Kandinsky painting *Pictures at an Exhibition* (and its relation to Mussorgsky's music; see figure 3.5). There are many parallels in the ways the sensory systems (vision and audition, for example) process information. These include the perception and processing of rudimentary stimuli such as visual gratings and auditory cadence. Perhaps, at a sufficiently abstract level, the physical world is known to us through a sensory system that is attuned to a limited number of elementary patterns. These patterns are collected by the peripheral sensory systems and sent on to a brain that is evolutionarily predisposed to receive and process them. If this reasoning is valid, and considerable evidence from both the behavioral and neurological sciences supports such a notion, then the seeing of complex visual forms, as when we view art, is a matter of sensing basic shapes, passing them along to a receptive brain, and combining the impression with our vast knowledge of the world from which inferences are fashioned.

SIMILARITY

Similar elements, shapes, sizes, and colors tend to be grouped together, as shown in figure 4.14. The inclination to see similar elements as belonging to the same class is so compelling that we interpret this illustration as three columns of two circles, or three lines of solid circles and three lines of open

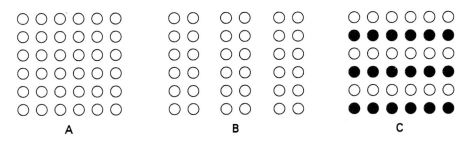

4.14 **Grouping by similarity. We tend to organize the circles in** *A* **as three columns of two circles.**

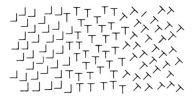

4.15 **Grouping by similarity. The T's in the center are perceived as belonging to a different class of objects. From Beck (1966).**

circles—although the latter impression is far less salient due to the solid circles being seen as figure. Many other common examples of **grouping by similarity** can be found in everyday life—such as the above boldface type, which seems to belong together while the remaining type belongs to another category.

A slightly more complex example of the ability of the perceptual system to organize stimuli by similarity is shown in figure 4.15, in which the group of T's in the center stand out from the rest—even though the physical energy reaching the retina is nearly identical for each of the three sets of information.

Similar patterns have also been used in art to organize a viewer's perception of an object. One such example is shown in figure 4.16, a portrait of Queen Elizabeth I, in which the artist (perhaps unconsciously) uses grouping by similar pattern to focus the viewer's attention. Take a moment and look at the small portrait. Notice how you naturally tend to organize the features of the subject's collar into a circular pattern. The similar qualities in Elizabeth's hair are grouped in pairs, and the pairs are organized into a larger pattern surrounding her face. All of these organizational patterns accentuate

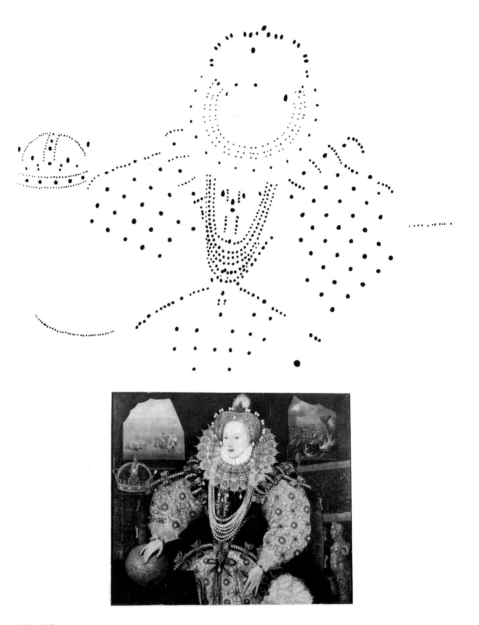

4.16 The Armada portrait of Queen Elizabeth I. The use of similar objects, beads, jewels, and collar material compels the viewer to organize these common features. Schematic drawing from Malins (1980).

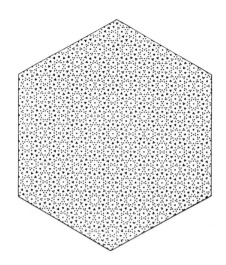

4.17   Rival organization of patterns. The tendency to see unstable circles is caused by features being parts of more than a single organizational scheme. From Marr (1982).

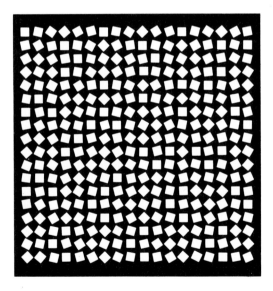

4.18   Another example of conflicting organizational patterns. As you look at this figure you will notice that once you establish one pattern of circles, another circle captures some of the elements of the first circle. This continual visual competition makes for a dynamic and (to many) interesting piece of art. (Design by Leonard Kitts.)

the features of the face—the focal point of the painting. Other examples of grouping by similarities are shown in the diagram above the painting.

A more complex visual example is shown in figure 4.17, in which rival organizations compete for our attention. There is a strong inducement to see a number of circles formed by certain common elements; but then some of these elements are parts of other circles as well. The psychological effect, in which the object becomes "alive" with changing formations, is a result of perceptual rivalry between two natural organizational patterns (circles). The object has a dynamic tension that makes it difficult to see a stable form. Many types of op art, discussed earlier, and geometric clothing patterns take advantage of the tendency to organize ambiguous features in one direction and then to see the same features as part of another pattern.

CONTINUATION

Objects that flow "naturally" in one direction are likely to be seen as belonging together. Our eyes seem to go with the flow. An example of continuation is shown in figure 4.19A. What do you see? It is probable that you see this figure as a straight line through which a curved line has been drawn, rather than as two "awkward" figures (B). It may be that this strong visual tendency (and the related principle of "common fate") is related to the physics of moving objects. We see things in motion as, more or less, keeping on course rather than making oblique angular changes in midcourse. Indeed, living in

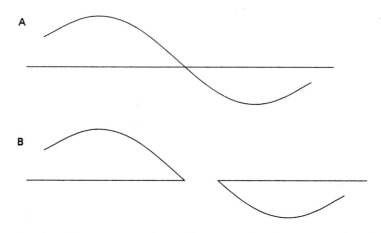

4.19 Continuation. We see two continuous lines (A) rather than two "awkward" lines (B).

a three-dimensional, potentially dangerous world, governed by laws of the physical universe (e.g., gravity, conservation of momentum), it is vital that we be able to predict trajectories (on which the law of continuation seems to be partially based) in order to avoid falling branches, spears, and left hooks. It seems that we now use those ancient abilities to hit a baseball, avoid fast-moving cars on the freeway, and predict the location of a golf ball badly hooked.

CLOSURE

Related to the law of continuation is closure—or the tendency to see figures as unitary, enclosed wholes. In figure 4.20A we "see" a figure of a circle. Technically, a circle is an *enclosed* round figure. This figure is not exactly a circle, and yet, if we saw this object momentarily projected (as in a tachistoscopic presentation), we would be certain that it was a true circle. And, generally speaking, in informal usage we commonly consider a wide class of visual objects "circles" if they are close to being circles.

In figure 4.20B we may be able to "see" the composite figure of a knight and his horse, not a series of unconnected shapes. Yet any one of these shapes

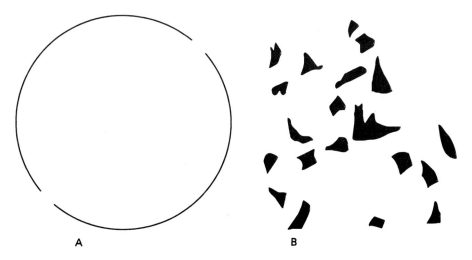

A   B

4.20   Closure. We see a circle (*A*) even though technically it is two separate lines. In *B* we may see a whole pattern of a knight and horse, not unassociated black dabs. Psychological tests of mental ability and organic brain damage have been devised using lacunary stimuli such as these.

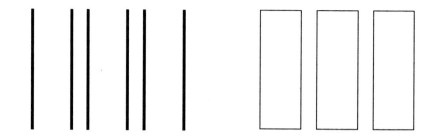

4.21 "Weak" and "strong" forms.

alone is empty of meaning. Only when we gain closure is the object recognizable and its components become an integral part of the whole.

Another example of closure and its psychological impact is seen in figure 4.21. Here we see six vertical lines on the left; at right, with the addition of top and bottom lines, we see a much different form. Such closed figures seem somehow to be "better" or "stronger." In general, the more basic the closed figure, the more psychologically salient it is (a topic closely related to *Prägnanz*). Thus, a rectangle is more "significant" than open lines, a square more "significant" than a rectangle, and a circle more "significant" than a square.

PRÄGNANZ

The German word *Prägnanz* translates into English as "pregnant with meaning," and is one of the more controversial aspects of Gestalt theory. Figures with *Prägnanz* are said to have "good shapes." This somewhat slippery concept (e.g., good to whom?) is applied to typical, geometrically regular configurations, such as a circle, square, triangle, or hexagon. The psychological implication of *Prägnanz* is that our mind seeks stable, regular figures in the environment and that we may feel uneasy if unable to find such objects, frequently without knowing the source of our discomfort. Artists and film makers capitalize on this tendency by creating scenes pregnant with "bad" (unstable) gestalts that are visually factious and crave stability. A similar phenomenon is found in music, in which unresolved musical patterns cry out for resolution. During the 1960s, folk singers would frequently end a tune with an open chord or unresolved chord, poignantly positing a type of musical question, "What?, Why?, Where?, When?" "What have they done to the rain?" A geometric example of conflicting "good" forms is shown in figure

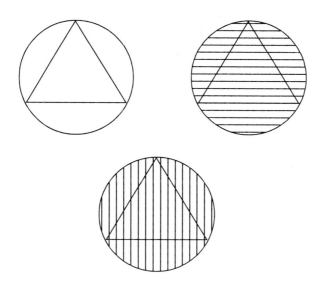

4.22   Competing stable forms.

4.22, in which an equilateral triangle is shown on the left and then embedded in a circle with parallel lines on the right. The stronger tendency is to see the parallel lines here and not the triangle. If the competition between the two stable forms is removed, as in the bottom figure, the triangle becomes visible.

Yet another way to understand the notion of *Prägnanz* is to consider the figures in figure 4.23. Spend a few moments looking at object *A*. What do you see? It is possible to see a three-dimensional figure, but it is likely that you see a two-dimensional hexagon. As a matter of fact, once you see the three-dimensional cube in this figure, it is hard to hold it; the tendency is to slip back to a two-dimensional figure. Now, consider the remaining figures. Objects *B* and *D* seem to be three-dimensional—it is difficult to see two-dimensional forms in these examples—while object *C* switches between two- and three-dimensionality. In all these examples, our perception of these ambiguous figures reverts to the most stable forms (those with *Prägnanz*). You might try this observation with a friend by exposing each of the four figures independently for about 30 seconds. (Cover up the other figures and show one form at a time.) While the observer looks at each figure, record whether he or she experiences two dimensions or three dimensions. (The observer could indicate his or her perception by holding up two or three fingers.)

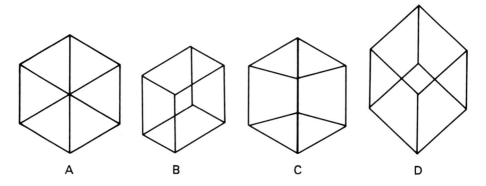

4.23   **Two- and three-dimensional-appearing figures that seek stability or** *Prägnanz.*

Typically, people see *A* and *C* as more two-dimensional and *B* and *D* as three-dimensional. There is a strong tendency for each of us to see stable forms in these objects, whether the stable form is expressed in two or three dimensions.

Finally, we see an example of *Prägnanz* in figure 4.24, in which a compound object (*A*) can be decomposed and explained in several ways. It could be that it is composed of two overlapping independent forms, as shown in *B* (and this is the "best" *Prägnanz*), or it could be that there are two nonoverlapping figures, as shown in *C,* or that three forms are used, as shown in *D.* The most parsimonious explanation is that there are two overlapping forms, and this explanation seems most "natural." We have an inclination to find more fundamental explanations for percepts, rather than "unnatural" interpretations.

To many cognitive psychologists (including your author), the work of the early perceptual psychologists is significant for two reasons. First, they identified fundamental forms that are processed similarly by all human observers; and second, they advocated a doctrine that was at odds with the environmentally determinist approach that dominated psychological theory during this period. The idea that objects, forms, and shapes were "naturally" processed in similar ways by all members of the same species was anathema to many academic psychologists during the early part of this century. While these Gestalt concepts are now important parts of cognitive psychology, the influence of radical behaviorism, as expressed by John Watson and others, has been sharply reduced. Presently, cognitive psychologists are searching for universal laws and principles of how the mind perceives reality, stores infor-

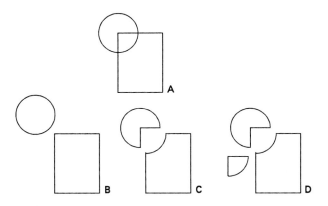

4.24 **Overlapping figures or three objects combined to make one: an illustration of** *Prägnanz*.

mation, and reacts to environmental forces. Curiously, the perception of simple forms is now seen as an important link in the chain of knowledge, which—in its idealized form—is expressed in a unified theory of cognition. At present such megatheories are immature, but serious efforts are being made to develop them.

The Gestalt laws of perceptual organization were fertile ground in which the aspirations of modern cognitive psychologists could grow. Other psychologists, notably perceptual psychologists, suggested that other laws of perceptual organization, which are generally simpler, less subjective, and more demonstrable empirically, could better account for the perception of forms. There is little disagreement, however, that the patterns of perceptual organization discussed in this chapter are major factors in determining how objects are perceived. And, for the purpose of understanding the perception of art, I would propose that the comprehension of complex visual stimuli, such as those exhibited in art, begins by distinguishing salient featural components that are then recombined in the mind's eye. The aesthetic experience is greater than the sum of the parts, but it begins with parts.

★The droodle in figure 4.3 is either "Casper the Ghost watching TV" or "A view of a scrubwoman and her pail."

5 Context, Cognition, and Art

> *This life's five windows of the soul*
> *Distorts the Heavens from pole to pole,*
> *And leads you to believe a lie*
> *When you see with, not thro', the eye.*

—*William Blake*

Art is always viewed in context. To the layperson, context is the location of the art—such as the Metropolitan Museum of Art or the National Gallery—and one's companions—Aunt Betty from Sun City, your roommate from college, a new boyfriend. To the cognitive scientist, however, context includes two additional features: the physical composition of the visual field and the personal history of the viewer.

The first of these was mentioned in previous chapters. Because the physical composition of the visual field is an important part of the scientific study of context, we shall extend our previous discussion and see how physical factors *interact* with other contextual features in a visual display. Basic perception is fixed by physiological structures that are jointly enjoyed by all members of the species. These invariant structures are an essential element in the understanding of the initial stages of visual perception. As personally portentous as most of us believe we are, the laws of physics and physiology do not wrap themselves around us; rather we wrap our impressions of the world around the laws of nature. Both individual psychology *and* common physiology contribute to the perception of art.

Another type of context will be introduced in this chapter, the context provided by an observer's rich personal knowledge as he or she views art. Sometimes this type of perception is called higher-order cognition, as it engages past knowledge and the social/political setting in the interpretation of art. Each of us approaches an art object with significantly different perspectives because of our unique personal history and social experiences. Knowledge is not haphazardly arranged in the brain, but is systematically organized around themes, or schemes, that are important structures in the understanding of art as well as all of reality. We will learn more about this intriguing topic in this chapter, but now consider how physiology and psychology function in the seeing and understanding of a classic piece of art.

Mona Lisa: **A Case Study**

When you visit the Louvre in Paris and see Leonardo's portrait *Mona Lisa,* you will see the physical features of that painting essentially identically to how all other humans see them—because the light reflected from the painting and the initial processing by one's neurophysiology are fixed by physical laws. In this example, notice the misty ambience that permeates the painting. Leonardo created this effect by *sfumato,* the subtle transition of tones that gives a hazy softness to the contours. In addition, you can clearly see certain contours, note figure-ground relationships, detect colors, discover contrasts and "good gestalts," and so on. Basic visual information is similarly organized by all people.

The *meaning,* or semantic value, derived from these basic forms, however, is subject to wide individual differences. When *you* see Mona Lisa's enigmatic smile, you see it differently than might your companion, or I, or Marcel Duchamp, or indeed Leonardo. But for centuries, the painting and especially the smile have been evocative.

The "message," meaning, and interpretation of art depend on your previous specialized knowledge of painting and related phenomena. That knowledge, plus your vast idiosyncratic knowledge of the world, contribute to the (internal) context in which art is viewed. If you know something of the history of Renaissance art, the work and personal life of Leonardo, the religious dogmas of the time, the medium used, and so on, then when you actually see *Mona Lisa* you have already formed an opinion about what you are seeing. Even if you slept through Art 1, you look out at the world with a thousand hypotheses—about people, fashion, landscapes, facial hair, smiling women, and the unique attributes of great art. Even now, as you read and think about art and cognition, your mind is alive with the formation of ideas about paintings in general, and *Mona Lisa* in specific. Actually seeing *Mona Lisa* is a test of your hypotheses about the world (the world as anticipated by

5.1 Leonardo Da Vinci, *Mona Lisa (La Gioconda)*.

your mind) and what the world is (as represented by your senses). The interplay between the internal (cognitive) representation of reality and the external (physical) representation is a fascinating problem in cognitive psychology, art, science, and philosophy.

If you have ever toured a gallery with a friend, you know that differences in the interpretation of art vary widely; even among professional art critics (those paragons of artistic judgment), sharp differences are commonplace. Each of us carries around with him or her a vast and unique mental storehouse of information about the world. And, since higher-order perception is determined by our past knowledge (a kind of personal "cerebral encyclopedia"), your view of Mona's smile is probably different from mine.

Physical Context

The physical context of visual objects has a substantial impact on basic perception. Things may appear bigger, smaller, brighter, darker, bluer, redder, closer, farther, clearer, hazier, and so on, than they actually are, depending on the nature of the object and the context in which it is placed. We begin our analysis of physical context with several simple examples, and then move to more complex examples including pieces of art.

BRIGHTNESS CONTRAST

First, consider the importance of physical context on perceived brightness, as shown in figure 5.3. In the sets of concentric squares at left, the two small gray squares are of identical intensity, yet the one at top appears much darker than

While working on The Battle of Anghiari, *Leonardo painted his most famous portrait, the* Mona Lisa. *The delicate* sfumato *of* The Virgin of the Rocks *is here so perfected that it seemed miraculous to the artist's contemporaries. The forms are built from layers of glazes so gossamer-thin that the entire panel seems to glow with a gentle light from within. But the fame of the* Mona Lisa *comes not from this pictorial subtlety alone; even more intriguing is the psychological fascination of the sitter's personality. Why, among all the smiling faces ever painted, has this particular one been singled out as "mysterious"? Perhaps the reason is that, as a portrait, the picture does not fit our expectations. The features are too individual for Leonardo to have simply depicted an ideal type, yet the element of idealization is so strong that it blurs the sitter's character. Once again the artist has brought two opposites into harmonious balance.*

—H. W. Janson

Mona-Leo

Leonardo da Vinci's *Mona Lisa* is probably the most thoroughly analyzed painting in the world. Critics have pointed out that the background is "impossible," and, if you look at the countryside behind the woman, the side on the left does not match the side on the right. Psychoanalytically inclined critics have suggested that Leonardo may have experienced an "Oedipus anxiety" caused by an unresolved sexual fantasy involving his mother, which was manifest in his portraits of women. Yet other critics suggest that in many of his portraits a self-portrait can be seen. Lillian Schwartz has shown us the combined faces of Mona Lisa and Leonardo, in a work called *Mona-Leo*. What do you think of this effort? Is Lisa actually Leo in drag? To my eyes there is a striking symmetry in this image. What alternative hypotheses might be supported by this observation?

5.2   Lillian Schwartz, *Mona-Leo*.

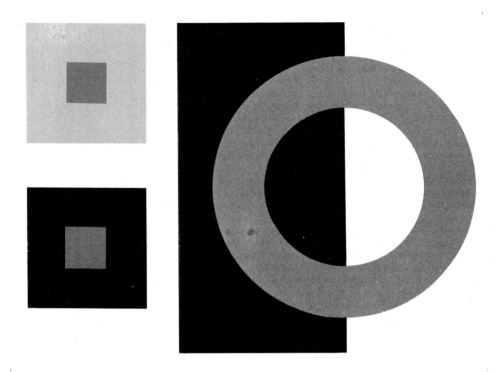

5.3 Two examples of perceived brightness and context.

the one at bottom. The effect is due to the context of the surrounding (darker or lighter) squares: the perception of brightness is determined, in part, by the contrast between a figure and contextual stimuli. An even more dramatic contextual effect is presented in the figure at right, in which a ring of uniform grayness appears lighter on the left-hand part of the display (where it is surrounded by a black field) than on the right (where it is surrounded by a white field).

The influence of context on the perceived intensity of an object is called brightness contrast, a condition in which a viewer tends to bias the light intensity of an object in an opposite direction from the background intensity. Thus, dark backgrounds tend to make enclosed figures lighter, and light backgrounds make enclosed figures darker. Since lightness and darkness are also cues we use for distance, it follows that context can also influence the apparent nearness of an object or, in some cases, whether a figure is concave or convex.

The contextual bias in brightness contrast is based on the same principles mentioned earlier in connection with contour perception and Mach bands (chapter 3). The anatomical explanation is based on lateral inhibition, in which when some retinal neurons are stimulated, adjacent neurons responding to contrasting features of the visual field are inhibited. Sometimes when we study the perception of art, it is easy to be deluded into thinking that these marvelously complex neurological components evolved for the sake of aesthetic felicity. This is wrong. They evolved over millions of years so our ancestors could see contours, differentiate objects, notice movement, and understand a three-dimensional physical world with an image cast upon a two-dimensional eye.

PERCEIVED CONTRASTS IN ART

Artists have known for centuries about these basic visual effects, though not about the psychological/physiological causes. One of the most sublime artistic uses of contextual contrast is seen in Georges de La Tour's *Joseph the Carpenter* (figure 5.4). On the surface, the scene is of a carpenter and a young boy holding a candle, the sole source of light. Almost instantly, our vast personal knowledge, logic, and emotions are called into play. Through higher-order processing the viewer realizes that if the carpenter is Joseph, then the lad must be Jesus. Here La Tour uses the technique of brightness contrast to illuminate the face of Jesus. By providing a dark background upon which the boy's image appears, the sacred face appears to be so radiant that it, not the candle, seems the source of light. The technique of using a single light source makes it possible to accentuate the effects of brightness contrast, as the illumination in the scene ranges from very bright to very dark.

The technique of creating dramatic lighting contrasts was well known among Dutch and French artists during the early part of the seventeenth century. Many of Rembrandt's paintings play on this theme (e.g., *The Blinding of Samson* (figure 5.5), *The Night Watch,* and *The Anatomy Lesson*). As early as the fifteenth century, Geertgen Tot Sint Jans had used a "radiant" Christ child as the single source of light in a Nativity scene, thereby controlling the brightness contrasts with stunning results. In another seventeenth-century example, in which the source of light is more diffused, Judith Leyster gives us her impression of a boy playing the flute (figure 5.6). She establishes brightness contrast by illuminating the scene from a natural source from the

5.4 Georges de La Tour, *Joseph the Carpenter.*

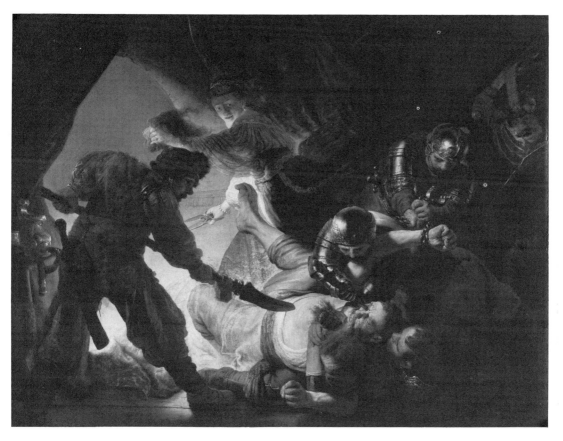

5.5   Rembrandt, *The Blinding of Samson.*

upper left, exaggerating the brightness of the boy's face. Leyster also uses subtle shading to enhance contours through Mach-like bands.

In these examples, it is easy to believe that the illusion of amplified brightness is a function of our knowledge of the characters in the scene, and so it is in part. After all, many representations of the Christ child show him blessed with a holy radiance or encircled by a halo. Therefore, when we see a painting of the boy Jesus we *expect* to see such luminescence. It would be hard to deny that a great deal of higher-order processing is involved in the viewing of these paintings, a topic to which we will now turn.

5.6 Judith Leyster, *Boy Playing a Flute.*

Top-Down Processing: Looking at the World with a Thousand Hypotheses

Humans actively seek answers to questions. We want to know the time the theater begins, what influences women's hair fashion, who discovered electricity, what is the origin of the universe, why stomach cancer is more widespread in Tokyo than in Nairobi, and how plants grow. These questions about the physical universe and ourselves are driven by knowledge. So prevalent is curiosity that some psychologists believe it to be a basic human motive. Hypotheses about the nature of reality are essential to top-down processing, and they frequently affect perception. When we read text, for example, we not only detect the letters and words, which are bottom-up features, but we also perceive these characters in terms of our expectations. The expectations are aroused by contextual components.

THE CAT

5.7 An example of context. The same stimulus is perceived as an H or an A depending on its context.

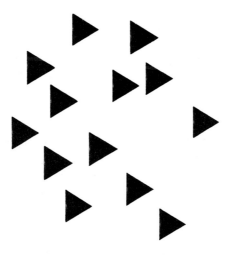

5.8 Look at the display of triangles. In which direction do they point? Look again. Does the direction change? Can you control the direction?

As an example, consider figure 5.7. When read, it is "THE CAT"; yet upon close inspection, the H in THE is the same figure as the A in CAT. If this H/A were presented in isolation, we would be confused as to its correct identity. The physical context provided by adjacent letters and our knowledge of the language determine our identification of it. The rules of reading are so much a part of our daily lives that they are applied automatically, as if we do not have to think about them. We process letters rapidly and with little conscious attention because we have experienced these patterns thousands and thousands of times.

Top-down processing also affects the way we see geometric figures, as in the case shown in figure 5.8. For many people the triangles seem to point to the right. But if we try to reorient them so they point upward and slightly left, we can do so with amazing ease. Or, we can will the triangles to point downward and left. The amazing mobility with which we can change their direction is achieved by entertaining a hypothesis about direction. That

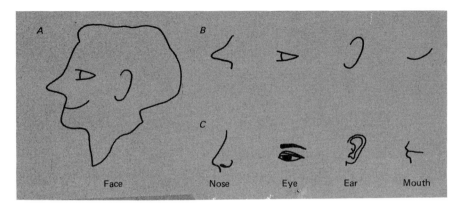

5.9   Facial features recognizable in context (*A*) are less recognizable out of context (*B*). Differentiated more fully and realistically (*C*), the features are more recognizable. From Palmer (1975).

hypothesis is so strong, in most viewers, that suddenly the whole flock of triangles fly in a specified direction.

When we process other types of more complex images, we do so in light of their context and the knowledge we have acquired through a lifetime of familiarization with the object. In an experiment that used complex visual displays (see Palmer 1975), it was found that facial features were easily identified when in context but poorly recognized when viewed out of context. In figure 5.9 we see an example of the facial features used in Palmer's experiment. Features out of context require more detailed information for correct identification. The principles demonstrated in "THE CAT" apply to more complex visual stimuli. Both experiments show the importance of context and past world knowledge on perception.

Further psychological experiments have extended these studies to environmental scenes. One study by Biederman, Glass, and Stacy (1973) showed subjects an everyday street scene (as shown in figure 5.10a) for a brief period of time. Then, immediately after the subjects had viewed the scene, a pointer appeared on the screen to indicate the place an object had appeared. The subjects in this experiment were asked to identify the object, such as the mailbox. As you might guess, this is not a very challenging task, and most subjects performed accurately. In a separate condition Biederman and his colleagues took the same scene, cut it into six different sections, and rearranged some of the sections (see figure 5.10b). Under these conditions, subjects had far greater difficulty in naming the designated object.

5.10 Scenes used in a study by Biederman, Glass, and Stacy (1973): a coherent scene (*A*) and a jumbled scene (*B*). It is more difficult to recognize the fire hydrant in the disorganized scene than in the conventional one.

Seeing Bit by Bit

5.11 **Paul Signac,** *The Dining Room.*

The French neoimpressionist Paul Signac used dabs of paint in a style called pointillism. Consider the enlarged details of this painting: the artist has composed a whole scene from bits and pieces. The technique is reminiscent of a refined mosaic style of art popular in the Middle Ages. (Roy Lichtenstein developed a similar technique in the twentieth century; see figure 2.9 for an example.)

The reason people have difficulty in remembering the object is because the context of the street scene is disturbed. When we look at an object, we see it in context, supported by immediate environmental cues and by our knowledge that makes those cues meaningful.

The human sensory system is constantly being stimulated by an enormous amount of information, some of which is important, some trivial, and

Signac's painting illustrates the way the human eye and brain interpret visual signals composed of a multitude of individual signals—dots and dabs of paint. When examined in detail, these signals are perceived to be mere dots, but when viewed from a distance or in some other way degraded, they become part of larger objects. Contours in such art are not usually produced by lines but by dots that are tightly clustered or darker. Through lateral inhibition, our eye "sees" lines. In addition, our brain organizes the dots and dabs into a whole pattern to which it can ascribe meaning. Our eye and brain search visual fields for some recognizable and/or stable forms ("good gestalts"). In Signac's painting we easily "see" a teacup in a dining room scene partly because we "expect" to see such an object there. We have an idealized image, or prototype, of what a teacup looks like and where it is likely to appear. Yet a detailed examination of this teacup shows it is merely a cluster of dabs of paint. Only when we relate these impressions to the context of the entire scene and combine that information with knowledge, stored in our long-term memory, do we "understand" the meaning of these paintings.

some worthless. If we processed all stimuli equally, it would not only be a wasteful allocation of energy but would overload a limited processing system. In order to make sense of our world, visual information must be processed rapidly and accurately. The human system is truly remarkable in the performance of this task. Human visual perception utilizes various pattern recognizers, such as those identified by Gestalt psychologists, in the basic organization of features. These features normally appear in context. The combination of features and context is detected by the eye and processed by the mind utilizing the brain's large compendium of knowledge about what the features in context mean.

The principles learned in the experimental laboratory may help us understand the processing of artistic information.

SCHEMATA

It appears that the human system has acquired a form of information processing based on the organization of information in long-term memory. The organization of this information and the rules that govern its use and combination are called schemata. Schemata represent the structure of an object, scene, or idea. When we look at a street scene, we activate the "street schema," which informs us of the features we might see and how they interact. We expect to see a fire hydrant near the street and not flying high in the air. When we view art, we also activate various schemata that expect certain objects and juxtapositions. The activation of schemata, in turn, allows us to make inferences about the art and to construct a larger interpretation and understanding of it. (See the discussion of schemes, canonic forms, and prototypes in chapter 9.) Most immediately activated are "art schemata," which are influenced by one's knowledge of the art.

The typical memory system used by humans involves the formation of abstract cognitive structures, or schemes. These schemes arise from prior encounters with the environment, as a result of which certain kinds of information have come to be organized in specific ways.

—Howard Gardner

If the painting, for example, is by Degas, we might further activate our "impressionism schema"; if by Andy Warhol, our "pop art schema"; if by Rubens, our "baroque schema"; and so on. Additional themes are also present that influence our perception. These schemata are part of our collective knowledge of the world and will be addressed in chapter 6.

Evidence of the influence of a schema on perception and memory is presented in a paper by Brewer and Treyens (1981). Subjects were asked to participate in an experiment and led into a college office, shown in figure 5.12. There they waited for 35 seconds, after which they were taken to a testing room and asked to write down everything they saw. Presumably, when the subjects were led into the office, they activated a kind of "college office

5.12 The experimental room used in the memory experiment of Brewer and Treyens (1981).

schema." If this is correct, then we would expect the subjects to recall conventional objects compatible with (and expected in) a college office. Furthermore, it is possible that subjects might invent objects that are highly compatible with the "college office schema" but not actually present in the office where they waited. These hypotheses were confirmed by the results obtained by Brewer and Treyens. Almost all the subjects recalled that the office had a chair, a desk, and walls. Only a few recalled that it had a bulletin board or a skull. But, most interestingly nearly one-third of the subjects *falsely* recalled that the college office had books, which it did not. Apparently, the college office schema was powerful enough to enhance the recall of compatible objects, diminish the recall of incompatible objects, and fabricate nonexisting objects.

INDIVIDUAL DIFFERENCES AND SCHEMATA

The subjects in Brewer and Treyens's experiment saw many of the same things, but they also saw different things depending on their intellectual

Developing and Using an Art Schema

Four different styles of art are arranged in chronological order in figure 5.13. The first is the tomb drawing of Nebamun from ancient Egypt (unknown artist), which on stylistic grounds can be identified as drawn during the reign of King Amenophis III (1417–1379 B.C., 18th Dynasty, New Kingdom). It is characterized by the lack of linear perspective, unique eyes, faces drawn in profile, and hieroglyphics in the background (which translate literally as "Taking recreation and seeing what is good in the place of eternity," or, my own unceremonious translation, "Capturing these birds is like heaven on earth!").

In the next painting we see Rubens's *The Raising of the Cross* (1609–1610), an example of baroque art characterized by a sophisticated arrangement of figures in which multiple and detailed parts blend into a unified design. Human figures are commonly shown well muscled and in agonizing poses. Religious themes then prevailed, and this example by Rubens (who is better known for his bountiful, if not corpulent, nudes) is part of an altarpiece.

5.13 Left to right: Egyptian tomb painting; Peter Paul Rubens, *The Raising of the Cross;* Auguste

Next we see Renoir's *Danse à la campagne* (1883), an impressionist painting. Here reality is captured by portraying the feeling of vibrancy and intimacy of a couple dancing. The impression is dreamlike, florid, with a hint of fantasy.

Finally we see an example of pop art, in which popular images are the theme. Andy Warhol, formerly a commercial artist, liked to point out the artistic merit of everyday images (such as a soup can), which he frequently showed in multiple copies, as in the case of Marilyn Monroe (1962).

With even this limited knowledge of these four art styles, a type of art schema has been learned. Should you be shown other exemplars from each of these periods, it is likely that you would be able to activate your (limited) art schema and correctly identify them by category. Of course, with greater experience of these types you would develop greater sensitivities within each classification, as well as a better appreciation for the prototypical examples. By learning some of the salient characteristics of an art period, you organize information in long-term memory and thus increase your memory load as well as your ability to think rationally about artistic concepts.

Renoir, *La Danse à la campagne;* Andy Warhol, *Four Marilyns.*

backgrounds. Our knowledge of the interaction between individual experiences and what we see in art (as well as in all sensory experience) has recently been formalized in schema theory. But as early as 1890, William James, a founder of American psychology, knew the importance of (unconscious) individual differences in perception and memory:

> Let four men make a tour of Europe. One will bring home only picturesque impressions—costumes and colors, parks and views and works of architecture, pictures and statues. To another all this will be non-existent; and distances and prices, populations and drainage arrangements, door and window fastenings, and other useful statistics will take their place. A third will give a rich account of the theaters, restaurants and public balls, and nought beside; whilst the fourth will perhaps have been so wrapped in his own subjective broodings as to tell little more than a few names of places through which he passed. (James 1890, p. 286)

Because each of the four men carries a unique mental structure of the importance of things, each sees and records different impressions.

Modern cognitive psychologists have conceptualized the way people organize the impressions of the world within a theory of schemata. Through our vast experience with the objects and ideas of the world, we form generalized impressions, or "idealized" forms, much like the Platonic forms. Thus, when I ask you to conjure up an image of, say, a teacup, it is likely that your image is one of a "standard" teacup, that is, more or less, an idealized image. If I showed you an odd-shaped teacup and asked you what it was, you would probably call it a teacup. You may never actually have seen the idealized image you conjure up (or the odd-shaped teacup either), yet the mental image is clear. These images reside in memory and derive from numerous experiences with a large variety of teacups. (See chapter 9 for more on teacups.)

The same cerebral vehicle is used when we think of a category of art. Rococo art is characterized as highly decorative, nonfunctional, and with too much attention to fussy little details; impressionist art as displaying natural objects that are vibrant and create a mood, or "feeling"; Egyptian art as consisting of clear lines, absence of linear perspective, people drawn in profile; and so on. Even though we have not previously seen a particular piece of art, we can easily identify it as belonging to one of these categories or to another category stored in memory. It is unlikely that we would mistake a painting by Renoir as belonging to Egyptian or rococo art. We have formed an impression, or an idealized image, of these art types through numerous experiences with paintings that share common features of the category.

Individual personalities also represent a type of idealized form, much like teacups. When you characterize the personality of a close friend or a popular figure, you select the salient and more or less permanent traits of that personality. Thus, you might recall the person's commitment to a belief or attitude. It is further possible to subdivide these traits into subordinate features, such as religious beliefs that are expressed zealously, or political attitudes that are displayed in support of a particular candidate. Further subdivisions are feasible until a composite structure of the personality is attained. These personality structures are particularly relevant to our discussion of the cognition of art as they influence what we see and remember, much as James's four visitors to Europe see and remember different things.

Experimental psychologists have demonstrated just how powerful individual perspectives are in determining top–down impressions of reality. In one experiment by Anderson and Pichert (1978) it was possible to create a type of personality schema that influenced perception. In the experiment, subjects were asked to assume the role of a certain individual. In one case some of the subjects were asked to assume they were thieves; in another case some were asked to assume the role of a prospective home buyer. In each case, an entire (imitated) structure of personality, or a schema, was activated. The two groups then read a brief story about a wealthy family home that included such details as the fireplace, the musty basement, leaky roof, silverware, coin collection, television, and so on. Afterward, the groups were tested for what they recalled from the story. Predictably, the "thieves" recalled the valuable items that could be stolen and the "home buyers" items related to the quality of the home. In this case the personal context influenced perception and memory.

We see art through a filter created by our personal schema, much as the "thieves" remembered things in which thieves are interested. Each person has formed a personality that is laden with attitudes about how the world should appear. But what if we see things that do not coincide with our expectations of how things should appear, such as in watching a magician or seeing a painting that is, in some way, distressing to our eyes? We have all had these experiences and each goes about resolving the conflict between what one sees and what one expects to see in a slightly different way. For generations, artists have known that people experience a type of psychological dissonance when the eye sees things incompatible with one's hypothesis about how the world actually is. Some modern and pop artists have shocked us by showing iconoclastic or scatological images (such as a contemporary photographer who showed one man urinating into another's mouth). While some of this art is dissonant only because it is clearly offensive, other pieces require a deeper interpretation to resolve their sense of dissonance.

Visual Dissonance

Visual dissonance is defined as a state of psychological tension caused when one experiences a disparity between what one expects to see and what one actually sees. The concept is related to a well-known phenomenon in social psychology called *cognitive dissonance,* which happens when we perceive a discrepancy between our attitudes and our behavior. Our eyes see the world of art with a thousand expectations based on our personality and our cognitive structure (knowledge system). Sometimes those expectations are fulfilled, sometimes not. In the case of unfulfilled expectations, the viewer is required to resolve his or her tension, or simply to abandon the piece and consider another. An important part of human motivation is found in dissonance reduction, in that people do not (normally) choose to live in a state of psychological tension. In psychological terms, such a state is aversive, to be avoided or resolved.

> *Every creative act involves . . .*
> *a new innocence of perception,*
> *liberated from the cataract of*
> *accepted belief.*
>
> *—Arthur Koestler*

The technique of producing unexpected visual forms is widely practiced by modern artists, who seek to gain our attention, and further intellectual effort, as we attempt to reconcile our expectations with what we see. Some may choose to resolve the conflict by simply turning away with the rhetorical rejoinder, "I can't believe what I saw." While denial of our sensory impressions may make a clam happy, most of us try to overcome the dissonance through cognitive means.

There are three basic means used to reduce visual dissonance: (1) reducing the importance of one of the dissonant elements, (2) reinterpreting one or both elements, or (3) changing one of the dissonant elements. We will illustrate these principles by considering a painting by the surrealist artist René Magritte (see figure 5.14). Look at this figure. What do you see? What does

5.14 René Magritte, *Not to Be Reproduced.*

it mean? Do you experience any visual dissonance? Perhaps your first reaction was the same as mine, namely, "Shouldn't the guy's *face* appear in the mirror?" (An alternative reaction is, "Shouldn't the guy be facing you, with the backside correctly reflected?") There is something radically "wrong" with this painting, or the laws of physics have suddenly been suspended. When one looks at this painting a type of visual dissonance develops, in the sense that what one "sees" is contrary to the "reflected image" schema that is part of our accumulated experience of the world. How can one work oneself out of this cognitive maze? Here are some common means of diminishing the dissonance.

The image of resemblance is what must be painted—if thought is to become visible in the world.

—René Magritte

• "The painting is not important." In this strategy visual dissonance is reduced by denying the importance of one of the elements. It is an easy solution, as the person may simply dismiss the painting as frivolous and move on to the next painting (if viewing this painting in a museum, for example). Another, more intellectually demanding version of the strategy is to deny the laws of reflected images or to invent new laws. For example, one could argue that Magritte had concocted a really wonderful mirror that showed the back side of the image.

• "The painting means more than is literally depicted." Here the viewer looks beyond the mere physical representation of the painting. Such interpretation could lead to a hypothesis about symbolic meaning and personal character, such as that the figure in the painting (or all of humanity) is so negative that he cannot even reflect his own frontal image. Deeper thoughts of the nihilistic nature of man might ensue.

• "This painting would be more consistent with my impression of the world if it truly reflected the person's image." In this case, an active person might repaint the painting with the frontal image. Or one could discard one's "reflected image schema" so that it now held that mirrors reflect the backside of whatever faces them.

Much of art has been purposely designed to generate a form of creative tension in the viewer that cries out for resolution. In many forms of classic art, the artist presented social issues that embarrassed the establishment, while many contemporary artists present visual statements about art, religion, psychoanalysis, as well as social conditions. All of these are intended to motivate the thinking person to find a deeper message in the art. Although these disturbing art forms may not be as comforting as viewing a Norman Rockwell illustration, they demand active participation in the construction of "reality."

Cognitive Dissonant Art—Mona Revisited

Another example of cognitive dissonant art is shown in figure 5.15. Here Marcel Duchamp shows us his *Mona Lisa,* who, unlike da Vinci's, is sporting facial hair. The title of Duchamp's Mona Lisa is *L.H.O.O.Q.,* which, pronounced letter by letter in French, means "She's got a hot ass." (Perhaps we can now understand the meaning behind Mona's enigmatic smile.) Duchamp thought art should function as a "cerebral pistol shot," and few can deny that

5.15   Marcel Duchamp, *L.H.O.O.Q.*

5.16 Andy Warhol, *Thirty Are Better Than One.*

the frivolous *L.H.O.O.Q.* gets our attention. The viewer sees something inconsistent with his or her expectation and is prompted to resolve the dissonance. One physical manifestation of this inner reaction is the movement of our eyes. We move them so they focus on the dissonant features, gawking unabashedly at the moustache and goatee.[1]

In ending this chapter, we show another variant version of Mona Lisa that further illustrates visual dissonance within a social context. When Leonardo painted his *Mona Lisa* it was an original, one of a kind, and intended to be viewed as such. Many consider it to be sacred, a hallowed icon not to be defaced as the graffitist Duchamp has. But since the original painting was done technological developments have occurred, including photography and mass reproductive techniques, that alter the social position of the work of art. All of these techniques have made "originals" available to a mass audience.

In figure 5.16 the pop artist Andy Warhol has taken the best-known portrait in the world and reproduced it 30 times, satirically calling it *Thirty Are Better Than One*. To many, Warhol's Mona is patently offensive, a banal reproduction of one of the world's greatest pieces of art. It is "common" and cheap. From another point of view, however, the viewer is forced to overcome his or her cognitive dissonance and look beyond Warhol's image. The viewer might consider the context of the twentieth century, which has trivialized the singular masterpieces of art, literature, and music through mass reproduction in which the counterfeit is usually a degraded imitation of the original. Many of these counterfeits are junk, like the popular kitsch art that might use the Venus de Milo as a timepiece, with a clock embedded in her belly; a visual diet that matches the gustatory diet of the masses. Such is the nature of the unreal world we have created. But such an interpretation requires a thinking brain filled with knowledge, not junk. We know these things initially through our eyes, the object of the next chapter.

6

The Eyes Have It:
Eye Movements and the Perception of Art

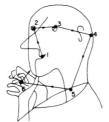

Eye movements can at very least be considered as tags or experimentally accessible quantities that scientists can observe to understand underlying processes of cognition.

—Lawrence Stark and Stephen Ellis

Of all the sensory organs the eye is the most active. Think about it: this restless little ball is constantly pivoting around its axes, and, if something of interest is outside its orbit, humans move the head for better focus. The reason this system is active is because its focal range is sharply limited (as compared with hearing, for example, whose compass is broad), and thus we need to look directly at an object to see it clearly.

As mentioned in chapter 1, humans see things distinctly only in the center of the visual field. This type of vision is called "foveal vision," as it is in the fovea that photoreceptor neurons are most densely clustered. The physical structure of the eye determines what we sense, while the rich storage of information about the world not only interprets these visual signals but, we now know, directs the eye to collect other, sometimes specialized, new information.

Foveal Vision and the Necessity of Eye Movements

The human eye is an enigmatic orb. At times it appears to be so poorly designed that one might think it could easily be improved. (Could an optical instrument that requires light energy to pass through a lens, two gunky humors, a network of capillaries, and a set of ganglion and bipolar cells *before* arriving at the place where photoreception takes place be an efficient organ? See figure 1.12 for an illustration.) At other times, however, the human eye

Eye-Tracking Exercise and *Christina's World*

6.1 Andrew Wyeth, *Christina's World.*

Christina's World, by the American artist Andrew Wyeth, is among the best-known contemporary works of art. Christina Olson, a friend of Wyeth's, lived on a farm in Maine; she was severely crippled but still managed to go outdoors by dragging herself by her hands. Wyeth wrote: "*Christina's World* is more than just her portrait. It really was her whole life and that is what she liked in it. She loved the feeling of being out in the field where she couldn't go, finally, at the end of her life . . . a lot of it came out of what she told me" (Piper 1991, p. 474).

Reexamine this piece with particular attention to where your eyes fixate. Try this simple exercise. Take a pencil, or other pointing device, and each time your eyes move to a new location move the pointer to that location. After a few seconds of viewing, retrace your eye movement patterns. On which object(s) did you spend the most time? Which did you revisit? Did your eyes move between features, such as the girl and the house? Were you trying to answer a question or establish a relationship? Did your eye movements mirror your interest and hypotheses about what story is being told?

appears to be so exquisitely fashioned that we might think it the world's most elegant object. One of the eye's curious attributes is central vision: visual acuity is best for objects focused in the center of the visual field and drops off substantially away from the center.

Visual acuity can be divided into three types, defined according to their angle from the axis of vision:

• foveal vision, which encompasses a visual angle of only about 1–2 degrees;

• parafoveal vision, which encompasses a visual angle of up to 10 degrees; and

• peripheral vision, which encompasses a visual angle beyond 10 degrees.

Of particular importance to our current discussion is foveal vision. The *fovea centralis* or *macula* is that small indentation near the center of the retina packed with numerous cones and connected to the brain by its own nerve fiber. A sample of the distribution of the rods and cones is shown in figure 6.2.

Only a moment's observation will confirm that we "see" clearly only within a narrow band. As you gaze at this WORD you see it rather clearly, but the words that surround it are less clear. Words further away are fuzzy, and those still further are not perceived at all. Take a moment and gaze at an object nearby—a lamp, a clock, a picture. As you continue to fix your eyes

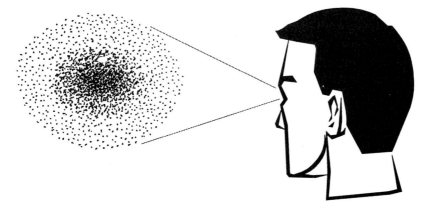

6.2 A sample of retinal neurons in the eye. Dots represent cones, which are concentrated in the center, or fovea, where typical vision is best. The number of cones away from the center is far less, and parafoveal vision (for illuminated objects) is correspondingly poorer.

on one feature, try to see objects outside the fixation point without moving your eyes. What type of information do you see? Do you see movement? Colors? Shapes? Lines? Details? Fine details? It is likely that the clarity of these things is in the order listed.

When we want to see an object clearly, we move our head or, more commonly, our eyeballs. The eyeball can move in each direction by means of three sets of extraocular muscles. These pairs work by means of highly sophisticated antagonistic muscle principles, so that, if the eye is to be moved in any specific direction (say to the right), then one muscle contracts and the opposing muscle in the pair relaxes. So routinely do we perform these actions that it appears to be an automatic function—and many eye movements are automatic, such as the ones you are now making in reading this text. However, directed eye movements are under conscious control and are affected by cognitive factors, such as specialized knowledge (a topic to be considered momentarily).

If our vision were equally sharp in all directions, we would not have to move our eyes or head to see objects well. However, the retina evolved in a resourceful way that both enhanced vision and minimized the amount of space required. This dual imperative necessitated a movable eye that could see things very clearly in a limited range, then shift to another location. Vertebrates solve the problem in various ways. Primates have one fovea in each eye. Other animals, such as some birds, may have two foveae, while others have a "strip" fovea in which objects are seen clearly through a wide band of the visual field. Still other animals see all parts of their visual field equally well (or poorly) and thus do not demonstrate saccadic eye movements. They gaze steadily at an object, in what we humans might assume to be an "anile stare."

A WINDOW TO THE MIND: THE EYE

Recently, eye movement has become a topic of immense interest to cognitive psychologists and other romantics. A roving eye in our culture is a social signal entreating further discourse. The original function of a roving eye was to move the eye so it could see things better; flirtation may be an affable by-product of this function. Perhaps the eyes are not the "mirror to the soul," as some would contend, but eye movements can be used to obtain valid measurements of a person's interests and cognitive processes. We look at interesting things.

Humans can control their eye movements, and that simple fact is of great interest to cognitive scientists. Conscious control over any body action, including the complex kinesthetic movements involved in an eye movement, is related to human volition, intention, and attention. The psychological significance of eye movements has been known for many centuries, but it was not until the end of the nineteenth century that serious experimental studies of eye movements were made in France and later in Russia and America. These experiments have been extended to the analysis of art.

Early scientific investigations in this field were slow to develop because eye movements occur very rapidly. The technical means of measuring eye movements (and the focus of the eye) were dependent on the development of motion picture cameras and electromagnetic field discoveries. The initial work in this domain is very interesting and attests to the considerable ingenuity of early scientists in refining data collection and equipment. Alas, we cannot pursue its history here. Currently, very sophisticated means exist, which use video recording apparatus and computers that precisely measure eye movements and fixations.

Eye Movements and Art

The cognitive theory of eye movements and art is based on the assumption that complex cognitive models of reality, which are already formed in a person's mind, control, consciously or unconsciously, the fixation and duration of eye movements. These models of reality, which all of us have, consist of hypotheses about the perceptual world that are constantly being tested against current visual sensations. Thus, when our contextual experiences lead us to "expect" to see an American flag and we actually perceive it, our internal (cognitive) world and our external (physical) world are in agreement. However, if we expect to see an American flag and an artist portrays it not with white and red stripes but with green and gray, we encounter conflict—a form of visual dissonance.

In the past, artists have used behavioral reactions to their work to guide their hands as they fashion visual objects. As early as the sixteenth century, scientists thought that eye movements were related to the appreciation of art. The French scholar and painter Roger de Piles, who may have been inspired by Descartes, observed the movement and fixations of eyes as a person viewed art, though refined observations and elegant cognitive models did not emerge during this period. However, with more advanced knowledge of the way the eye and brain process visual stimuli, including art, it is possible to formalize the operations of artists and viewers. With this in mind, we turn to experimental work tracking the movement of the eyes.

Eye-Tracking Studies

Eye movement is called saccadic movement, so named in 1878 by Emile Javal, the French scientist who observed that school children read text material by moving their eyes by small jumps (*par saccades*), then pause, then jump to another part of the text, pause, and so on. We view art in much the same way. Our attention is directed toward something interesting in the periphery, we move our eyes, pause, and then repeat the sequence. During the fixation period visual apprehension takes place. For the viewing of art, this period averages about 300 msec (an eye blink takes about 20 msec) but can vary widely. Fixations for reading tend to be shorter, but again with wide individual differences, depending on many factors including the ability of the reader.

Saccades occur very fast. A 2-degree saccade takes about 25 msec, a 5-degree saccade about 35 msec, and a 10-degree saccade about 45 msec, with some individual variation. During movement, vision is largely blurred ("visual smear"). When reading, the eye normally follows a linear track, as you are doing now. Occasionally the eye will backtrack if something is a bit odd or we want to reconsider a thought or word. Sometimes we pause on a word far longer than 300 msec, if it is interesting, puzzling, or difficult to understand, while other times our eyes fly through the material, capturing only salient words and phrases. We rush to the "good parts" of, say, a salacious pulp novel or a technical report, depending on our literary choice. The physical processing of visual information is very similar for all members of the species, though the content and interest of materials differs widely.

The perceptual concepts derived from the reading laboratory and visual research laboratory are directly applicable to the study of the perception of art. Art is viewed in context by fixating on one feature at a time for a brief period, moving the eyes, and then fixating on another feature. This scanning and fixating is not an entirely random pattern of activity. It may be that peripheral vision is constantly vigilant to the detection of interesting contextual features. Although the exact mechanisms involved in selective attention are not completely known, several general types of processes have been isolated that contribute to it.

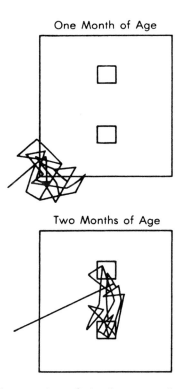

6.3 This figure shows the scanning of visual contours by one- and two-month-old infants. The stimulus consisted of two small boxes framed by a larger box. The erratic lines represent the infant's eye movements. Very young infants tend to concentrate on whatever field they initially select, such as the outer box, while older infants tend to scan the inner boxes, moving their eyes between them as though they are comparing them. Adapted from Salapatek (1975).

Eye movements are concentrated, even among infants. In a study of one- and two-month-old infants, Salapatek (1975) found that very young babies attend to some features of a visual field more than to others. (See figure 6.3.) Even at one month, an infant attends to a salient feature of a visual field (in this case, the lower left-hand-corner and the edge of the frame). The eye movements are not arbitrary, but directed at a specific section. By two months, an infant appears to spend more time looking at the central features and even switching attention between them, as if comparing the objects. As children mature, more multifarious motives control eye movements.

It is likely that visual attention in the human adult is driven by intention, interest, previous knowledge, movement, unconscious motivation, and context. When a provocative or interesting feature is detected, full attention may be allocated to it by moving the eyes or head in such a way that the object is focused on the fovea. There detailed examination is possible, if for only a few hundred milliseconds. The relentlessly probing eyes then move on to another feature, fixate for a brief period, and continue to move on, or perhaps revisit a formerly perceived feature for another look. This stratagem applies when we read, perceive art, or shop at a supermarket.

Yarbus (1967), working in Russia with early equipment, was one of the pioneers in the field of eye tracking and picture perception. In figure 6.4 we see two examples of his work, each recording the subject's eye movements and fixations over a three-minute interval. Yarbus believed that time is allocated to a feature in proportion to the information contained in it. In the present example, it appears that a large amount of time is spent observing the eyes, the mouth, and general shape of the face. These features are the most salient for the observer; and the record of his eye movements and fixations alone tell us something of his thoughts. They are rich in information that motivates action. These activities are so universally shared that it is possible to guess the identity of the object (a face) by looking only at the record of eye movements.

In another experiment, Yarbus isolated the factor of the intention of the observer. For this task he selected a painting by the Russian artist Repin and asked different questions of different subjects while recording their eye movements and fixations. The results of this experiment are shown in figure 6.5. In one condition he allowed the subjects to view the painting as they chose; in other conditions he asked about the economic conditions, age, activities, clothing, locations, and relationships of the people in the picture. The locus of eye fixations varied widely according to the type of information asked. Eye movements can thus provide a subtle means of measuring a viewer's intention and purpose. Also, the type of information gathered from a painting is directly related to the time allocated to specific features.

What the Brain Tells the Eye (and Vice Versa)

The eye and brain work together in collecting and processing information. This principle holds for the viewing of all sorts of visual stimuli, whether we are driving a car, playing tennis, or viewing art. Although much still needs

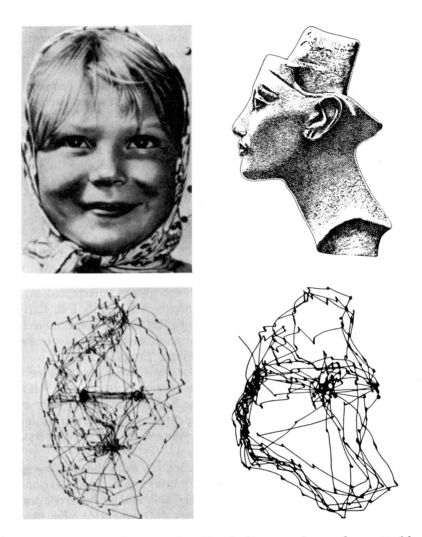

6.4 Eye movements and fixations of a subject looking at a picture of a young girl and at a profile of Queen Nefertiti. From Yarbus (1967).

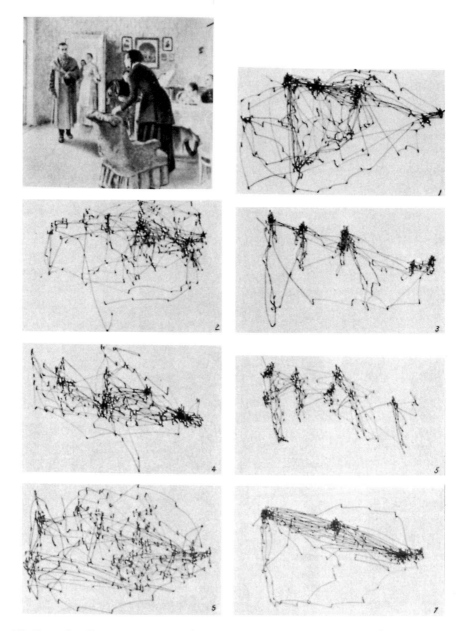

6.5 Records of eye movements of subjects examining a picture. Trace 1 was made when the subject examined the picture at will. Subsequent traces were made after the subject was asked to estimate the economic level of the people (trace 2); judge their ages (3); guess what they had been doing before the arrival of the visitor (4); remember their clothing (5); remember their position (and those of objects) in the room (6); and estimate how long it had been since the visitor had seen the family (7). From Yarbus (1967).

Eye Fixations and the Viewing of Art

The next time you visit a gallery, pay attention to where your eyes move and how much time you spend on each feature. Eye movements and fixations are usually driven by a person's intentionality. If you are looking for relationships, for example between two figures in a painting, then it is likely that your eyes will move to one figure and then to another and then back to the original figure. If you are looking for artistic technique, then your eyes will be directed toward composition, use of materials, skill in using media (e.g., oils, watercolors, acrylics, and so on), and innovation of method. Or if you are interested in the narrative a painting tells, your eyes may wander throughout the scene looking for visual fragments that, when combined in the brain, tell a story.

to be learned about the exquisite interplay between eye and brain, much is known. We know that the process of seeing involves a feedback loop between the eye and the brain. The process may begin with a hypothesis about the world or an "internal world" hypothesis. This hypothesis seeks confirmation in the physical or "external" world. The eye is then dispatched to find information related to the hypothesis. The eye collects visual information and passes it along to the brain, which processes it and then redirects the eye to scan other parts of the field. The process continues until resolution of the hypothesis is achieved or the topic is replaced with another hypothesis.

The eye-brain recursive loop is frequently internally controlled by intentionality, as in the case of setting out to find specific answers to a problem. An example of a goal-seeking recursive search was shown in the results of Yarbus's eye-tracking experiment, in which people were asked a series of questions about the characters in a painting. As noted above, fixations and eye movements were then *directed* toward specific features. A hypothesis is planted in the mind of the subject, who then seeks confirmation in the physical world by moving the eyes to selected areas. As the eye fixates on a feature, its message is fed to the brain, it is analyzed in light of the hypothesis, the eyes are redirected, another part of the puzzle is addressed, and so on, until the process is exhausted.

Perhaps the most remarkable part of the recursive loop principle is how rapidly these complex perceptual-cognitive tasks are executed. A person viewing a picture may fixate his or her gaze on a specific object for only a

Art Appreciation: Science and Art

Take a moment to look at this painting by the American artist Georgia O'Keeffe.

What eye movement took place when you viewed this painting? It is likely that your eyes focused on one feature; perhaps the feature just above the lower rose. Then your eye's focus probably darted off to another location, you examined it, and then, in less than a second, your eyes hastened to another part for a quick glimpse, and so on. This action (saccadic eye movement) is due to the eye's limited capacity to see clearly any more than a narrow field of vision. Thus, multiple impressions—a kind of multiple "snapshots"—are sampled from various parts of the painting, which, when combined in the brain, are interpreted and meaning is given to the painting.

What did you see? Most people see a stark skull of a horned animal with two flowers. Did you notice that the painting is divided into two nearly equal halves by the dark streak down the center? Did you notice that the horns nearly touch the frame? Did the painting remind you of a crucifixion? What meaning do you attach to this painting? Does the painting stir an emotional reaction in you? What do you know about the artist and her philosophy of painting? What might the flowers mean?

In O'Keeffe's *Cow's Skull with Calico Roses* we see both the limitation of the eye in visual perception and the expansiveness of the brain in determining meaning.

few hundred milliseconds and then move on to another, and then to another. During these brief frames of perception, information is fed to the brain where it is processed, and a new program of search is then initiated and executed.

Scanpaths and the Cognition of Art

Further eye-tracking experiments have produced interesting data regarding visual search procedures that bears on our understanding of the cognition of art. One series of experiments was conducted by Norton and Stark (1971), who coined the word "scanpaths" to describe the repetitive fixations and movements eyes make in viewing a scene. The basic idea behind their model of eye movements is that of a *feature ring,* an ensemble of alternating sensory-motor-sensory routines that are observable in eye movements (as shown in

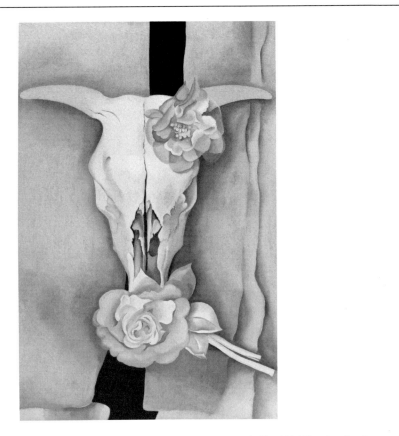

6.6   Georgia O'Keeffe, *Cow's Skull with Calico Roses,* 1932. **Photograph © 1993 The Art Institute of Chicago; all rights reserved.**

figure 6.7). A scanpath of the sort shown was observed in a subject who first viewed a picture. Norton and Stark found idiosyncratic scanpaths among subjects for the same picture—and even idiosyncratic scanpaths for the same person looking at different pictures. The driving force behind eye movements is the brain, which within its tangled network of neurons has constructed a schema, or a hypothesis about the picture and its contents. Once this schema is activated, the search begins.

THE TRAVELING SALESMAN PROBLEM

An intriguing part of the puzzle of eye movements and perception is the efficiency with which these operations are performed. By way of analogy, consider the so-called traveling salesman problem of having to choose the

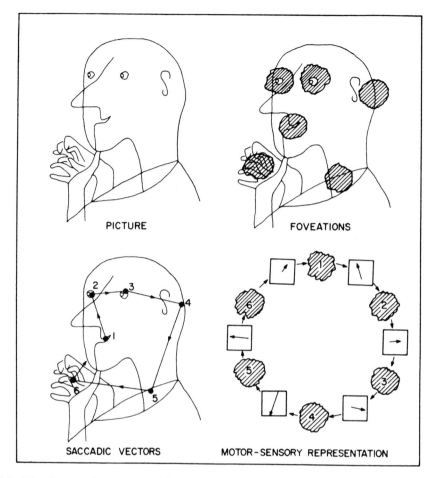

PICTURE   FOVEATIONS

SACCADIC VECTORS   MOTOR-SENSORY REPRESENTATION

6.7 The feature ring, proposed by Norton and Stark as a format for internal representations of a picture. Picture recognition follows the identification of a picture's subfeatures after successive saccades that make up the scanpath. The feature ring consists of brief visual memory traces plus the saccades of the scanpath. From Stark and Ellis (1981).

most efficient route between a number of cities. How can this problem be solved? One way would be to randomly connect the cities, much as you might do if you placed the city names in a hat and drew them out one by one. ("Let's see, I go to Atlanta, San Francisco, Pittsburgh, Seattle, Miami, and Reno.") Of course, this is a foolish system (but one that I suspect some travel agents use). A much more efficient path would minimize the route by organizing the cities in some geographic system and, coincidentally, would resemble the type of circular scanpath shown in figure 6.7 (say, from Reno to San Francisco, Seattle, Pittsburgh, Atlanta, and Miami). Determining the best route requires enormously complex cognitive processing. If the number of cities is 10, the number of routes possible soars to 3,628,800, and for a 100 cities . . . forget it! Yet finding a very good route is accomplished easily, even by school children, though it challenges sophisticated computers.

The human brain operates by massive parallelism: the immense number of individual neurons whose function is to process information do so by routines that engage many millions of other neurons that function simultaneously. Thus, a complex traveling salesman problem is solved in the human brain not by (stupidly) calculating all possible routes—a "brute force" search—but by understanding the problem and then estimating the best route. It may not be *the* best route, but it is likely to be a very good approximation, and *the* best route is beyond the capacity of the brain. Our physiological brain is thus capable of elaborate thought that can determine a "best guess" route, as well as what visual signals may mean.

Viewing art has some of the same features as the traveling salesman problem. When we look at Mona Lisa, for example (who bears a slight resemblance to the character in figure 6.7, which is a sketch by the artist Paul Klee), we could move our eyes in a random fashion, but such a strategy would be as inefficient as randomly selecting a geographic route. Or we could proceed with a systematic search of the portrait. Indeed, some scanpaths indicate that the route taken in the viewing of art appears to be a closed cyclic pattern that minimizes the total search pathway (see Stark and Ellis 1981). The maximum amount of visual information is gathered in the minimum amount of time. As the research of Nodine suggests (see below), the strategy used for eye movements and fixations is typically not at all random. It may be that the greater the specialized knowledge about a topic, the more educated the eye search.

Expert Viewing

In specialized fields that depend on visual skills (radiology and art, for example), experts are more efficient in their eye movements than nonexperts. There is evidence for this in the medical literature and, to some extent, in the art literature. The pattern of eye movements produced by expert radiologists as they make a diagnosis from an X ray is far more parsimonious than that of novices. This fact is important to professors of medicine, as identifying eye movements and fixations of skilled physicians (which ultimately reflect underlying cognitive activities) may prove to be beneficial in the training of

Visual Search in Art and Medical Diagnosis

Calvin Nodine and his associates have used eye-tracking instruments to learn more about the way experts go about the visual search for pertinent information in a visual scene—be that an art object or an X ray of a patient with a disease, as in the case of suspected lung cancer. The search for the hidden NINA in an Al Hirschfeld cartoon (figure 6.8, top) is similar to the search for abnormalities in X-ray images. This has led Nodine and associates to an overall model of the visual search (figure 6.8, bottom), which has similarities to the viewing process used in looking at art.

In this model, an initial glance at a visual scene gives a global impression of the scene. This is followed by more directed viewing (focal attention) and interpretive decision making.

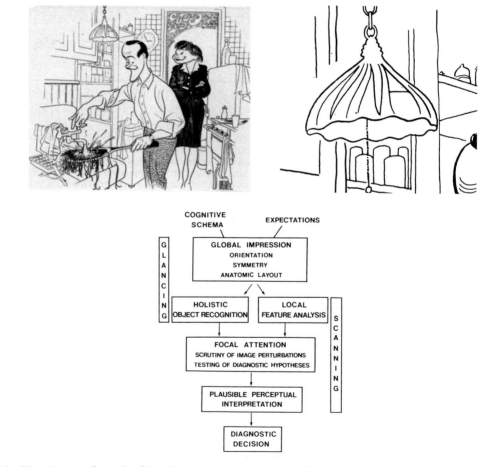

6.8 *Top:* A scene from the film *The Apartment* by Al Hirschfeld, with Hirschfeld's daughter's name **NINA embedded in a detail of the scene (enlarged at top right).** *Bottom:* Nodine et al.'s model of **the visual search. From Nodine and Kundel (1987).**

new physicians. Interestingly, many of the same cognitive/perceptual ingredients seem to be brought into play when a radiologist searches for a lung tumor as when an art critic looks at a painting, which suggests that underlying these search procedures is a cognitive schema, in the form of a cancer prototype for example, based on specialized experience that directs eye movements and fixations.

Studies of the behavior of experts in the field of art (art critics, students of art, and artists) is based on the postulate that art can best be understood by observing those trained to view it. In other endeavors, such as medical diagnosis of X rays by expert radiologists, memory of chess pieces by grand masters, and map reading by skilled cartographers,[1] technical knowledge significantly enhances what is seen and how the material is remembered. It is reasonable to suppose that the perception of art follows the same underlying psychological laws, and that eye-tracking experiments are a likely way to reveal some of these laws. What sets the viewing (and evaluation) of art apart from medical diagnosis, chess problems, and map reading is that in those fields objectively determined standards may be ascertained—the evaluation of an X ray by a physician may be validated by other diagnostic methods, and by the course of events. In art, the standards and values are largely subjective.

Diversive Exploration and Specific Exploration

In his theory of psychoaesthetics, Berlyne (1971) identified two types of perceptual exploration in the aesthetic response to art: diversive and specific exploration. Diversive exploration occurs as a hunt for stimulation without regard for content, while specific exploration is aroused in the viewer by incomplete knowledge that seeks out specific information. Each of these types of visual exploration has its distinctive ocular "signature," which can be discerned in eye-tracking data. For example, diversive exploratory behavior is typically widely dispersed, with sparsely populated clusters of fixations in which information is sampled. Conversely, when a subject concentrates on a specific location, it suggests that he or she is interested in the informational properties of that section and is exhibiting specific exploratory behavior. The distinction has proved useful in studying eye movement patterns of radiologists (see Nodine and Kundel, 1987). Let's examine this distinction among people looking at art.

In one study (Locher and Nodine, 1987), the lengths of fixations were measured for initial viewing of a piece of art and for subsequent viewing. The results indicated that initially, subjects tend to exhibit widely dispersed fixations of short duration (less than 300 msec), suggesting a type of global viewing of the artwork indicative of diversive exploration. As viewing continues, however, there is a significant increase in the number of longer fixations (greater than 400 msec), which suggests a shift to more specific, information-gathering activity. It should be pointed out that aesthetic evaluation is based on both types of exploration. It would seem that our eyes, like early pioneers on the American frontier, first send out scouting expeditions that briefly reconnoiter the topography, and then inspect the interesting sights at greater length.

ART TRAINING AND THE PERCEPTION OF ART

Does formal training in art education change the nature of the visual exploration of art? In a recent paper on this topic, Nodine, Locher, and Krupinski (1993) examined the eye fixations of art-trained and untrained viewers as they looked at pairs of paintings that differed in terms of their composition, balance, and symmetry.

Artists have always had some sense of balance and symmetry in their work, and this seemingly natural proclivity has been formalized in art education courses.[2] The deep psychological reason for the predisposition engages theories of the universal attributes of the mind as it interacts with the physical world. At every opportunity we humans form taxonomies; we like to believe that the universe is organized in some systemic pattern and that we scientists are intrepid explorers searching to find its logic. (Perhaps it is, or perhaps it is simply the mind that invents order, which it understands, and rejects chaos, which it does not.) Symmetry is one of the techniques used by artists to achieve a pleasing design. However, visual symmetry involves much more than simple balance. A *perfectly* balanced painting would be rather boring, as would a perfectly balanced building, face, or even personality. While we understand order, we find minor visual dislocations interesting and invest greater effort in investigating them. (Perhaps we choose to add our own organization to seemingly maverick pictures and people.)

The stable, harmonious whole of *Prägnanz* is also an important part of Gestalt psychology (see chapter 4). Some idealistic art scholars maintain that idealized forms exist in a type of abstract utopia and that terrestrial forms are only counterfeit representations, each of which, more or less accurately, mimics the ideal. One measure of the merit of art is its approximation to the ideal. Others, more socially or behaviorally oriented, insist that art appreciation is learned and is based on social and environmental factors. While the debate cannot be resolved here (and the ideas are not quite mutually exclusive), it is generally agreed that art education teaches principles of balance, proportion, and symmetry as powerful forces in pictorial composition, and that artists for centuries (especially Western artists) have faithfully applied these principles in their work.

It is possible to alter balanced pictures to make them unbalanced and observe the eye movements of trained and untrained viewers. Figure 6.9 shows works by Seurat, Mondrian, and Gauguin in their normal, balanced form (on the left) and then in their distorted, unbalanced form (on the right). Since exploratory eye movement (diversive exploration) is motivated by curiosity, we might expect sophisticated subjects to exhibit more diversive exploration when viewing an unusual work—one in which the canons of portion and symmetry have been defiled.

The results obtained by Nodine et al. did show a difference between the eye movements of art-trained people and those of untrained viewers in these conditions. Trained viewers spent relatively more time in diversive exploration than in specific exploration when viewing the altered pictures, while untrained viewers performed just the opposite. (Examples of scanpaths are shown in figure 6.10.) Additionally, it was found that those subjects who had had extensive art training tended to concentrate on finding thematic patterns among compositional elements, while the untrained subjects tended to concentrate on representational and semantic use of picture elements. Nodine et al. concluded that "untrained viewers failed to recognize the perceptual organizing functions of symmetry, focusing attention instead on the representational issue of how accurately individual elements conveyed 'objective' reality. . . . Art training seems to teach viewers to appreciate paintings not because, in Levi-Strauss's words, 'they are good to see,' but because they are 'good to think.' This suggests that beauty is less in the eye, and more in the mind of the beholder." This insightful analysis is perfectly attuned to current theories in visual perception (as well as aligning exactly with my views) stressing the *cognitive* basis of art. We "think" art as much as, no, even more than, we "see" art.

Original (Balanced)   **Altered (Unbalanced)**

6.9 Compositions shown formally balanced (left) and altered to make them unbalanced (right). Top to bottom: Georges Seurat, *Les Poseuses;* Piet Mondrian, *Composition with Red, Yellow, and Blue;* Paul Gauguin, *Jour de Dieu.* From Nodine, Locher, and Krupinski (1993).

Unbalanced (Altered)   Balanced (Original)

Trained
Viewers

Untrained
Viewers

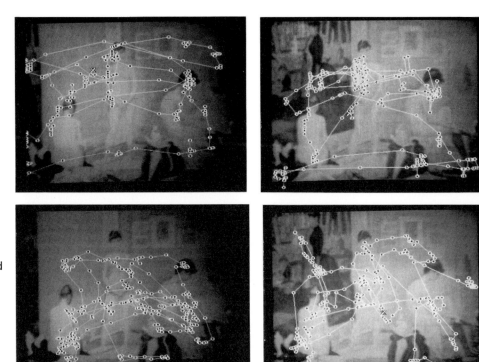

6.10   Scanpaths of trained and untrained viewers of Seurat's *Les Poseuses* in its unbalanced and balanced form. Note the more sweeping eye scan for trained viewers in the unbalanced condition (upper left) than for the untrained viewers (lower left). From Nodine, Locher, and Krupinski (1993).

Centralized Viewing

The most frequently explored part of visual art is the center, although contextual factors can shift the focus of attention to peripheral areas. Several research papers have confirmed the idea that more time is spent on objects that are in the "center of gravity" of a visual scene (see Kaufman and Richards 1969, for example). The center of gravity of a visual scene is determined by estimating the "perceptual weight" of each element in the field. The system seems to work well with nondiscrepant visual elements, though there is some controversy as to how perceptual weight should be determined in art. Obviously, artworks are not collections of uniformly weighted "elements" but are composed of richly combined asymmetrical forms and colors. Nevertheless, center weighing of a painting seems to be a general rule that applies to art perception.

I will offer a physiological explanation of center weighing. Imagine the way the eye sees the world to be a screen upon which visual information is played. The screen is oblong and is variable in clarity. The features in the center (foveal vision) are far clearer than those even a few degrees off-center. Because of the location of the fovea and the (limited) latitude of movement of the muscles that control the eye, the range of visual search is restricted. The muscles of the eye can, however, move in such a way that peripheral stimuli can be made central, or so that the image cast by peripheral information falls on the fovea. These physiological realities are invariant and play a fundamental role in visual perception, including the perception of art.

Now, consider the pathways taken when the eye scans a field (or painting). Because of the physiological limitations, the eye sweeps across the elliptical field, stopping at one element for a few hundred milliseconds, then darting off in another direction, stopping, and so on. Given the natural course of eye movements, which region of the visual field would receive the greatest amount of traffic? The center would. This discovery required empirical confirmation by twentieth-century scientists, but artists for centuries were aware of the natural tendency for humans to focus on central features more than peripheral ones. As a consequence, artists placed important features in or near the center, and less important features in the periphery. This general rule, of course, has exceptions; otherwise, art would become terribly predictable and ultimately boring. While some artists may choose to place important features in the center (the "centralists"), others may require their viewers to search a wider compass of the field to find important features (the "peripheralists"). In artistic composition, salient figures are often placed in the upper, lower, left, or right third of a scene.

Art and Eye Movements

As Yarbus demonstrated, intentionality influences eye movements and fixations. Further investigation has refined the scope of these studies, examining differences in the ways trained viewers search for meaning and for aesthetic qualities in the fine arts.

In a study reported by Molnar (1981), two groups of fine arts students in Paris were asked to view art pieces and be prepared to answer questions regarding either their meaning or their aesthetic qualities. One of the examples was *The Anatomy Lesson* by Rembrandt; figure 6.11 illustrates the scanpaths of a student from each group. We see some differences between these scanpaths, but the remarkable feature is that the two are very similar. There were some differences between the fixation times (versus the paths traced by eye movements), in that the aesthetic group held their fixations longer than the semantic group. The average length of the fixation for the aesthetic group was 365 msec, versus 315 msec for the semantic group ($p < .01$). The homogeneity of scanpaths may be due to the homogeneity of the sample of subjects: fine arts students who share common aesthetic backgrounds. The shorter fixation times for the semantic group might have been a reflection of the subjects' need to examine many different areas of the picture and not linger too long on any fixation. These scanpaths also indicate that fixations, for both groups, corresponded to "important" elements—the faces of the anatomy professor and his students. Some attention is given to contours, which help identify forms, but these art students gave little attention to the cadaver stretched out in the lower part of the painting. (My guess is that eye fixations for medical students, undertakers, werewolves, and Count Dracula would be directed at the more macabre details of Rembrandt's masterpiece, which would reflect their specialized appetites.)

To uncover the reasons behind eye fixations and movements, Molnar derived a measurement of eye fixations that is based on a regional rather than a point-by-point analysis. Take the example shown in figure 6.12. In this case, the work is Manet's (then scandalous) *Olympia,* a picture of a matter-of-fact whore who is celebrated not only for her nudity but because she is looking out of the canvas directly into the viewer's eyes. There is nothing subtle about her message.[3] To many, her eyes, embarrassingly frank, are "interesting" features. If we examine the art students' point-by-point eye scans of this painting, however, we see that no fixations occur directly on her eyes.

Several (nonindependent) reasons may account for this.

• First, it may be that subjects do not find this feature interesting (contrary to what some art critics may tell us).

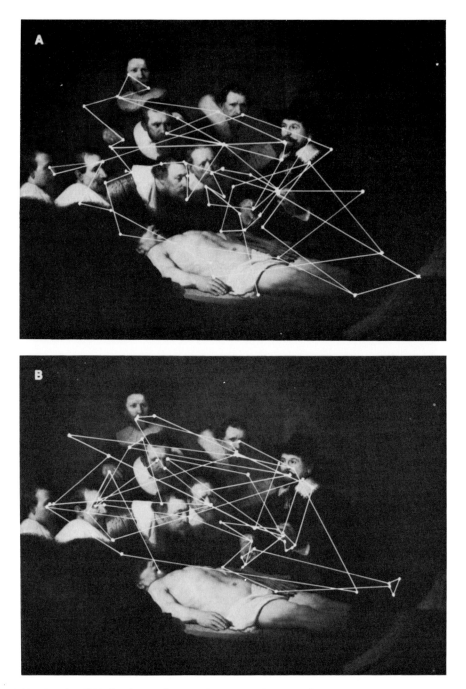

6.11 Graph of 60 fixations of two subjects viewing Rembrandt's *Anatomy Lesson:* (*A*) aesthetic group; (*B*) semantic group. From Molnar (1981).

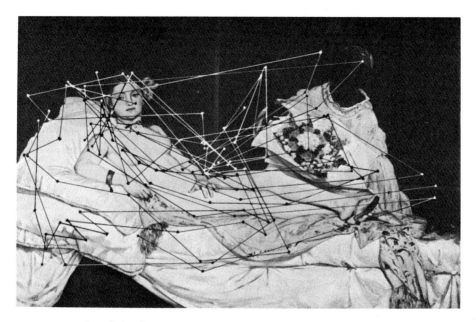

6.12   Scanpaths of the first 10 eye movements of several subjects looking at Manet's *Olympia.* **From Molnar (1981).**

• Second, eye movements and fixations rarely find the dead center of the "interesting" part of a visual display. Frequently our aim is poor; our eyes alight at a point a little too far, too near, too high, or too low for the feature to fall directly on the fovea.

• Third, other parts of the display compete for attention, and the reader may find his or her own partiality through introspection.

• Fourth, regional analysis, of the aggregate eye fixations falling in the same neighborhood, may be a more sophisticated measure of intentionality than point by point analysis.

An analysis of visual neighborhoods yields some interesting information (figure 6.13). Here the results of a large number of fixations have been consolidated in five different regions. These are (1) the head and bust, (2) the left hand and legs, (3) the maid, (4) the feet, and (5) a cat, scarcely visible. The aggregate shares of fixations by region were:[4]

Region	1	2	3	4	5
% of fixations	18	21	15	14	4

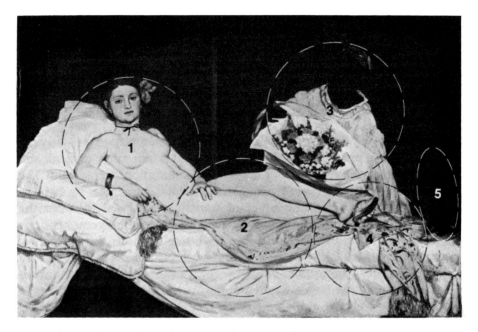

6.13 Schema of a partition of Manet's *Olympia* into five areas. From Molnar (1981).

These results show that viewers focus attention on the head and bust (region 1), but allocate greater viewing effort to the hand and legs (region 2). These results are reliable after only about 25 observations, and remain stable over longer viewing times. Two things can be learned from these data: features that are rich in information command attention, and attention tends to be weighted toward the center of the picture.

Evidence also suggests that different styles and periods of art produce different kinds of eye movements and fixations. In an earlier paper, Molnar (1974) pointed out the relationship between certain stylistic aspects of a picture and eye movements. For this study, examples from the classical works of the high Renaissance were compared to examples from the mannerist and baroque periods that followed (which Molnar collectively labeled "baroque"). Molnar found that classical art produces eye movements that are large and slow, reflecting the expansive nature of that style, while baroque paintings involve small and quick eye movements, reflecting the dense, animated character of that form. The distribution of fixation times between baroque and classical art is shown in figure 6.14. The mean duration of eye fixations for baroque art was about 60 msec briefer than for classical art.

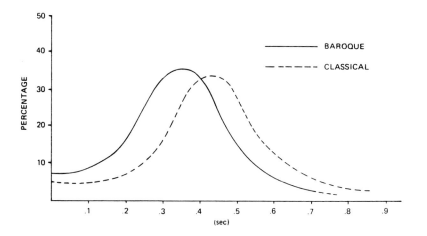

6.14 Distribution of the durations of fixations on a classical picture (Titian's *Venus*) and on a "baroque" picture (Tintoretto's *Origin of the Milky Way*). From Molnar (1981).

The general rule suggested by these data is that more complex pictures produce shorter eye fixations than less complex forms. This hypothesis has gained further support in another study by Molnar (reported in Molnar 1981), in which art experts were asked to judge the complexity of various types of art. Judgments were made of baroque pictures, classical paintings, and the art of Vasarely (see figure 4.11 for an example), Pollock, and Mondrian (see figure 9.23 for an example). A high degree of agreement was found among the experts as to what constituted complexity. Baroque paintings were judged to be more complex than classical paintings, and Pollock and Vasarely judged to be more complex than Mondrian. Eye fixations then follow the general rule stated above; complex pictures, such as baroque paintings, produce shorter fixation times than simple pictures. It may be that such complex art, which is densely packed with details, demands that attention be given to a large number of visual elements. This demand can be satisfied by allocating shorter fixation times to each feature. Simple figures, such as those created by many modern abstract artists, have far fewer features vying for attention, and therefore more time is allocated to each feature. Also, one could argue that in viewing abstract paintings, the viewer is trying to find a "deeper" meaning in each of the limited number of features—and thus spends more time on each.

7 A Truly Marvelous Feast: Visual Perspective

Oh, what a lovely thing is this perspective!

—*Paolo Uccello*

Long before humans used their eyes, brains, and muscles to guide complex sensory-motor actions, such as assembling a delicate watch or threading a tiny needle, our distant ancestors used the same instruments to hunt elusive antelopes, pick berries, avoid low-hanging branches, judge distances over an expansive plain, and remove small thorns from their feet. These were all matters of life and death. It was not enough to know *what* an object was (although it was important to know one's mate from a rock, eatable berries from poisonous ones, and so on). It was also important to know *where* it was. Much of the concern with the cognition of art has been directed toward visual localization and the perception of depth. How our ancient ancestors (and we) perform each of the common acts mentioned above is a difficult question requiring a complex answer. However, a large part of the problem deals with being able to see things "in depth." The native propensity to see, to understand, and to guide one's behavior is contingent on the reciprocal action of the eye and brain as they differentiate near objects from distant objects—a topic called visual perspective, the theme of this chapter.

Seeing a 3-D World with a 2-D Eye

The world has three physical dimensions—height, width, and depth—plus the dimension of time. Visual signals from the physical dimensions enter the eye and are recorded on the retina, which has but two dimensions: height and width. We human animals are two-dimensional visual creatures seemingly trapped in a three-dimensional world by the geometry of the retina.

Nevertheless, the brain interprets two-dimensional visual images as having three dimensions by use of contextual cues and knowledge of the world as gained through a lifetime of experience. Thus, a three-dimensional world is recorded by a two-dimensional eye and then interpreted as three dimensions by the brain (the "3-D/2-D/3-D" problem). We may have a 2-D eye, but there is no doubt that we have a brain that sees in 3-D and beyond. These facts have baffled and bemused philosophers and scientists for centuries (see Berkeley for interesting philosophic considerations). Only within this century have scientists unraveled some of the mysteries surrounding the 3-D/2-D/3-D problem.

So compelling is the predisposition to "see" the world in 3-D that our eye and mind constantly decode flat stimuli as having depth. It seems that artists have, from the very beginning, known how the eye and brain use information to create the illusion of depth. One of the techniques used by artists is perspective—a method of representing a three-dimensional object on a two-dimensional surface, such as an artist's canvas.

UCCELLO'S PERSPECTIVE: A WORKSHOP IN A DEVELOPING TECHNIQUE

Contemplate *The Battle of San Romano* by Paolo Uccello in figure 7.1. Uccello, who was obsessed with creating three-dimensional figures on a two-dimensional canvas, lures the viewer into this painting by a number of visual illusions, of which linear perspective is but one. Notice the use of larger figures in the foreground and smaller objects in the background, and how closer objects cover (occlude) distant objects. Careful inspection reveals two distinct scenes separated by a hedgerow: one, in the foreground, where soldiers are engaged in a battle, and another scene in the background in which bucolic characters romp seemingly oblivious to the riot. There is little attention to middle distances, and thus the background appears to be flat, as if only a backdrop to the central action taking place in the foreground.

Pay particular attention to the fallen warrior at the very bottom left of the painting (see detail). Here Uccello has used the technique of fore-shortening (illustrating an object shorter than it is to create a three-dimensional illusion). It looks, more or less, natural—the way our eyes might see a recumbent figure.

The fallen warrior is important for another reason. Many of the salient figures in the foreground are generally oriented toward one central point, which is an important feature of linear perspective. The fallen soldier is

7.1   Paolo Uccello, *The Battle of San Romano* (National Gallery, London), with detail.

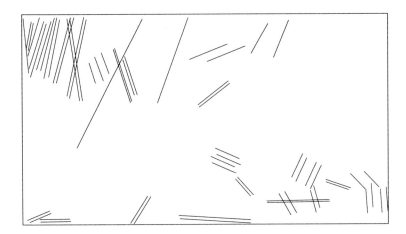

7.2 Parallel forces in *The Battle of San Romano.*

aligned with other strong visual cues, for example the lances that are parallel to the body (see figure 7.2). From our discussion in chapter 4 of Gestalt psychology, we learned that the mind's eye organizes these prominent features on the basis of similarity. The overall effect of similarly aligned features is to create an unconscious sensation that the entire scene is oriented toward an imaginary single point of reference. The eye organizes the real world by finding similar lines, which are interpreted as depth cues. So, too, does the eye achieve a sense of depth in this picture.

Uccello, as well as other Renaissance painters, employed other visual techniques to create an impression of depth. These include making distant objects smaller and higher than near objects, covering background objects with near objects, and making objects in the background seem less distinct than foreground objects. While one can see clearly the details of the bridle on the center horse, the features in the background are obscure. In addition, the artist has used bold contours in the foreground, fuzzy contours in the background; warm colors (reds and yellows) in the foreground, which seem to advance, and cool colors (blues and greens) in the background, which seem to recede. While it is clear that Uccello didn't get it just right (the men in the background would be the size of Goliaths if they appeared in the foreground at the same scale), this early attempt to use several perspective techniques does, nevertheless, create a sense of depth.

7.3   Chalice perspective: a study by Uccello.

Principles of Depth Perception: Where Is It?

Comprehension of physical objects is based on our knowledge of what the object is, what it is doing, and where it is. The initial process of visual identification of an object is based on its shape or contours, as we learned in our discussion of form perception (see chapters 3, 4, and 5). We know *where* an object is largely because of visual depth perception, which we will consider next. In a later section we will discuss the third question of what an object is doing (see the discussion of kinetic cues below). In everyday perception, from which we learn what the world is really like, all of these cues seem to be processed together, as if they were each a beautifully crafted musical instrument designed to play its part well but always attuned to the other instruments.

Binocular and Monocular Cues

In recent years, perceptual psychologists have analyzed the types of perspective that have been used by artists to create a sense of depth. There are two general types of cues involved, binocular and monocular, and within each of these classes are several subclasses (figure 7.4).

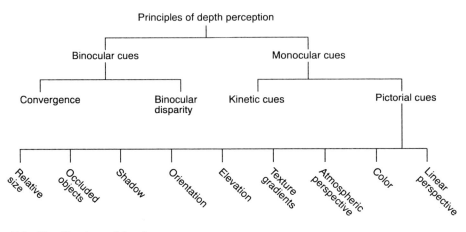

7.4   Classification of depth cues.

Binocular cues are those derived from the use of two eyes. Images that fall on one retina are not identical to the images that fall on the other, and information regarding this disparity is translated by the brain as a depth cue. Binocular perception of depth is particularly important in working with objects close to the eyes but, contrary to common opinion, is not critical for most forms of depth perception. People who, through accidents or disease, are left with only one good eye drive cars, play baseball (several major league players have been blind in one eye), and "see" most forms of art very much like you do. Furthermore, people with only one good eye from birth also have a good sense of depth. However, close work requiring depth perception is markedly impaired with single-eye vision. Try this little experiment. Remove and replace the lead in a mechanical pencil. (Do not use any other aids, such as steadying your hands by touching them.) Now close one eye and try to do this. (Threading a needle will produce the same effect.)[1] Chances are you had difficulty doing fine work with only one eye.

The ability to perform this simple hand-eye coordinated act is based, in part, on binocular disparity (sometimes called binocular parallax), in which the image that falls on one eye is (slightly) displaced on the other eye, and on convergence, the action of the ocular muscles as they move the eyes while focusing on an object. In figure 7.5 we can see how the pencil and lead fall on different parts of each retina. Furthermore, the disparity between eyes is shown in the differences between distances (represented by the line segments

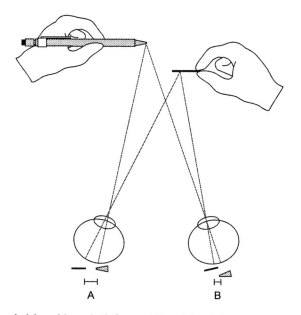

7.5 Area subtended by objects in left eye (*A*) and in right eye (*B*).

over A and B). These differences (for close objects), although small in actual span on the retina, are powerful depth cues for the brain. By the laws of simple geometry, we can easily see that more distant objects subtend visual space of very nearly identical size on each retina (the retinal disparity becomes less disparate) and thus the effect largely disappears. The science of binocular vision is important in perceptual psychology and in seeing some modern forms of op art, but for the most part the viewing of traditional two–dimensional art is more reliant on monocular cues.

Monocular cues are those that require only one eye, though they normally also involve both eyes (despite the name). Among monocular cues are visual stimuli available from the inspection of a stationary visual scene, such as the scene represented by an artist on canvas. Sometimes the term *pictorial* cues is applied to this type of scene, in distinction from another class of monocular cues that are based on motion. Movement cues, called *kinetic* cues, work when either the observer or the scene is in motion. Thus, when I look out my window and hold my head still, I know that the tree in the foreground is closer to me than the river, or the park, or the distant snow-capped mountains because of the pictorial cues available. If I move my head from

Perceived Distances and Familiarity

Given the perception that these five faces range from close to far, which face is at the
same distance as the ball? The answer depends on how large the ball is. Suppose the ball
is a basketball. Which face is on the same plane? Now suppose the ball is a Ping-Pong
ball. Distance judgments are made on the basis of size as reflected on a person's retina
(bottom-up processing) and on knowledge of the object (top-down processing).

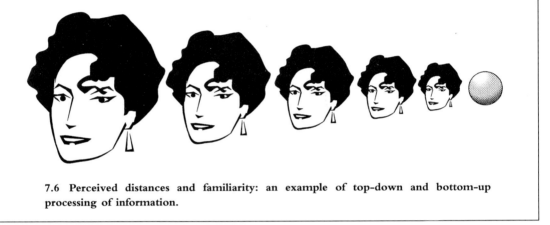

**7.6 Perceived distances and familiarity: an example of top-down and bottom-up
processing of information.**

side to side the relationships between near objects changes slightly. The tree
in the foreground covers a part of the river and uncovers another part.
Sometimes this monocular depth cue is called *motion parallax,* as motion
provides the essential information on which depth perception is based. These
cues to depth perception are essentially the same for one eye alone or two
eyes functioning together and will be discussed later.

Monocular depth cues abound in art and everyday life. We learn, at a
very young age, to use these cues to judge the relative location of objects. So
powerful are these cues that it is possible to create an illusion of depth by
presenting them on a two-dimensional surface. Psychologists have recently
classified these cues, but for centuries artists have used the full range of
monocular cues to indicate depth.

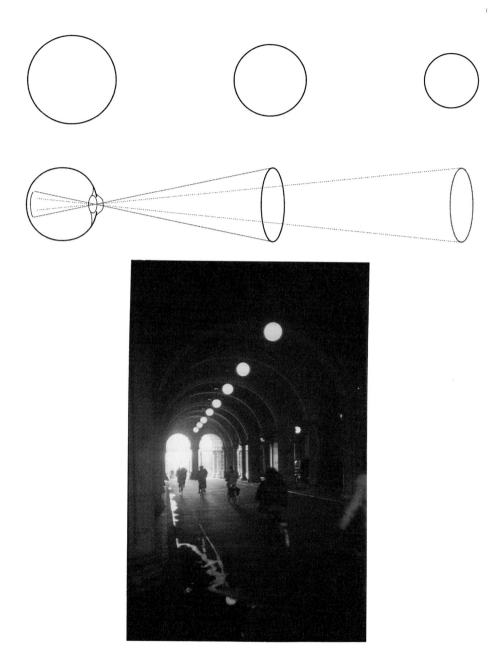

7.7 Which of the circles is most distant? In the lower drawing, the inverse relationship between object distance and retinal size is shown. (Compare the receding line of globes in the photo.)

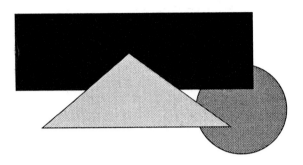

7.8   Which object is nearest? Farthest? Why?

RELATIVE SIZE

The size of the retinal image varies in inverse proportion to the distance of an object. Near objects appear larger than far objects because they occupy more space on the retina. In the perception of real world stimuli, an object 5 feet away casts an image on the retina twice the size as the same object viewed from 10 feet. Correspondingly, artists represent distances by the same geometric proportions, with near objects larger than distant ones. Relative size is a compelling depth cue, as shown by the drawing in figure 7.7. We immediately sense that these three circles may "in reality" be the same size, but located at three different distances. However, if you are told that the first circle is the size of a half-dollar, the second of a quarter, and the third of a dime, then the three circles appear to be of different size but located on the same plane. This feature of size is called *familiar* size and is based on our knowledge of the dimensions of well-known objects. In the parlance of an earlier discussion, these objects are processed in a top–down fashion.

OCCLUDED OBJECTS

Another type of depth perspective is obtained by the use of occluded objects (also known as interposition), in which foreground objects cover, or partly cover, distant objects. In figure 7.8 three geometric forms are shown all on the same plane, yet the impression is that the triangle is partly on top of the rectangle and circle and that the rectangle partly covers the circle. Hence, we infer that the triangle is the form closest to us, the circle the most distant. It is possible, of course, that we have it all wrong. Perhaps the "circle" is not a circle at all, but a weirdly shaped form with slots and wedges cut out that coincide perfectly with the seemingly interposing rectangular and triangular forms. It is much more likely that we "see" a whole circle that is simply behind (and therefore more distant than) two other forms.

SHADOW

Depth can be ascertained by shadows, such as the way a shadow may be cast on the underside of a ball, which suggests a solid, three-dimensional object as contrasted with a flat two-dimensional object. The interpretation of these depth cues has proved to be a tricky and complex matter. Consider the disks in figure 7.9. Our mind and eye interpret these as being members of two classes, one class concave and the other convex. Those circles, or hemispheres, that "jump out" from the page are those that are light on the top and dark on the bottom. It seems our brain interprets these signals as if light were shining on a three-dimensional object from above. That makes sense. Most natural light appears from above. Therefore, a dark shadow on the underside (even if it's the "underside" of a two-dimensional object) suggests to an observer that this is a three-dimensional object, something like half of a ball. If you rotate this figure 90 degrees, the illusion frequently disappears (although you can hold onto the image in that rotated orientation, and even

7.9 Depth cues supplied by shading. If the tops of the circles are light, they look like bumps. If the bottoms are light, they look like depressions. From Ramachandran (1988).

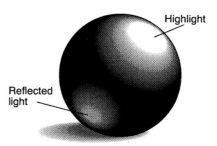

7.10   Light and shadow on a ball.

7.11   Shadow as a cue for depth. Turn the photo upside down and the crater becomes a hill.

beyond). If you continue to rotate the picture to 180 degrees, the formerly convex circles become concave and the formerly concave circles become convex! This object is fun to experiment with, and there are no prohibitions against twisting it every which way.

The illusion created by shadows is compelling. Take the rather pedestrian photograph shown in figure 7.11. Here the object looks like the crater that it is. However, if the picture is rotated 180 degrees, the crater suddenly becomes a mountain. This visual misinterpretation may seem quite benign, unless, of course you are navigating a space probe on some pock-marked surface, like the moon. There, determining if an object is a mountain or a hole in the ground is likely to be critical.

When you view art, be aware of the powerful effects light and shadow have on our interpretation of scenes. Artists during the Renaissance and the impressionist period were sensitive to the effects shadows produced and used them skillfully.

ORIENTATION

Related to shadow effects, but decidedly different, is the effect that orientation, or the alignment of an object, has on depth perception. Many two-dimensional forms are seen as having three dimensions when viewed from one orientation, but only two when viewed from another. Consider the objects in figure 7.12. Most people see object A to be "flat" and describe it as "two diamonds hanging on a bar," while object B appears to be a cube—a three-dimensional object. Yet if you rotate the page 45 degrees clockwise, you will see that the objects are identical except for orientation. This somewhat baffling phenomenon is largely ignored by perceptual psychologists and, as far as I can tell, has never been addressed seriously by artists. Yet the effect, as shown in this illustration, is compelling. I suspect the effect may have something to do with the strong vertical bar upon which the diamonds are hung. Another plausible cause is our familiarity with boxlike three-dimensional objects oriented at right angles to the ground. This effect is particularly forceful when accompanied with a verbal label (as your author has not so subtly supplied in this case). Thus, the effect of orientation seems to be largely due to top-down processing in which our eye and brain seek out images that remind us of something else we have seen. Since three-dimensional boxes are

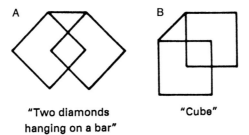

A

B

"Two diamonds
hanging on a bar"

"Cube"

7.12   **The effect of orientation on perception. Which of these objects appears to be a three-dimensional figure? From Solso (1991).**

commonly seen, it is likely that we have a strong "box prototype" (see chapter 9 for a discussion of canonic forms). Thus, when we look at object B we interpret it in terms of the object in memory that it best approximates.

ELEVATION

By elevation I mean the relative vertical position of objects within a picture frame. Close objects appear toward the bottom of a painting, distant ones toward the top. Art simply reflects reality, in this case. Children represent distant objects by use of elevation without (it appears) any instruction. It is the way they see the world. It is the way they represent the world. From prehistoric to Egyptian to Asian to Renaissance to impressionist to (some) modern art, elevation has been used as an indication of depth, sometimes without regard to size or linear perspective. (See the discussion of Asian art below.)

TEXTURE GRADIENTS

A very robust set of pictorial cues that produce the sense of depth are those associated with texture. Consider the river stones shown in figure 7.13. The image that is projected on the retina is of a few "large" stones in the foreground, fanning out to numerous "small" stones in the background. The image shows a continuous change, a textural gradient, that depends on the spatial layout of the relevant surfaces; and we use this textural gradient as a cue for depth perception.

ATMOSPHERIC PERSPECTIVE

Another type of pictorial cue is based on atmospheric perspective, in which distant objects are represented as we might see them distorted in the physical world. Distant objects appear to be less precise, small details are lost, and colors become paler. The effect is caused by the way the atmosphere distorts objects. For example, colors shift in vividness and become softer, with a hint of blue tone. This effect is due to characteristics of the troposphere, or the air near the earth, which is filled with stuff. In Los Angeles, for example, the "stuff" is called "smog," a mixture of smoke (or, more generally, hydrocarbon exhaust) and fog (or, more generally, water particles). This "stuff" distorts distant objects in a way most humans find obnoxious. There appears to be a

7.13 Stones in a river bed.

gunky pall over the city, and distant objects, rather than shifted toward the bluish end of the visual spectrum, are shifted to a kind of a dirty brown. In distant "clean" mountain regions, Lake Tahoe for example, distant objects are distorted but in a different way. Here water vapor in the air filters the light from distant objects, much as when we look through sunglasses, in a way that shifts the reflected light to the blue end of the spectrum (see figure 7.14). Different climatic conditions, regions of the world, and even times of day each have their own distinguishing

When painters of architectural scenes wish to show colors of things seen at a distance they employ veiling airs.

*—Ptolemy
(2nd century A.D.)*

7.14 In atmospheric perspective, water particles and other substances in the atmosphere distort light reflected from distant objects. In the case illustrated here, shorter wavelengths are reflected back to the person's eye, which thus perceives the distant mountain to be a hazy, soft blue.

atmospheric "signatures," which have been captured by landscape artists since Uccello and before. These cues, subtle as they may seem, tell the viewer much about a scene, depth information being but one of the several messages conveyed.

The artists of the Renaissance, neoclassicism, romanticism, and impressionism often used atmospheric perspective with much greater finesse than in the example by Uccello. Interestingly, during the later of these periods the strict use of linear perspective, which presents a rather stiff image, was eased, and a softer, more gracious effect was achieved without losing a sense of depth.

COLOR

In the real world of daily visual perception and processing of information, we experience the natural shift in colors of objects of varying closeness, and an object's color is an additional component of the process of knowing where the object is. In keeping with the effects of atmospheric perspective, warm colors seem to advance while cold colors recede. For example, an orange or yellow object (warm colors) placed on a blue or green background (cold colors) seems to stand closer to the observer. This generalization is likely related to the way we see these colors in the real world, in which atmospheric distortion has a cooling effect on colors proportional to their distance from the viewer (largely due to the refracting effect of water vapor in the atmosphere).

In addition to this environmental reason, some theorists (e.g., Wright 1983) suggest a physical basis for colors acting as cues to depth, in that different colors come into focus at slightly different distances from our eye. To illustrate this, look at a color transparency, such as a common 35 mm slide. When viewed in a bright light (not projected), the reds seem to stand closer while the cool colors (e.g., blues) seem to stand farther away.

> *If in painting you wished to make one seem more distant than the other it is necessary to represent the air as a little hazy. . . . Paint the first building its true color; the next in distance make less sharp in outline and bluer; another which you wish to place an equal distance away, paint correspondingly bluer still; and one which you wish to show as five times more distant, make five times bluer.*
>
> —*Leonardo da Vinci*

LINEAR PERSPECTIVE

Of the many different techniques used to create visual perspective, linear perspective is mathematically most interesting. In linear perspective, the overall geometry of a painting suggests that its salient features converge on a single point, called the *vanishing point* (see figure 7.15), near the back center. We are so used to seeing these cues of visual perspective that artists incorporated them in their drawings. Uccello, who was one of the earliest of the Italian painters to experiment with perspective, did not calculate the precise linear coordinates in composing *The Battle of San Romano;* and hence we get the impression that something is not quite square with this painting. Later Italian painters, especially during the later Renaissance, became so obsessed with the geometric correctness of their compositions that many paintings look like architectural renderings.

KINETIC CUES: WHAT IS IT DOING?

The most ecologically powerful depth cue is movement. Along with other cues, it tells us what something is doing. Things close to our eyes seem to

7.15 Visual cues of depth showing a vanishing point.

dart by quickly, while distant things seem to move slower. Look at a high-flying jet as it slowly moves across the sky. Although its speed may approach 600 mph, because it is far from our eyes and therefore subtends a smaller visual angle it appears to move slowly. Now, consider a fast-moving automobile close to your eyes. The subjective experience is that the near object is moving much faster than the distant airplane.[2] The principle involved is called motion parallax and is one of the most powerful cues for three-dimensionality.

   Motion parallax is missing in traditional art forms, although some very interesting experiments are being done with computer graphics that simulate many of the effects of motion parallax.[3] Its absence in two-dimensional art is important for our consideration of perspective. As absorbing as painting is, and as correct from a perspective viewpoint, it never completely fools the eye.[4] This failure has everything to do with motion parallax. All you have to do to break the mesmerizing effect of perfectly drawn pictures is move your head . . . oh, ever so slightly. (More distant paintings, such as ceilings painted in large churches, require somewhat greater motion.) On a two-dimensional

Motion Parallax in Milan

In everyday life we are frequently reminded of depth perception through motion parallax, in which the relative motion of near objects seems more rapid than that of distant objects. In figure 7.16, the figures near the observer are blurred with movement, while distant objects (even if moving) are not.

7.16 Motion parallax: people moving.

canvas, the relative position of near and far objects remains the same. In real life, relationships among visual objects change all the time due to our head/eye movements and movements of the objects themselves (see figure 7.16).

Depth perception, which is very important for creatures living in a three-dimensional world, is achieved in large part through kinetic cues. This is evident through the nearly continuous motion of our eyes, and, if that were not enough, our head swivels around with the slightest of excuses. I believe these motions serve to tell us where we are and where things in our view are. Much has been written about the techniques used by artists (especially Renaissance artists) to create a three-dimensional illusion. But few scholars even mention what appears to me to be the most important depth cue *not* available to these artists, motion parallax. The importance of relative motion as a powerful depth cue is, however, central to perceptual theorists, such as J. J. Gibson (1950, 1979), who suggest that most of our knowledge of the three-dimensional structure of the world is derived from the way an impression moves across the retina during locomotion.

Digesting Perspective: Illusions and Constancy

Showing things as they really are requires an understanding of the trigonometry of linear perspective—the way that objects and images are distorted as a function of a person's point of view. The mathematical laws that describe linear perspective are reasonably straightforward and were known to Renaissance scholars. To illustrate the way the eye distorts reality, consider a simple object, such as a rectangular table top. If you view this object from a slightly elevated angle, the retinal sensation is foreshortened, which is to say that the visual impression is one in which the actual figure is compressed. While the signal from the eye to the brain indicates a compressed object, the mind does not for an instant believe the object is actually of that shape. Likewise, when we see a person approach us, we do not believe that he or she is growing larger. The evolution of the central nervous system and the eye produced cognitive machinery that comprehends a wide variety of sensory exemplars as belonging to a superordinate class of objects. All sorts of "distorted" rectangular objects are projected onto the retina, and the brain understands them as "rectangular objects." As simple as this is, the deception proved to be difficult to practice for Renaissance artists, and is no less difficult today.

Artists such as Uccello used a type of linear perspective called *one-point* perspective, as all the lines (more or less) converge on a single vanishing point. We also saw an example of this method of representing depth in the photograph of globes (figure 7.7) and will see another in Roger Shepard's "two-sized" monsters (figure 7.20). Other forms of perspective are also commonly used by artists, including *two-point* perspective and sometimes *three-point* perspective. These forms use multiple vanishing points, as in the case of the "basic" box.

The Basic Box

The most elementary three-dimensional object beginning artists draw is the cube or box. Almost everyone can draw a three-dimensional box, but if it is properly constructed the simple box has two vanishing points (imaginary points on which features drawn in perspective converge). In figure 7.17 the structural components of two-point perspective are shown using a box. Here all the salient features—the "horizontal" edges of the box—if extended focus on a vanishing point. We are compelled to view this two-dimensional drawing as having depth. This two-point perspective could become a three-point perspective view if the vertical lines of the box also converged.

Even if a box is degraded in some way, such as having some features missing as in figure 7.18A, our brain decodes the impression as having three dimensions. A very similar "cube" is shown in figure 7.18B, but with one small difference that immediately transforms the object into a two-dimensional form—a sort of assemblage of mixed Y's. What changes were made in the bottom figure?[5]

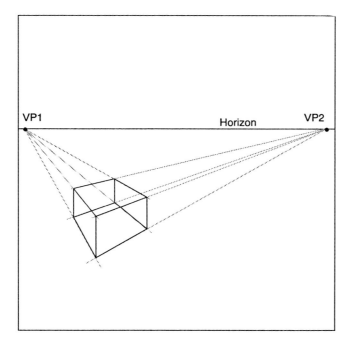

7.17 Vanishing points of a box.

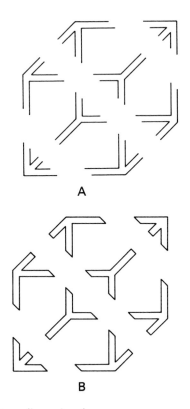

7.18   Cubes: three- and two-dimensional.

The cube and other rectangular shapes can be so compellingly organized as three-dimensional objects that artists frequently use them as models for all sorts of drawings, even those that use curved lines in their composition. (See figure 7.19.)

In these examples, one of the principles of linear perspective illustrated is that distant objects are diminished. Careful inspection of the farther edges of the cube in figure 7.17 reveals that they are smaller than the closer edges. In figure 7.20 we see two monsters, the smaller one being chased down a tunnel by the larger one. Look again. Which is really the larger? In fact, the two figures are the same size. Measure them. The illusion is compelling, even though we have empirical proof that the perception is but an illusion. We are led to this perception by the context of converging lines that make up the vault and floor of the tunnel. (One way to check illusions based on linear

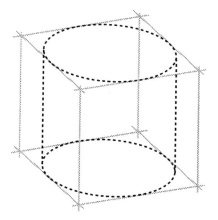

7.19   From a cube to a cylinder.

7.20   Which monster is larger? From Shepard (1990).

perspective is to make a cylinder, such as a rolled up sheet of paper, and view with one eye an object without visual context. Look at the head of one monster in figure 7.20 through a tube. Now look at the other monster's head. Take your "illusion buster" along when you visit a gallery. Act cool.)

Visual illusions that play on our strong tendency to use depth cues to judge the size of an object are not restricted to scenes having obvious diminishing points, as in the preceding example, but also apply to more subtle dimensions of geometric objects. In figure 7.21 we clearly perceive two tables, one long and narrow and the other short and fat. Yet, surprisingly, the shapes of the two table tops are identical in this figure. Measure them.

Many artists have used rectangular forms to create powerful depth cues. In figure 7.22 we see a sketch of how an artist might formulate his or her composition. Notice that the effects are drawn in relation to the eye level and to a vanishing point. One artist who has taken advantage of these cues in the modern artist Paul Klee, whose *Uncomposed Objects in Space* is shown in figure 7.23. By the use of numerous rectangles, all more or less drawn in perspective with a diminishing point, we are drawn in to the painting and convinced of its three-dimensional quality. It may well be that Klee is pointing out one of the basic paradoxes of 2-D humans functioning in a 3-D world: note the two-dimensional people in the lower right and lower center.

7.21 A tale of two tables. From Shepard (1990).

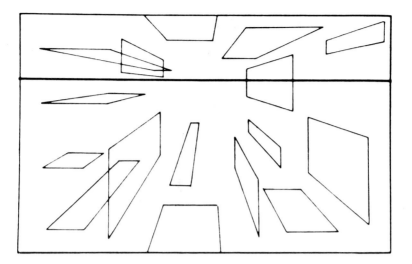

7.22 Artist's sketch of main compositional objects drawn in perspective. From Malins (1980).

Recumbent Figures: Why They Are So Hard to Draw

Buildings and other geometrically regular forms are relatively easy to show in perspective, and artists since the early Renaissance have amazed their audiences with exquisitely drawn pictures of these objects. Painters sometimes created surprising visual effects by producing unusual angles of view, called *scorci*. Drawing figures in perspective, however, proved to be more challenging, and recumbent or unusually positioned figures were nearly impossible. This problem was faced by Uccello, whose fallen warrior was illustrated in figure 7.1. Undoubtedly Uccello struggled with this figure and drew a good approximation of how a fallen warrior would appear. In figure 7.24 we have redrawn the fallen man as an upright figure, given the best estimate of the overall perspective presented in the painting, with somewhat surprising results. As shown, the warrior is diminutive when standing up. Had a true perspective been used, the figure would be in scale with other upright people in the painting. Because we see people standing more often than we see them lying down, the problem of drawing a foreshortened recumbent figure is even more difficult. The artist, then, has two cognitive/perceptual problems to overcome: he or she must draw a reclining figure "in (geometric) perspec-

7.23 Paul Klee, *Uncomposed Objects in Space.*

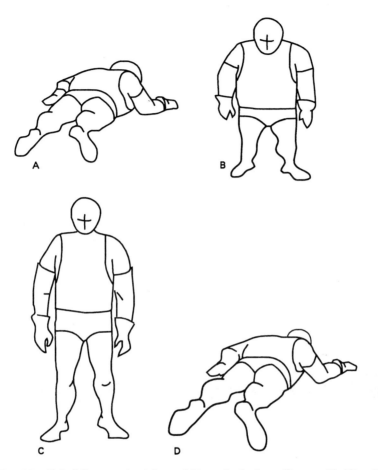

7.24 How Uccello's fallen warrior (*A*) would have looked standing up (*B*). How Uccello should have drawn the warrior using accurate perspective techniques (*D*). We have had this fellow stand up (*C*), and he is more realistic than Uccello's man.

tive" and must overcome the archetypal image of how people look when commonly perceived.

One means of drawing recumbent figures in perspective is to imagine (or even sketch) a "three-dimensional" rectangular frame in which principal body parts can be arranged (see figure 7.25). This technique was used in early teaching manuals for artists, as shown in figure 7.26. Here schematic heads ("block heads") are shown in such a way that the artist can see the geometric relationships between facial features from different orientations.

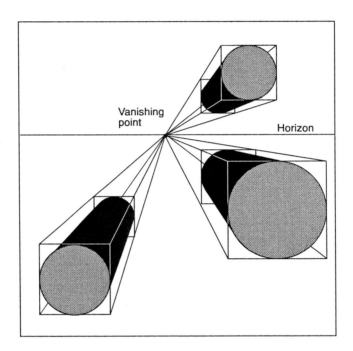

7.25 **The use of three-dimensional rectangular and cylindrical forms to guide an artist in drawing objects in perspective.**

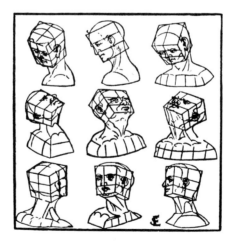

7.26 **An early teaching manual for drawing heads. From Gombrich (1963).**

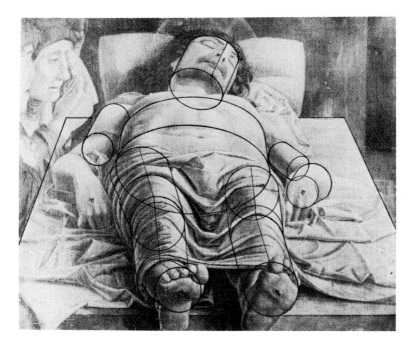

7.27 Andrea Mantegna, *Dead Christ,* with added schematics. The use of cylinders to gain perspective is an artists' technique. Acute foreshortening problems can be overcome by superimposing cylinders or rectangles.

The use of this technique may be applied to the best-known example of extreme foreshortening, Mantegna's *Dead Christ* (see figure 7.27). The artist selected an unusual vantage point from which to portray the recumbent Christ. From this perspective all of the features of the body appear to be distorted. In figure 7.28 we see the original rendition (at bottom) and two copies made sometime later. These copies have altered the original perspective so that the Christ figure is more accurately shown. In spite of his intellectual appreciation of the mathematical laws of linear perspective, Mantegna's previous experience with recumbent figures and his respect for his subject persuaded him to use artistic license. Hence the facial features of the dead Christ are out of proportion to his feet. By violating the strict canons of linear perspective, Mantegna presented a far more powerful image of the dead Jesus, giving the viewer an intimacy and shocking proximity to the body, and especially to the face. Look at the reproduction at top right. The overall

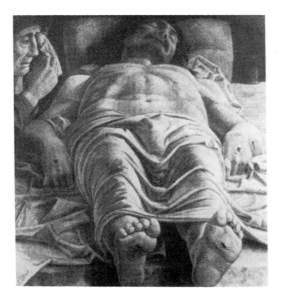
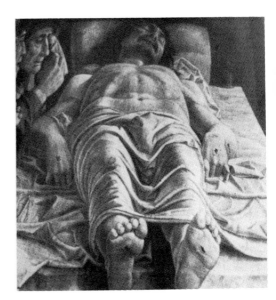
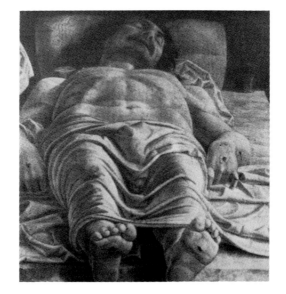

7.28 Mantegna's painting (bottom) and two later copyists' "corrected" versions. Note the relative size of the head in the three versions.

feeling one has from this rendering is of remoteness, distance, and aloofness, as contrasted with the almost voyeuristic image below.

These figures were hard to draw, not because the laws of linear perspective were unknown (they were not) nor because the artist lacked technical skill (he did not), but because our *perception* of the world is swayed by our concept of how things *should* appear. Lurking in the brain of all normal humans is a collective image or prototype of people, objects, things, ideas, and the like. We see the world through a thousand hypotheses. We see things that fit well within our preconceived notion of how things should appear, not necessarily as they actually do appear. The way we acquire the idea of "how things should appear" is one of the most fascinating chapters in the cognition of art. We have a pretty good idea of the psychological experiences that are the ingredients of prototype memories. Those exciting new discoveries are waiting for you in chapter 9. First we will conclude our discussion of perspective and art by tracing its history.

8   Perspective and the History of Art

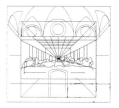

The apparent diminution of objects with increasing distance was noted at least as long ago as the seventh century B.C. when—according to a story on tablets from Assyria—one Etana, being carried up by an eagle to the heavenly throne of the goddess Ishtar, was so clear-headed in emergency as to observe that the earth became smaller and smaller until it reached a vanishing point.

—Lawrence Wright

Perspective is important to you and me as we move through a three-dimensional world, but it was also important to an evolving creature as it helped answer one of the riddles of sight: "Where is an object?" Ecological cues, which have been on earth far longer than humans have, convey certain specific types of information. These include contours, colors, shapes, movement, distance, and the like. In the course of its evolution, the human sensory/cognitive system developed receptiveness to those stimuli that allowed people to know where and what an object was as well as what it was doing. Professional artists have understood, at least at some level, these natural cues and how the eye sees them. They have incorporated natural cues into their paintings, and we, armed with an eye calibrated to see natural stimuli and a brain attuned to make sense of them, more or less understand these artistic expressions. In this chapter we will apply the principles of cognition and perception to the historical use of perspective in order to better understand both the psychology and the artistry involved.

The Technology of Perspective

Early in the Renaissance, artists devised a method of drawing an object "in perfect linear perspective." One technique for doing this was developed by

8.1 Albrecht Dürer, *Draughtsman Making a Perspective Drawing of a Woman.*

Albrecht Dürer and is illustrated in figure 8.1. Dürer's device consisted of a frame with vertical and horizontal wires strung across its opening to form a grid. The artist had a fixed viewing location (see the vertical marker in figure 8.1) from which he looked through a grid at a figure to be drawn. On the drawing table a canvas or paper was placed, about the same size as the frame and similarly marked with a faint grid. The artist copied what he saw through the grid onto the canvas. He may have noticed, for example, that the left knee of the model fell in a certain cell of the grid, the tip of the nose near an intersection of the grid, and so on. A reconstructed version of what Dürer saw is shown in figure 8.2. The effect is similar to that of taking a transparent sheet, holding it against a glass window, and tracing the perceived image exactly as it appears on the sheet. In the present example, the reconstructed illustration will show an image in which all of the linear cues will be of "correct" proportion. Artists found this device helpful but cumbersome[1] in getting their paintings in perspective. A much more versatile technique involved taking a sighting, as with a pencil, measuring the relative size of objects, and then copying those proportions onto a canvas—a technique still used today.

Well before Dürer's window, artists had practiced some form of perspective drawing; a sample of the techniques used is shown in table 8.1. During each period various artists treated perspective somewhat idiosyncratically—especially during the impressionist and modern periods—so exceptions may be found to this taxonomy. Nevertheless, table 8.1 will serve as a general guide to the next section.

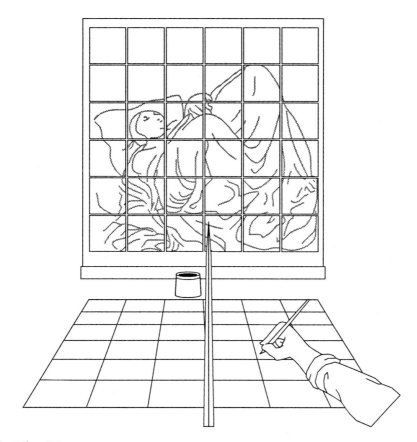

8.2 **What Dürer saw.**

Prehistoric Art and Perspective

The common impression that Renaissance artists invented perspective is wrong. Renaissance painters did richly develop linear perspective and its geometry. From the very beginning of visual art, however, artists have used some type of perspective to give their creations a realistic appearance.

Near the French village of Montignac, in the valley of the Vézère river, the cave of Lascaux was discovered by a group of children in 1940. The narrative tells that, while they were playing around an uprooted tree with their dog, the pet ran away. The children found the dog in a cave and stumbled onto one of the richest troves of prehistoric art yet seen. In this

Table 8.1
Perspective Typically Practiced in Various Periods of the History of Art

Period	Relative size	Occluded objects	Shadow	Elevation	Texture gradients	Atmospheric perspective	Linear perspective
Prehistoric	Yes	Yes	Limited	Yes	Not generally	No	No
Egyptian	No	Yes	Not generally	Yes	No	No	No
Greek	Limited	Yes	No	Limited	No	Limited	Limited
Roman	Yes	Yes	Yes	Yes	Limited	No	Limited
Renaissance	Yes	Yes	Yes	Yes	Yes	Limited	Yes
Impressionist	Yes	Yes	Yes	Yes	Yes	Yes	Limited
Modern	Sometimes	Yes	Sometimes	Limited	Not generally	Not generally	Not generally

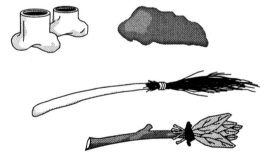

8.3 The prehistoric "paint box."

underground cavern hundreds of wall and ceiling paintings of deer, horses, ibexes, cows, bulls, stags, humans, and geometric patterns are displayed, fashioned by the hands of people of the Upper Paleolithic period about 15,000 years ago. It has been reliably determined that these early painters used soils mixed with blood, fat, and/or juices from plants to make red, yellow, and brown pigments. These paints were then stored in hollow bones and applied with moss or brushes made of animal fur, sticks, or leaves. Simple lamps of

animal fat in stone or clay vessels, or burning torches, provided meager light
for the artist to work by.

These magnificent examples of prehistoric art are remarkably unmo-
lested. (And the French authorities are determined to keep it that way.
Entrance to the caves is forbidden except for selected scholarly excursions.)
Figure 8.4 is a bull, painted on the limestone wall of the cave at Lascaux.
The total length of the bull is about 13 feet. Of particular significance for our

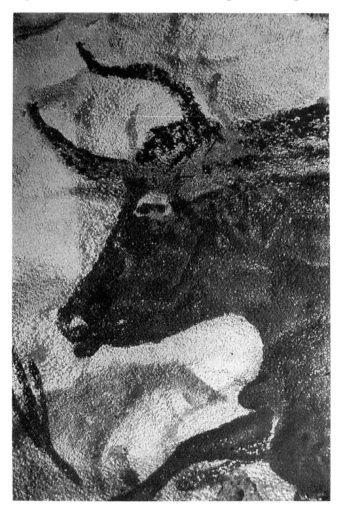

8.4 **Black bull, c. 16,000–14,000 B.C., from Lascaux, France.**

discussion is the use of a type of linear perspective in which nearer objects are larger than distant objects. Here, an example of linear perspective can be seen in the length of the animal's horns. The near horn is *longer* than the distant one, although the illusion created by the human eye and brain is that the distant horn may be slightly longer. It is not. Measure them. Notice, too, that the farther horn is partly occluded by the nearer forehead of the beast. Look at the shadowy figure under the bull's head. This distant horse (?) is less clear than the bull and is smaller. Yet we interpret the real size of the distant figure as about the same as the near object. Even if these two figures were drawn at different times, the rendition is consistent with modern theories of linear perspective.

Egyptian Art: In Perspective

Ancient Egyptian art persisted with remarkably little stylistic change for 3,000 years. The commonly accepted idea that Egyptian art was without perspective

DRAWING BY ALAIN © 1955 THE NEW YORKER MAGAZINE, INC.

8.5 From the tomb of Nebamun (18th Dynasty), Thebes. The impression of depth is (partially) achieved through occluded objects rather than by linear perspective.

is wrong. Depth, in Egyptian art, was indicated by occluded objects, and to a lesser degree by representing distant objects with fewer details than close objects. Also, in many examples from ancient Egypt, close objects were placed at the bottom of the surface and distant ones higher up, much as in Asian art. The use of *linear* perspective was carefully avoided in two-dimensional art forms, although there is ample evidence that the ancient Egyptians knew of these effects, as exhibited in the sophisticated use of three-dimensional perspective in sculpture, bas-relief, and (in some rare instances) in tomb paintings. The prohibition against using linear perspective seems more attributable to artistic dogma than to ignorance.

Figure 8.5 shows an example of the use of occluded (but not linear) perspective in Egyptian art. This drawing is from the tomb of Nebamun, a scribe and grain counter who lived in Thebes during the 18th Dynasty, a period of particularly rich artistic achievement. In the top panel a herd of short-horned cattle is shown, in the bottom a herd of long-horned. Egyptian wall art commonly depicted scenes in a series of rows, much like a Sunday cartoon; in place of balloons, a strip or scroll of hieroglyphics conveys the dialogue. In this case, the cowboy holding a lariat in the center of the painting is saying "Come, hurry up, do not speak in front of the praised one [Nebamun]! People speaking are his abomination." It is also likely that the account-ant Nebamun wanted to see exactly how many head of cattle he had in his herd, and the artist(s) obliged by showing the exact number in the first row

8.6 A magnificent bust from the Amarna period (18th Dynasty) of Egypt, showing remarkable technical skill in three-dimensional sculpture. This bust, widely believed to be of Nefertiti, wife of Akhenaten, is more likely an idealized model, maybe fashioned after one of the daughters of the royal couple.

(5), complete with an exact number of front legs (10). The purpose of this painting, and of many others from this period, is as much a matter of accounting as it is of decoration.

These rows of cows look curious to our eyes because the drawing does not follow the rules of linear perspective and, more importantly, does not present objects in a manner our eyes are accustomed to seeing. However, at least one form of perspective is maintained: the use of occluded objects to show which objects are closer and which are further from the viewer. Had the artist decided to depict the distant cattle in perspective (a violation of Egyptian artistic practice), he would have had to make them smaller, and, from what we know of Nebamun's own perspective on life, the owner would have seen this as meaning that he owned some normal-sized cattle, some small ones, and some very small ones. (He might then have demanded a reassessment, or the head of the artist.) In this sense, depicting cows without the diminishing limbs demanded by linear perspective is a perfectly valid way of showing reality.

Egyptian art was orthodox to the point of being imperious. Conventions for geometric proportions were laid down during the Early Dynastic Period (3000–2780 B.C.) and continued, with little modification, over a span of 3,000 years. The rigid control over the ratio of body parts in a drawing of a human, for example, was maintained by a matrix, or grid, that served as a guide for the artist. In actual practice, grids were drawn on the surface, then the figures were drawn, usually by apprentice craftsmen, and finished by skilled draftsmen and painters. (In some Egyptian tombs the process was not completed before the tomb was sealed, so a clear record of the process is preserved to this day.) Proportions within the grid were prescribed, irrespective of the overall scale of the grid (figure 8.7). Not only were the body proportions specified, but also such conventions as the distance between the kilt and the ground, the girth of the waist, and the width of the shoulders.

Egyptian figures appear awkward to our eyes, what some would label artless, because of strict adherence to an artistic standard that shows a frontal body (with correspondingly massive shoulders) and a head in profile. Both legs are usually shown (see the gaggle of differently marked legs in figure 8.5), which requires one leg to be extended, and, in many instances, in order that the big toe be clearly shown, two left (or right) feet will be shown attached to one person. Size, which in Renaissance art varies as a function of the proximity of the viewer, plays a much different role in Egyptian art. It is a matter of status. Thus, a Pharaoh may be immense, his wife a bit smaller, and his children appropriately diminutive.

The Egyptian mode of depicting size doubtless conveyed very significant information. To use linear perspective would have destroyed the formula for understanding. The knowledgeable eye of an ancient Egyptian "saw" things invisible to many. But to assert, as some learned critics have, that Egyptian art is unsophisticated is in itself a sophomoric claim. In modern cognitive terms, the Egyptians employed top-down processing of signals. Interestingly, some artists in the latter part of the nineteenth century and throughout the twentieth century returned to a nonlinear mode of representation, which has the effect of creating a dynamic tension in the viewer. (See Van Gogh, Cézanne, Picasso, and many others for examples.)

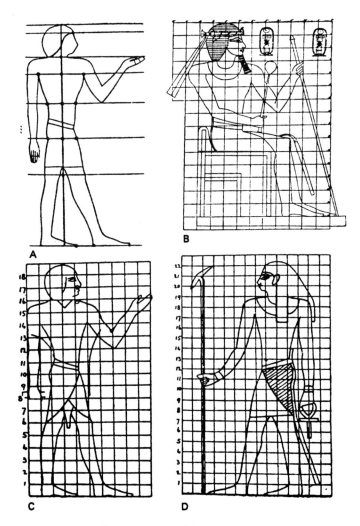

8.7 The Egyptian canon of proportion: Old Kingdom (*A*), New Kingdom (*B*), late period (*C, D*). From Sporre (1989).

8.8   The use of linear perspective in Greek art: *Hercules and Telephos* **(Roman copy of a Greek work of the second century B.C.).**

Greek and Roman Art: Gaining Perspective

Very early Greek artists, prior to 500 B.C., mimicked Egyptian art conventions. The artist was restrained by a predetermined formula and many of the drawings and sculptures from this period look very "Egyptian." However, with the emergence of classical Greek society and state, there developed a more democratic, humanistic, and naturalistic mode of representation. One of the most conspicuous departures from Egyptian art was the orientation of human figures. Faces were shown in three-quarters view, eyes were shown in reference to the head, feet were not always parallel, and objects began to be foreshortened. We also find in representations of buildings that parallel lines began to converge. In figure 8.8 we see an example of the use of

8.9 Fragment of a crater from Taranto, c. 350 B.C. Except in the door, receding lines do not converge.

perspective in Greek art, from the second century B.C. Notice how relaxed the people seem. One does not mistake this drawing for Egyptian art. An even more precise use of linear perspective is shown in figure 8.9, although the geometric parameters are ill defined.

During the fourth century B.C., the laws of linear perspective were defined by Democritus and Anaxagoras. Vitruvius (cited in Wright 1984, p. 35) later commented on the development of perspective drawing:

> Given a certain central point, the lines should correspond as they do in nature to the point of sight and the projection of the visual rays, so that from an unclear object a clear representation of the appearance of buildings might be given in painted scenery . . . so . . . some parts may seem to be withdrawing into the background and others to be protruding in front.

8.10 *Lady Playing the Cithara,* Roman (c. 50 B.C.), showing the use of linear perspective.

Even though the essential intellectual qualities of linear perspective were known during this time, the application of those principles still proved problematic for many Greek and Roman artists.

Although most two-dimensional Roman art has been destroyed, there are some specimens that indicate perspective. Some of the best examples are from Pompeii, which was preserved under several meters of ash spewed out of Mount Vesuvius. Roman art, especially during the early period of that style, imitates Greek art, as early Greek art imitates Egyptian art. Roman art frequently depicted classic forms of the human figure, as shown in figure 8.10. Here, visual perspective is attempted with only half success. While the angles on the chair seem almost right, the furthest leg of the chair is identical in length to the near leg; it is not shorter, as we would expect. A somewhat more convincing example of linear perspective is shown in figure 8.11. In this case, all of the features are oriented toward a single point, or vanishing point. Other examples from this period also verify not only that Roman and Greek artists knew the principles of perspective, but that a few possessed the ability to portray two-dimensional art as if it had a third dimension. Full development of the style did not appear until the Renaissance.

Asian Art

About the same time as the high Renaissance in Europe, Japanese, Korean, and Chinese artists of great skill and refinement were producing ink paintings of fine quality. Some form of perspective is used in nearly all of these paintings, although much less attention is given to the geometric correctness of linear perspective, the trademark of Renaissance painters. We see in the paintings of the Chinese artist Tang Yin (c. 1500) a use of linear perspective applied to architectural forms and furniture—walls, tables, and chairs are shown in (crude) perspective—while people are shown in proportion to their status—important people are larger than less important people. In one of Tang Yin's paintings, *A Poet and Two Courtesans,* the seated poet is nearly twice the height of his female concubines.

Artists from these regions were particularly adept with atmospheric perspective, in which distant objects were shown as more diffused than near objects. Many of these works are landscape scenes and bear such dreamy titles as *Traveling among the Mountains and Streams* (Fan Kuan, eleventh century, China), *Spring Mountains, Clouds, and Pine Trees* (Mi Fei, eleventh century, China), *The Dream of the Peach Blossom Garden* (An Kyon, fifteenth century,

8.11 Cubiculum from a Roman villa at Boscoreale (c. 50 B.C.), showing skillful use of linear perspective.

Korea), and *Autumn Landscape* (Sesshu, fifteenth century, Japan). Figure 8.12 shows a particularly exquisite example of Japanese art in *Maple Viewers* (Kanō Hideyori, c. 1560). Here visual perspective is achieved through the vertical placement of figures, distant objects toward the top of the scene and near objects at the bottom. The size of people in Asian art does not follow the laws of linear perspective but appears to be based on status, with central

8.12 *Maple Viewers*. Kanō Hideyori, Muromachi period, c. 1560.

Giotto

During the late Middle Ages, from about the twelfth to the fifteenth centuries, journey-man artists in Europe plied their trade by painting frescoes, altar panels, and manuscripts. Art of this time generally lacked depth, both in terms of the physical representations of a third dimension and in terms of the subject matter. The Florentine artist Giotto (1266–1337) broke with the convention of the time and portrayed people as they actually appeared. He drew expressions and actions as none of his contemporaries even attempted. He also thought deeply about the geometry of paintings and how they could be designed to look real.

One of his paintings is *The Angel Appearing to St. Anne* (figure 8.13). In this painting we see how Giotto reintroduced the use of linear perspective to create a sense of realism. Notice how this scene is reminiscent of a stage on which players perform. The people have genuine expressions and freedom to move about in a three-dimensional space. This illusion of three-dimensional space is based on three-dimensional perspective; the main lines of convergence are shown.

8.13   Giotto, *The Angel Appearing to St. Anne,* as diagrammed in Malins (1980).

figures proportionally larger than peripheral figures. Size of people seems, more or less, independent of their proximity to the viewer. Geometric objects, such as the low table and box at lower right in figure 8.12 as well as the distant pagoda, show some signs of linear perspective. Also, the artist uses occluded objects as a depth cue.

The Renaissance: Visual "Truth"

Art of the Renaissance strove for a precise visual realism: a painting should look much like an object viewed through a window. A painter's canvas, then, became a type of window frame upon which the world was displayed. Artists used many techniques in trying to create the illusion of reality, the most important being perspective.

For an example, consider a work not from Italian art (which dominated much of the science of perspective during this period) but by the Flemish artist Jan van Eyck, described by his contemporaries as "the prince of our age." Van Eyck's wedding portrait *The Betrothal of the Arnolfini* (figure 8.14) is as marvelous today as it was stunning to art critics over 550 years ago. The sheer technical skill is astonishingly refined. The rich details of the dress, the subtle portrayal of light as it embraces the figures, and even the sheen of the little dog's fur rival paintings of the high Renaissance. On the wall (above the mirror) the artist has written "Johannes de eyck fuit hic 1434" (Jan van Eyck was here, 1434). To van Eyck is attributed the first use of oil paints, and his meticulous attention to textures and details was achieved with this new medium. For centuries art critics have pondered the theme of the painting, some inferring that the bride-to-be is pregnant.

Perspective is of such a nature that it makes what is flat appear in relief, and what is in relief appear flat.

—Leonardo da Vinci

Of particular interest to students of perspective is the artist's ability to create an illusion of three dimensions. The illusion is created, in part, by the use of linear perspective, and yet, if we study this painting in detail, there is an uneasy impression that it is not entirely "square." Further analysis reveals that the artist used at least four vanishing points in the painting, as shown in figure 8.14, but the discrepancy is so slight that we don't immediately notice it, and are otherwise impressed with the fastidious attention to details that gives the painting a photographic quality.

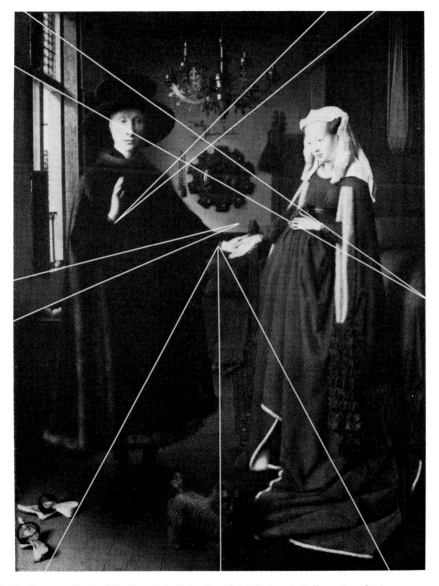

8.14 Jan van Eyck, *The Betrothal of the Arnolfini* (National Gallery, London).

8.15   Masaccio, *The Holy Trinity.*

About the same time in Italy, artists were absorbed in perspective, especially linear perspective. Brunelleschi was laboring over the mathematical principles of perspective (some say he "invented" it), Alberti was concerned with the "practical" side of perspective that dealt with producing a geometrically correct painting, and Masaccio was busy doing two-dimensional church paintings that looked as if they were in three dimensions. Such is Masaccio's visually precise rendition of *The Holy Trinity* (figure 8.15), which is found in the church of Santa Maria Novella, just opposite the train station in Florence. This two-dimensional painting, like many emerging at this time, has a carefully calculated linear scheme in which the lines converge on a single point. The illusion is as compelling as Bramante's false apse (see figure 8.17). The painting has six figures that appear to be located at various distances from the observer, with some of the figures set back in a niche in the wall. Closest

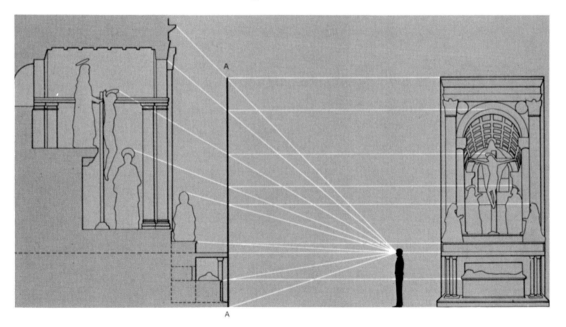

8.16 The logic of Masaccio's perspective. The figures are placed back in explicitly defined layers of depth. The line AA marks the picture plane, the window through which the viewer sees the illusion, standing a few paces back. The observer's viewpoint is precisely level with the top of the altar. The skeleton under it is seen from above. The figures, however, are all of the same size and all seem to press against the picture plane. From Piper (1991, p. 105).

Bramante's *Trompe-l'oeil*

Tourists to Milan are usually so busy visiting the magnificent cathedral, the church of Santa Maria delle Grazie, and the famous opera house of La Scala that they overlook a small church only a five-minute walk from the cathedral in the center of the city. The church of San Satiro was designed by Donato Bramante near the beginning of the sixteenth century, although the campanile dates from the ninth century and the facade from 1871. Bramante, who is better known for submitting the original plan for St. Peter's in Rome, faced a problem in the planning of San Satiro. A city street blocked extension of the aspe (that part of the main sanctuary that extends beyond the transept and in which some liturgical ceremonies take place). Specifically, it was impossible to build a

8.17 Church of San Satiro, Milan, and ground plan showing the actual depth of the apse in Bramante's *trompe-l'oeil*.

church deep enough both to be aesthetically pleasing and to accommodate the parishioners. Bramante solved the problem by creating a magnificent *trompe-l'oeil,* a visual deception based on false linear perspective, in the apse. The result, as shown in figure 8.17, looks like any number of other churches. However, what appears to be an apse of 6 or more meters has been condensed into a tiny space, with the altar constructed in scale and placed in front of the false apse. The illusion is created by painting in false pillars of diminishing heights and a vaulted ceiling orientated toward a vanishing point, and, in general, converging all other major visual cues to a distant point. Compare the photograph with the ground plan and especially notice the arrow. This column is the *same* column as shown by the arrow in the photograph! The altar is actually in front of this column. As convincing as this illusion is upon entering the church, it soon disappears as you move forward, and the deception is totally destroyed if you view the apse from the transept. Don't miss it if you visit Milan. (Send a postcard.)

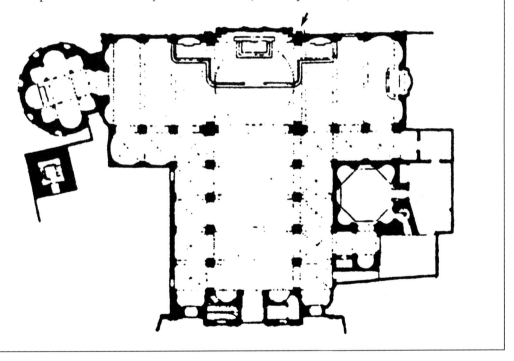

to the viewer are the patrons who commissioned the work. On the next plane we see the Virgin and St. John on about the same level with the outcrop of rock in which the cross is inserted. Then Christ, behind whom is God the Father, looking out and the only figure shown in a full frontal view. These figures appear to be naturally positioned along a continuous field of visual cues all suggesting depth. In figure 8.16 a schematic diagram of the illusion shows how the artist may have used a window frame (see Dürer, beginning of the chapter) upon which to create the illusion.

In 1488 Carlo Crivelli painted the *Annunciation* shown in figure 8.18. Here the use of linear perspective is so overwhelming—our eye is drawn to the miniature painting framed by the distant arch—that we lose sight of the important features. The foreground seems to be so close to the viewer that it appears to extend beyond the picture plane and "gets in the viewer's face." By the mid-fifteenth century, Italian painters had solved most of the major geometric problems associated with linear perspective, and their art was nothing short of spectacular.

The most celebrated and enigmatic of all *trompe-l'oeils* may be Leonardo da Vinci's *Last Supper,* painted between 1495 and 1498 on the refectory wall of Santa Maria delle Grazie in Milan. The last supper of Christ had been a recurrent theme in the history of Western art, but no previous artist had achieved the artistry and mathematical precision shown by Leonardo. (For an example of a less artful rendition, in which the artist seems unconcerned not only with the principles of perspective but with the need to plan ahead, see figure 8.19.) Volumes have been written about Leonardo's masterpiece, some of which have concentrated on his use of linear perspective. When dealing with the geometry of visual perspective, unfortunately, many critics have been only half-right and some have been downright wrong.

Let's decipher the mystery of the *Last Supper's* problem of perspective.[2] A photograph of the wall painting and its natural context is shown in figure 8.20. The painting was done in an eating hall for monks and one can only imagine the impact it had on the row after row of solemn diners when it was first unveiled. The present painting is badly damaged through centuries of neglect, bombing in World War II, alterations in the building (a doorway was punched through the wall), amateur repair, and decay of the surface (some critics have suggested that the surface was so unstable, due to the humidity in the refectory, that the painting began to deteriorate even before it was completed). The wall is on the north side, further contributing to the humidity problem. The medium was an oil-tempera pigment that did not adhere

8.18   Carlo Crivelli, *The Annunciation*. Note the attention to perspective detail, such as roofs and arches extending to the back of the painting.

well to the wall. However, during the late fifteenth century, the monks dined in the intimate splendor of Leonardo's masterpiece. The emphasis on the monks and where they sat is not trivial, for if we are to understand the geometry of *The Last Supper* we must begin with the point of view of its audience, for whom the painting was designed. Leonardo did. He spent three years making preparatory sketches of the painting.

The monks' initial reaction to the then brilliantly colored work is likely to have been astonishment, because of the painting's realism. The imaginary room in which Christ and his disciples sup appears to be a natural extension of the refectory itself, and yet one cannot quite grasp the visual dynamics that are working to create this illusion. The powerful intimacy one feels is even more remarkable when one considers the painting's vertical elevation. Christ's face, a focal point of the painting, is about 15 feet from the floor of the hall, or some 10 feet above the eye level of a standing spectator and even higher above the eye of a seated diner.

Christ was to celebrate his last supper, among the Dominicans, at Milan.

—Goethe

8.19 The Last Supper, miniature from a Syrian codex, twelfth century.

8.20 Leonardo da Vinci, *The Last Supper,* wall painting in the refectory of the monastery of Santa Maria delle Grazie, Milan.

After the initial reaction to the intimacy and realism of the painting, the viewer may have considered the narrative told by it. The moment frozen in time by Leonardo is when Christ said, "Verily I say unto you, that one of you shall betray me," and the disciples replied, "Lord, is it I?" The twelve disciples are arranged in four clusters of three disciples each, and our eyes organize the like visual features of heads into four groups (see the discussion of Gestalt organization in chapter 4). One of the disciples is isolated and ambiguous: Judas, fourth from the left, who clutches his bag of silver. Leonardo painted a scene designed to embrace the audience in such a way that they felt very much a part of the last supper of Christ. The effect of visual involvement is largely dependent on the skillful application of the laws of perspective.

Painting the *Last Supper* well above the eye level of the seated monk was enormously practical. Everyone in the room could see it clearly. But it also proved to be a problem for the artist. Proper prospective of a picture placed high above the eye of a viewer would render a painting along the lines shown in figure 8.21A. Such a viewpoint would have made the mural seem remote, detached, monumental, aloof, and ultimately uninteresting. From this perspective one would look, for example, at the underside of the table and be denied a look at the expressive hands. The solution to this problem was to orient the perspective to an imaginary viewpoint from which a horizontal line of sight runs to the faces of Christ and the disciples. This point is about 15 feet above the actual floor of the refectory, yet Leonardo achieves the illusion of this point of view from every seat in the dining hall. A lesser artist might have required the viewer to see the painting from an elevated point of view (one that might be achieved by having one monk stand on the shoulders of another).

The dimensions of the imaginary room in which the last supper is depicted are important for both aesthetic and symbolic reasons, but calculating its dimensions is problematic. The perceived vertical depth of the room *recedes* as one approaches the painting and *grows deeper* as one steps back from the painting. So compelling is this illusion that one can see it in the two sketches in figure 8.21. If one knew where to stand (or sit) when viewing the painting, then one could calculate the room's intended dimensions; if one knew the intended dimensions, then one could know where to stand. Experts have disputed the issue for centuries, with some suggesting a close viewpoint (viewing angle about 125 degrees) and thus a shallow room (see Arnheim 1974) while others suggest a far viewpoint (viewing angle about 45 degrees) and thus a very long room with the proportions of a church (see Pedretti 1973). Still others (see Wright 1983) suggest the room to be a cube.

There are some subtle cues Leonardo left with which we can solve the two unknown parts of the formula. The first of these cues is in the dimensions of the back wall. We can see that the height of the wall is equal to its width—it is a perfect square. This alone does not indicate depth, but does hint that the artist had regular features in mind. Other evidence comes from the orientation of the diagonal vanishing points, which strike a point behind the head of Jesus. These lines, if extended, form the crossbars of a perfect square (see figure 8.21B), which is consistent with Leonardo's concern for

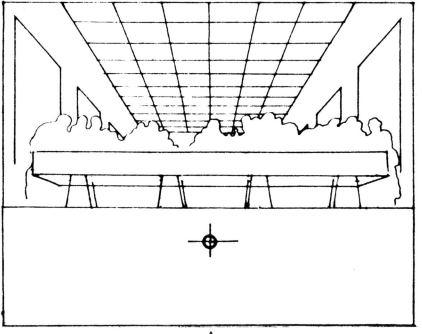

A

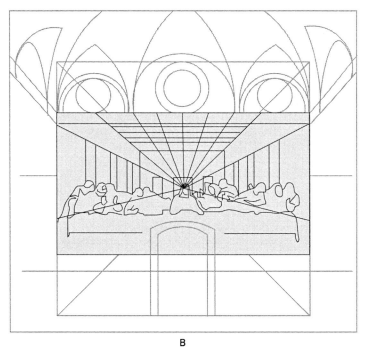

B

8.21 How the painting would have appeared if da Vinci had assumed the point of view of a seated monk (*A*, from Wright 1983). The use of converging lines gives a sense of depth and focuses one's attention on Jesus (*B*).

regular, geometrically harmonious figures. Further evidence can be found in the table top and its dimensions, which are geometrically proportional to the major perspective lines. The width of the table is a very important depth cue, for if that distance can be reliably estimated, then by simple trigonometric functions the depth of the room can be estimated. In this regard, look at the figure farthest to the right (the apostle Simon) and the shape of the plate in front of him. Assuming that both he and his plate are of normal size, we can estimate the width of the table and apply that measure to the depth of the room. My calculations of the dimensions of the table, assuming a 90-degree viewing angle, make it about 3+ feet wide, which is consistent with the space occupied by Simon. The panels on the right and left side walls also appear to be rectangular and in proportion to the back windows. The ceiling tile is a bit problematic, as we might assume it to be made up of squares. If our hypothesis is correct that the room is a cube, then these panels would have to be rectangular—a ceiling style not unusual, but somewhat inconsistent with the other geometric features of the painting.

If we carry out the major lines and ratios of panels and windows, we can deduce that the depicted room was a perfect cube. The "perfect" viewing distance (i.e., the one in which all of the major visual cues are consistent with a cubicle room) would be one in which the visual angle subtends a 90-degree view, although all viewing conditions embody the intimacy of the painting. Since the width of the painting is about 28 feet 10 inches and a 90-degree angle of view is prescribed, the geometric shape formed by the painting (on the hypotenuse) and the viewer (at the intersection of the two legs) is a perfect isosceles triangle. I calculate the "proper" viewing distance (i.e., one in which the room looks to be a cube) to be about 14 feet 5 inches directly in front of Christ.

The Renaissance produced scores of geometrically pristine paintings by Giotto, Raphael, Michelangelo, Bellini, Titian, Crivelli, and many others, including Uccello. To record these achievements in detail would take us too far afield, but a study of these artists in the context of cognitive psychology would be a worthy venture. Alas, our selective review of perspective in art must omit much of the baroque, rococo, classical, and romantic periods. We will, however, move to impressionist and modern artists, who treat perspective much differently than the Renaissance painters.

8.22 William Hogarth, frontispiece to *Dr. Brook Taylor's Method of Perspective* (1754). Hogarth's engraving shows a playful impression of perspective gone awry. Fishing lines are crossed, a woman lights the pipe of a man on a distant hill, and an outsized crow perches on a distant tree.

Impressionism

The impressionist and postimpressionist artists of the last part of the nineteenth century—such characters as Manet, Monet, Morisot, Degas, Renoir, Cassatt, Seurat, Signac, Pissarro, Cézanne, Gauguin, van Gogh, Toulouse-Lautrec, and Matisse[3]—developed a new way of representing art in which the psychological perception of reality was captured by colors, movement, and aerial perspective, among other techniques. In one sense, as Greek art shucked off the rigid canons of Egyptian art, impressionism abandoned the dogma of linear perspective and realism established during the Renaissance. One school of thought suggests that impressionist art emerged in reaction to the newly invented camera, which portrayed real scenes with startling fidelity. Painters could do no better, and developed instead a new style of art in which the principal effect is obtained through one's emotional reaction to a painting, rather than through one's sense of visual correctness. Other factors surely contributed as well, including the increasing personal freedom and wealth of the period, greater understanding of the interactive qualities of colors, and the invention of new products such as tin tubes that kept oil paints fresh for days and thereby allowed artists greater mobility. Many painted outside in natural settings. Then, there were the extraordinary artists and their personal outlook on life—not trifling factors.

Linear perspective, essential in recreating a church's facade, was only marginally effective in recreating a field of poppies or people gathered at a picnic. Furthermore, harsh application of the geometric laws of linear perspective depicted a world of inflexible, restrained, and immobile objects inhabited by people frozen in time and space. Such a view was antithetical to the free-spirited bohemians who lived, loved, and painted in Paris during the latter part of the nineteenth century. Aerial perspective worked better for their view of the world and humanity. It created a dreamy, softer, warmer view of their subjects.

Only a small sample of the rich collection of impressionist and postimpressionist art will be presented here, but the principles exhibited should serve as a cognitive template through which you can view all sorts of impressionist paintings. They are beautiful, and a large part of their beauty is derived from the way the artists used perspective.

In general, impressionist art distorted the laws of linear perspective. The idea that all lines should be oriented toward a single vanishing point was abandoned in favor of a code of perspective that created a dynamic tension.

Consider the well-know example of the way van Gogh painted his bedroom at Arles a short time before his death (figure 8.23). Something is radically "wrong" with this painting and would be sure to drive a Renaissance painter or critic mad. The lines do not converge, and it would be impossible to fit a real bed into the space it occupies in the painting. The chairs are not "right," especially if one compares them with the table top. A schematic representation shows this painting redrawn in proper perspec-

There are two things in the painter; the eye and the mind. Each of them should aid the other.

—Paul Cézanne

tive. While this version is largely correct from a linear perspective standpoint, it is less interesting than van Gogh's interpretation, which causes a dynamic tension among viewers.

A creative use of linear perspective is shown in figure 8.24, Cézanne's *Still Life with Fruit Basket,* in which the artist shows forms of fruit and objects on a table. If viewed literally, the fruit, basket, wine, and all would slip, under the influence of gravity, onto the floor. Notice particularly the surface of the table: if the lower left line is continued, it would not line up with the exposed portion on the right side (see the diagram in figure 8.24). In this painting, as well as other works by Cézanne, several viewpoints are represented simultaneously. This pioneering technique was later embraced by cubist painters, especially Picasso and Braque (see chapter 9). Loran's (1943) analysis of the use of perspective in Cézanne's still life is particularly revealing: "The first eye level, marked I, takes in, roughly, the front plane of the fruit basket, the sugar bowl, and the smaller pitcher. . . . The second eye level, much higher, marked II, looks down on the ginger jar, and the top of the basket." Also shown in this diagram are the eye positions at Ia and IIb, which show two other points of view. The multiplicity of viewpoints suggests that we can see around these objects—that they have a dimensionality created by the mobility of the viewer. A kind of motion parallax has been ingeniously created by Cézanne on a stationary two-dimensional canvas viewed by an observer who sees from a single fixed position.

In Monet's *Field of Poppies* (figure 8.25), perhaps his best-known work, we can see most of the elements of perspective discussed in chapter 7. The schematic diagrams indicates the use of atmospheric perspective, the shift in colors with depth, and the use of occluded objects to show location; the use of texture and distinctiveness, with distant flowers more numerous,

8.23 Vincent van Gogh, *Van Gogh's Bedroom at Arles,* and a schematic representation of the painting drawn in perspective.

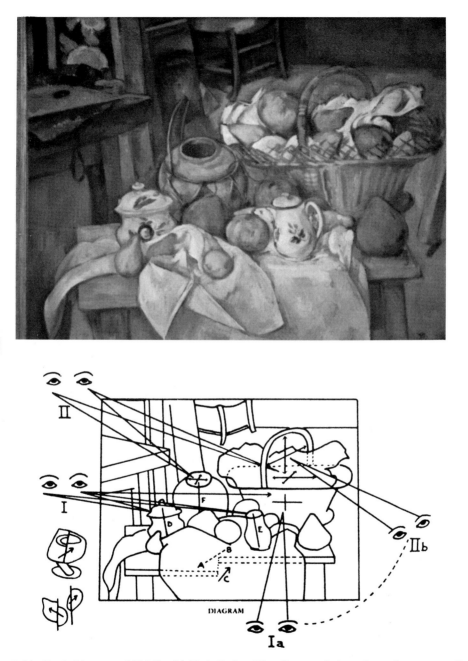

DIAGRAM

Ia

8.24 Paul Cézanne, *Still Life with Fruit Basket*. The diagram below shows how parts of the painting are in correct perspective for eyes situated at different heights (I and II) and at different angles of observation (Ia and IIb). Diagram from Loran (1943).

8.25 Claude Monet, *Field of Poppies*. The diagrams at right show the different elements of perspective used in the painting.

smaller, and less detailed than close flowers; and the use of size, linear perspective, and elevation as cues to depth.

Modern Art

If impressionism is experimental art, then modern art is revolutionary. Modern art, insofar as one can fit a dozen or more styles under a single label, is characterized by breaking all the rules of art. Linear perspective, illusions of depth, representational art, and even the subject matter of art were thrown

Atmosphere, colors, shading, and occluded objects

Texture and distinctiveness

Size, linear perspective, and elevation

away in favor of an art searching for a theory. As Euclidian mathematics, Newtonian physics, and linear perspective dominated the intellectual thought of the previous generations, the twentieth century saw fundamental challenges to all of these traditional views.

No longer would the degree of linear correctness be the measure of a painter, as many modern artists created a sensation of depth in revolutionary new ways. Consider the work of Pablo Picasso, who painted *Seated Nude* (figure 8.26) during his cubist period. Here the observer is confronted by a montage of strong visual lines, but, unlike in Renaissance paintings, the lines point in all sorts of directions. No vanishing point here.

Return to this painting and inspect it for possible depth cues. After a while people see the seated nude in 3-D—sort of. Suddenly her breasts stand out from the canvas, the forearm is closer, and the features of the face are lively with depth. One way to think of this painting is to imagine a perfect representation of a seated nude painted on a plane of glass. It is shattered and the shards are put together to form only an approximation of the original painting. This reconstructed painting may contain most of the parts of the original, but the painting is not the same. Yet this new view might show different parts of the seated nude: subtleties intellectually invisible in the representational painting. Picasso takes this analogy one step further. Not only does he show us parts, but sometimes he shows parts from different perspectives. Thus, in one painting we may see an eye drawn from the frontal perspective and a nose in profile. Strong linear cues that suggest a type of vanishing point appear in the same painting with other linear cues that suggest another vanishing point. Picasso has broken the rules of conventional artistic practice and reconstructed his image of reality with a new set of rules.

Other modern artists even mocked the conventions of the past, as in the popular illustrations by M. C. Escher. In figure 8.27 we see a playful interpretation of monks ascending and descending a staircase that has no end. The visual cues in this illustration are based on our tendency to organize shadows and elevations as shown in the small figure at upper right. Here we organize the immediate stimulus of the stairs in a series of local schemata. If we take a visual walk on these stairs, our eye follows the cues presented by the steps and risers—it does not matter whether we are ascending or descending. Although our rational brain may tell us that it is impossible to continually go up or down a staircase, we fail at first to look at the overall elevation of the walls that support the stairs and consider alternative organizations.

8.26   Pablo Picasso, *Seated Nude.*

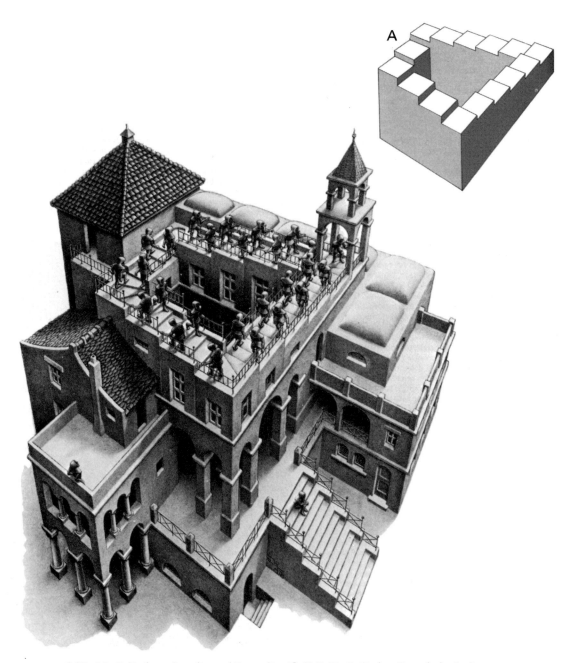

8.27   M. C. Escher, *Ascending and Descending* (© 1960 M. C. Escher Foundation). At upper right is the drawing on which Escher based his lithograph.

It is possible to demystify this figure if we "see" the staircase as not being continuous but having a large gap between the walls at A. Think of the middle step as being separated from the far wall by a large distance. Stare at that block until you see it as closer and *higher* than the square to its upward right. (This exercise may be difficult, but continue to work on the illusion from this perspective. It may help if you place a pencil over the center step. If you see it, you will be rewarded by understanding a key feature of Escher's work and will no longer be mute when reading an Escher T-shirt.)

Finally, two examples of how contemporary artists use some form of perspective in their work. The first is *Preparedness* by Roy Lichtenstein (figure 8.28), which uses linear perspective, occluded objects, and diminishing size. The second example is Peter Max's *Traveling through Darkness* (figure 8.29), in which illumination, colors, and a hint of visual perception (see the feet) are enough to give us the impression that this fireball is hurtling through the darkness of space, which is in the distance.

It isn't that modern artists have repealed the laws of visual perspective—they have not, as to do so would require that the laws of physiological sensation and brain processing be repealed—but that they have used them in creative ways. Our eyes and brain, long adapted to using visual cues to see things in perspective, react to the visual cues used by all artists in essentially the same way as our ancestors reacted to the environmental cues essential for

8.28 Roy Lichtenstein, *Preparedness.*

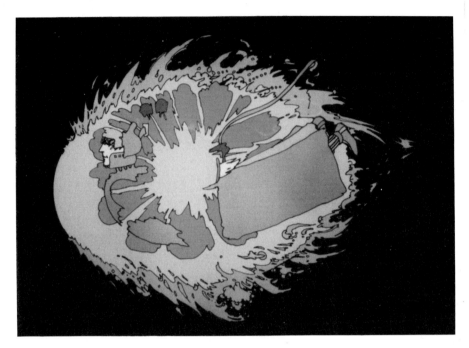

8.29 Peter Max, *Traveling through Darkness.*

their life, love, and survival. Artists through the ages have chosen to emphasize one or another aspect of the rules of visual perception in the way they portray their impression of the world and its people. In this chapter we have only sampled the history of these artists and the visual rules of perspective each has emphasized. It remains for you to apply this knowledge to the myriad different art styles you will encounter throughout your lifetime.

9 Connections: Canonic Representations, Memory, and the Cognition of Art

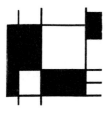

The lowest form of thinking is the bare recognition of the object. The highest, the comprehensive intuition of the man who sees all things as part of a system.

—*Plato*

With me, a picture is a sum of destructions. I make the picture, and proceed to destroy it. But in the end nothing is lost—the red I have removed from one part shows up in another.

—*Picasso*

Different styles of art affect people differently. While some prefer the near-photographic realism of modern illustrators, others choose the misty perspective of impressionist art. Still others enjoy the "unconventional" art of ancient Egypt, or the surrealist qualities of some modern artists, or the "correct" art of the Renaissance. Each style reflects the aesthetics of the artist as he or she attempts to touch the mind and soul of humanity.

Representational Art—Abstract Art

All art is representational . . . at least partly. In the case of "realistic" art, as in illustrations by Norman Rockwell, a depicted object is made nearly identical with what the eye senses. Here a pumpkin looks like a pumpkin, a man like a man, a woman like a woman, and a chair like a chair . . . almost, for even in really "realistic" art, the pumpkin, man, woman, and chair—although thoroughly recognizable—are somehow slightly "idealized," especially in the scenes shown in figure 9.1.

9.1 Prototypic views of people and of an American scene by Norman Rockwell.

ROCKWELL

In the left-hand picture, people from various races and nationalities are shown in quasi-photographic realism. While the folks in this painting are definitely shown as individuals, they are also drawn to be idealized representatives of categories of people. Psychologists call these best examples *prototypes.* The American working man near the center is likely a farmer (note the suntanned face and light forehead—distinctive features of farmers, who work out-of-doors and wear hats). He embodies all the conspicuous features of that group: strong, rough hands, well-worn blue shirt, tousled hair, an "honest" face, and so on. The illustration is worth study (although some art critics may dismiss such paintings as mere illustrations or "calendar art," not "serious art"),[1] and from the perspective of a cognitive psychologist it has much to tell.

The theme in the second illustration is familiar: it is the personification of home, Thanksgiving, Mom, patriotism, and "the American way"—a place, a symbol, and a sentiment that represent an idealized portrait of more abstract concepts. There is an American archetypical theme in this picture that is derived from the understanding of features. This is Rockwell at his best. He shows people as they like to be seen and as we like to see them. Even though objects and people are generally shown as they appear to the eye (the wicker chair is drawn in perfect perspective, not like van Gogh's chair in figure 8.23; the table holds things squarely, not like Cézanne's misaligned table in figure 8.24), Rockwell's things are somehow slightly better than they are in real life. The artist has taken some license with this slice of Americana and shown a hint of abstraction. He has shown us people, places, and things as we wish they appeared and has captured epitomized images—those that we all hold in our long-term memory. For these reasons the people are "familiar." Perhaps they are like people in our own family, or like people we know—someone who might live in our town—or someone we wish to know, or perhaps they have features of people we know.

Everyone can invent a story to go with these illustrations. Return to *Thanksgiving*. Notice the small details (Rockwell did): his shoes, their hands, how he sits on the chair, her look, their features, the perspective of the tablecloth, the wallpaper. Who are these people and what are they saying to each other? (Think about your eye movements and fixations as you consider these matters. See chapter 6.) The storymaking of these *Post* covers went on each month in many American homes for decades, and the story enhanced the picture and vice versa.

On the opposite end of the representational continuum is abstract art. All art is abstract, more or less, as was shown in the scenes by Rockwell. That is, art is not reality[2] but always a representation of something else, whether an object, a person, a feeling, or even an idea. In figure 9.3 we show two specimens of a more overtly abstract art. In much abstract art no subject is identifiable or intended; it is impossible to see a person, a tree, a potato, nor are we meant to. Doing away with a tangible subject was thought by some to "free" art from earthly conventions that inhibited expression. Music provided an excellent model for many painters (Kandinsky for example; see figure 3.5) of an aesthetic expression that could be achieved without semantic content. So too, some reasoned, a type of visual euphony could be created purely from the effects of color, lines, and shapes. Doing away with a physically recognizable subject, however, does not mean that these paintings are without a theme.

This Is Not a Pipe

What does Magritte mean when he writes "This is not a pipe?" Of course it is! What is reality? Is this *really* a pipe? Of course not, it is a picture of a pipe. Magritte has drawn a visual "gotcha" *while* posing a serious question of reality.

9.2 René Magritte, *The Betrayal of Images.*

LÉGER

In the first of these works, Fernand Léger's *Woman Holding a Vase,* the painting is clearly of a woman holding a vase (although we need to apply more imagination to see these things than we would had Normal Rockwell drawn them). Léger shows us but half a vase and balances it with the circular breast of the woman. The composition is far less a photographic impression than an expression of the artist's version of the essential emotive aspects of

9.3 Fernand Léger, *Woman Holding a Vase;* Wassily Kandinsky, *Cossacks*.

the subject. The painting is distinguished by its "chunkiness," and forms are tightly controlled within definite boundaries.

KANDINSKY

Kandinsky's *Cossacks* is more typical of abstract art, and a naive viewer would be hard pressed to make sense out of these few lines seemingly carelessly strewn across the canvas. Indeed, the artist intended to produce a type of visual music in which one senses the psychological effects of pure colors. The reds should strike the eye and brain like a piercing arrow. The artist gives us a clue to the subject in the title, *Cossacks* (sometimes called *Battle*). With this verbal label, we can begin to make out the headgear, muskets, and movement associated with those warriors. In both of these examples we see the application of top-down processing, in which the viewer adds his or her interpretation to what you might call an artistic Rorschach test. It is cerebral art, which means that the viewer must apply his or her intellect to appreciate it fully. These abstract works, because they require interpretation, are susceptible to misunderstanding and controversy. Yet however ambiguous they are, there remains a central theme in each. An underlying reality of womanhood or cossacks can be found (or invented) in the mind of the beholder.

Reality: Two Views
A story is told about Picasso and an American soldier at the end of World War II. The G.I. complained that he could not understand Picasso's portraits because everything was distorted; the eyes were misplaced, the nose misshapen, the mouth twisted, and so on. "What should a picture look like?" inquired Picasso. The G.I. whipped out his wallet and produced a photograph of his comely girlfriend. "Like this!" Picasso looked carefully at the photograph and then said, "She's kind of small, isn't she?"

Each of the paintings shown in figures 9.1 and 9.3 contain a central theme of some sort. Psychologists have been intensely interested in the cognitive aspects of topics related to themes, including the topic of canonic representations.

Canonic Representations

Canonic representations of a given concept or class of things are memories that best represent that concept or class. They are "central" views, whether the view is of an object, a person, an emotion, or an idea. Canonic representations may be expressed in mental images activated when a theme or subject is mentioned. Thus, when you are asked to image a typewriter, a woman, a clock, or a book, your mental image is likely to be a central image of these objects. They may also be expressed in artistic production, as in the case of Rockwell's faces of the world (see figure 9.1).

Canonic representations are formed through experience with members of a category, called exemplars. Recently, I asked the members of a class in the cognition of art to "draw a cup and saucer." The results are shown in figure 9.4. Although this is an awful hodgepodge of drawings reflecting individual differences in sketching ability, the remarkable feature is that almost all students drew "prototypic" cups and saucers. Surely the students have seen numerous cups and saucers from all different angles, and yet they chose to draw them from a similar perspective. Why?

One explanation is that throughout one's lifetime, experiences with common objects are stored in permanent memory—not as singular instances, but as items organized around a central theme. We have all seen thousands of cups and saucers, but we have not stored all of them in memory. We have stored some; but more importantly, we have formed a generalized impression of this class of objects that serves as a type of master model to which new items may be compared. We recognize and classify a variety of disparate objects (cups and saucers) as members of a class by rapidly comparing them with an "idealized" image of the class. We recognize a German shepherd as a dog, not only because we might have seen that dog before but because it embodies all of the essential features of the superordinate category DOG and the subordinate category GERMAN SHEPHERD. It is the idealized image, or prototype, of an object, person, feeling, or idea that is stored in our long-term memory. Figure 9.5 shows a collection of cups and saucers. While each is different, each has certain distinctive characteristics of "cupness and saucerness" that allow us to discover the cerebral category of "cup and saucer."

In our introductory examples, Rockwell shows us visual prototypes of people, things, and feelings, while the abstract artists Léger and Kandinsky show us conceptual prototypes of people, things, and feelings. All these examples, as well as all art, are thematically supported by concepts centered in the heart and mind of the artist.

9.4 Canonic representations of cups and saucers.

9.5   A collection of cups and saucers.

Early Canonic Views

Several early canonic representations are illustrated in figures 9.6 and 9.7, in which early Egyptian artists view a pond. Of particular interest in these drawings is the orientation of objects. Trees, for example, are shown as they would look as perpendicular objects viewed straight on. Fish (see figure 9.7) are shown in the same orientation, but the pond is seen from a bird's-eye point of view. Egyptians were not much concerned with such inconsistencies and chose to show each object from its most "natural" position. Egyptian artists drew what they knew to be the most prominent and characteristic attribute of an object. Perhaps this is why their paintings of people look so odd to our eyes: an arm might be shown in one perspective, the shoulders in another, and the eyes in a third.

This treatment of objects raises the interesting issue of time and art. While we have all seen the objects represented in these Egyptian drawings, we have not seen them in these orientations at the same time. In one sense, the Egyptian artist was emancipated from time constraints, and thus saw no

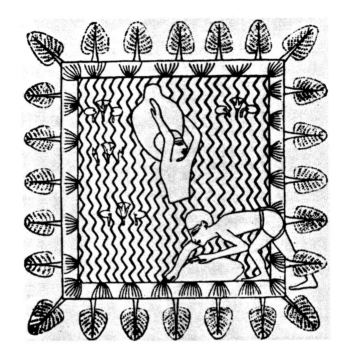

9.6 Egyptian style of representing a pond, trees, and people. From Gombrich (1982).

inconsistency in showing canonic forms of objects simultaneously. The artist drew TREE, FISH, and POND, not a tree, a fish, and a pond—and selected the view of each that carried the central theme.

There is a remarkable parallel between these early examples of art and children's art. In figure 9.8 a 12-year-old gives his version of a town square. Never mind that this is an "unrealistic" picture—the lad had not been indoctrinated with the rules of artistic convention—the objects are shown as representing commonly seen people, buildings, and trees. These views are windows to the artist's mind and tell us a great deal about his or her memory for classes of objects.

Experimental Studies of Canonic Forms

Experimental data confirms the saliency of canonic forms as memory representatives. In one experiment by Palmer, Rosch, and Chase (1981) a series of photographs of common objects, such as a horse (see figure 9.9), were

9.7 **A pool in the garden of Nebamun in Thebes, 18th Dynasty, Egypt.**

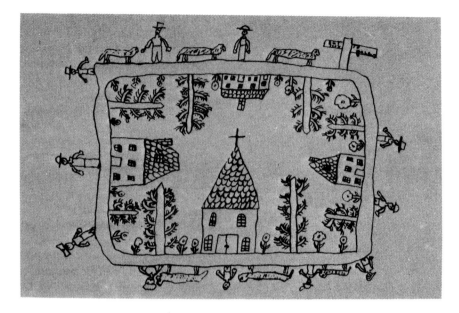

9.8 A child's canonic drawing: a town square in Connecticut drawn by a 12-year-old boy. From Lewis (1966).

shown to people, who were asked to rate them for typicality. In a second part of the experiment subjects were shown the photographs and asked to name the object as rapidly as possible. Not surprisingly, the reaction times (which indicate how accessible an item is in memory) reflected the rated typicality of the object. The horse in the upper left-hand part of figure 9.9, the canonic horse, was most rapidly named, while the less typical views (top view and hindquarters view) took significantly longer to name. Several possible explanations of this phenomenon are: (1) more important parts of the object are shown in the canonic view; (2) the canonic view is more frequently seen; (3) the canonic view best fits our idealized impression of the object. All three of these explanations have merit, but the one that carries the greatest weight is the third. Our memory for common objects is based on the storage of important features of the class of objects. These frequently experienced features are restructured and stored as an abstraction that is the canonic form.

The freedom to express individual features from different canonic views, within the same painting, was brilliantly demonstrated in the art of Pablo Picasso and the cubist painters of the early part of the twentieth century.

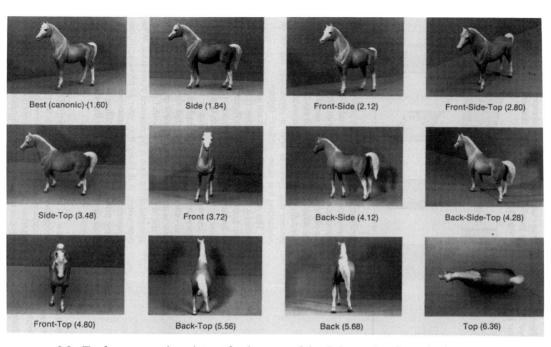

Best (canonic) (1.60)   Side (1.84)   Front-Side (2.12)   Front-Side-Top (2.80)

Side-Top (3.48)   Front (3.72)   Back-Side (4.12)   Back-Side-Top (4.28)

Front-Top (4.80)   Back-Top (5.56)   Back (5.68)   Top (6.36)

9.9 Twelve perspective views of a horse used by Palmer, Rosch, and Chase (1981), with mean "goodness" ratings of the views.

THE PICASSO CONNECTION: SEEING "EYE TO EYE" WITH THE PHARAOH

The use of different viewpoints for various canonic figures in the same painting did not begin with Cézanne or van Gogh, but was part of Egyptian tomb art. However, this technique reached dazzling heights during the brief period of cubism and throughout much of modern art. The uncontested master of cubism was Picasso, who drew partially recognizable features from different views on the same canvas. He experimented with perspective, space, colors, and time in creative ways with splendid artistic skill, while collecting praise from many critics and unparalleled scorn and ridicule from others.

Picasso was influenced by Cézanne, the impressionist who chose not to square his table. Cézanne wrote to the young Picasso advising him to look at nature in terms of cones, cylinders, and spheres, as he believed a painting should be organized by those "basic" forms. Picasso took the advice literally and began to experiment with building a picture from basic forms. Within

Subverted Canons

In the "Fur Cup" (as this *objet d'art* is affectionately known) Meret Oppenheim exhibits a version of a cup, saucer, and spoon that, to most viewers, presents an interesting psychological problem. On one hand, the cup and saucer resemble canonic forms, but on the other hand, wrapping these common objects in animal fur seems weird. Furthermore, cups are used to drink from, and an imaginary sip from this cup is most distasteful. Think about it. Fur caressing our skin is pleasant; in our drinking cup, disgusting. Some critics, noting the proclivity of many surrealist artists to embrace Freudian psychoanalysis, have interpreted this work in terms of sexual symbolism, in which the spoon becomes a phallus and the cup a vagina, both covered with pubic hair libidinously linking the two. Such conjectures are left to the reader to judge. What is certain is that this object demands our attention, and one reason is because a canonic form (cup) is given new meaning through the use of conflicting contextual cues (fur).

9.10   Meret Oppenheim, *Object: Luncheon in Fur* (1936).

these forms elements are added, not as visual reproductions of objects but as we might conceptualize objects. A painting of a violin or woman should be a reflection of our brain as much as of our eye. When we conceptualize a violin or a woman, we are free to see it from all different angles, to color it oddly, to think of other objects, and to emphasize certain features and de-emphasize others. Violins and women have more than one side.

African art for Matisse was the exotic or naive, and for Picasso the Spaniard was something natural, immediate and dignified.

This principle of picture construction bears a close resemblance to what has been discovered about human information process-ing of visual events. Our memory for a person, say a woman, is not based on a series of "cere-bral snapshots" of women we have neatly filed away in memory stores, but on salient and meaningful features of women that are stored, in memory, as an abstract representation of that class. For each person these storage systems contain some unique elements, but there are remarkable similarities between people. Your cerebral woman and mine are not identical but are probably very similar.

—Gertrude Stein

Picasso's work abounds with basic, or canonic, forms used in unusual ways. Consider how he drew body parts and faces in *Les demoiselles d'Avignon* (figure 9.11). Body parts are distorted, profile views and frontal views appear within the same figure, details are forgotten or emphasized, and features are twisted in sometimes grotesque ways. Yet there remains a theme that holds the entire picture together. These representations are similar to the way human memory functions. When we perceive objects—horses, violins, peo-ple—the features may be distorted, forgotten, or exaggerated, but our collec-tive memory is of the most representative form, which embodies all of our impressions.

The technique of pluralistic forms of representation has precedents in the art of Africa and Egypt, although the level of refinement—both concep-tually and artistically—is expressed differently. Figure 9.12 shows an African mask and the faces of two Egyptian women. Compare the mask with the woman in the upper right-hand part of *Les demoiselles d'Avignon*. Now, compare the eye of the woman on the left edge of Picasso's painting with the eyes of the Egyptian women. One explanation for the striking similarity is that Picasso was familiar with these older art techniques, especially African

9.11   Pablo Picasso, *Les demoiselles d'Avignon* **(1907).**

art, and imitated the style.[3] There is a deeper reason. Both Picasso and the African and Egyptian artists chose to represent objects not as they appear to the eye but as they appear to the mind. And the mind is capable of plural views of things. If such a hypothesis is correct, then these art objects are windows to the mind of their creators. Insofar as we are all able to respond to them, they are windows to the minds of all humans.

ART AND SCIENCE: TWO SIDES OF THE SAME COIN

Picasso was fond of saying that he "did not search, he found." Such a notion is compatible with the idea that artists do not invent art, but find expressions

9.12 African masks and Egyptian women.

9.13 Connection: Picasso and African art.

of reality that are compatible with basic structures of the mind. We naturally understand real art. In this regard, there is a stunning parallel between two disparate spheres of knowledge: art and natural science. Artists do not invent art any more than physicists invent physics, or physiologists invent physiology, or psychologists invent scientific psychology. Art, physics, physiology, and even scientific psychology are worlds waiting to be discovered by a mind. And valid discoveries (in art, science, and psychology) are those that are exquisitely calibrated to stimulate the human neural system in ways consistent with its sensory/cognitive architecture, acquired through the course of evolution. These disciplines of art and science may differ in superficial traits but are linked together at a deeper level.

The common denominator between art and science is the degree to which expressions in each domain are compatible with the human mind. Einstein's elegant theories of the universe are true (and beautiful) because they are consistent with the capability of the human mind to understand such ideas. Picasso's application of new techniques, juxtapositions, and perspective are beautiful (and true) because they see the mind: they are consistent with the capacity of the human mind to understanding these visual stimuli. As scientists discover laws of the universe that are congruent with mind, artists discover visual images of the world that are harmonious with mind. Both explore the truth and beauty of the mind and, at an abstract cognitive level, are identical.

Memory and the Comprehension of Art

Memory was once conceptualized as a type of recording device that stored impressions and produced responses. The strength of these stored impressions (and the accuracy of recall) was thought to be a function of the number of times a person perceived an item and/or the vividness of an item. This model, developed during the last century, bears a resemblance to the storage system of a modern computer or camcorder, in which data is input, stored, and recalled. The storage of information in these models was passive.

The passive memory model has been replaced by a dynamic model in which perceived impressions are associated or connected with other impressions and organized in more or less meaningful memory units. These units and their associations or memory nodes constitute our long-term memory. While they are not identical with input stimuli, they serve as good representatives of stimuli.

Recent studies in memory and brain sciences have given us an appreciation of the process of information storage and visual memory. The story is kind of a good news/bad news tale. First, the bad news. The neurochemistry of the human brain is sluggish, especially when compared to computers. Electrochemical messages wend their way through the cortex connected by a series of neurons. Between each neuron is a type of switch, or synapse. It takes about 100,000 times longer to close a neural switch than a computer switch. The good news is that the human brain has a great many neurons that conduct the brain's business. The precise number of neurons is unknown, but a good estimate is that it is more than 100 billion. However impressive that number is, the number of potential connections between neurons is even more impressive: each neuron is connected to 1,000 (or more—some estimates go as high as 100,000) other neurons. If neural transmission is parallel (i.e., if a neural message can be transmitted to a variety of neurons, each of which has the potential to pass the impulse to many others, and all of them operate simultaneously) then the number of neural units activated within a few hundred milliseconds is huge, multiplying logarithmically across time. With massive numbers of neurons processing information over brief periods of time, the human brain can perform truly amazing feats. Of particular interest is how memory recognizes and reacts to visual forms (art, for example). We can recognize an old professor, a famous politician, or a rock star, or distinguish Rockwell from Kandinsky, in a few hundred milliseconds. We do all this with ease because the architecture of the brain allows us to process information by means of massive parallelism, in which basic visual patterns engage countless millions of neurons simultaneously.

Another feature of the human brain that determines the way visual information is processed is its proclivity to organize information in terms of categories, prototypes, and schemata. While we *may* recognize a Rockwell painting because we have seen it before, it is more likely that we "recognize" a Rockwell painting because it contains many of the salient features of the category of Rockwell-like paintings. And, as we saw at the beginning of this chapter, within his paintings prototypic images often appear, viz. the farmer, the mother, the returning soldier, and so on. These internal representations can be thought of as the "hidden units" of art—a theme to be developed shortly.

Other categories seem to be part of our brain—colors for example. The perception of red is the result of the visual detection of electromagnetic energy with wavelengths in the area of 700 nanometers, but it is also the result of neurons in the brain firing at specific rates. Our brains access the category "red" in response to a limited range of wavelengths. Of course, some reddish colors may be similarly classified, but the "best" reds are restricted to a limited range. Such central colors are called "foveal colors" and are prototypical.

Prototypes

Prototypes are abstractions of stimuli against which similar patterns are judged. They serve a very practical need. Even with the billions of cortical neurons working in parallel, it is impossible to store *all* the sights and sounds (and other sensations) of this teeming world. It is possible, and far more economical, to store impressions that embody the most frequently experienced features of a class of objects. Experimental work on prototypes has shown how powerful they are and how they can be formed.

In one experiment I conducted with Judy McCarthy (Solso and McCarthy, 1981), we created a series of visual stimuli (faces) that were derived from a prototype face. For the sake of internal consistency we composed a face from the plastic cells in a police identification kit. These kits contain an assortment of features; for example, there are several dozen styles of hair, noses, lips, eyes, and other features. After the prototype face was constructed, a series of exemplar faces were put together in which some of the prototype's features were included. Figure 9.14 shows one of the prototype faces and samples of exemplars. The exemplar faces were shown for a few seconds to subjects who volunteered to participate in the study. Then they were given a recognition test that included some of the original set of faces, some new faces, and the prototype face. We expected that some subjects would falsely recognize the prototype face (which they had never seen before) as an "old" face, but were unprepared for the robustness of this false alarm. An overwhelming number of people not only identified the prototype face as a previously seen face, but also gave confidence ratings that indicated they were more confident of their decision than they were for any of the other faces, even more confident than they were for faces they had actually seen. We called this phenomenon "pseudomemory," as the memory for the prototype face was stronger than the memory for actually perceived faces and was derived from frequently seen features rather than from a single face that contained all the features.[4] Since the original experiment the results have been replicated using differently composed faces, with young children, with a six-week delay between the presentation of original faces and test faces, and with students from Stanford University, the University of Nevada, and Moscow State University (Russia), all with very similar results.

This form of memory, which I am convinced is the predominant way information is stored in long-term memory, is important in the conceptuali-

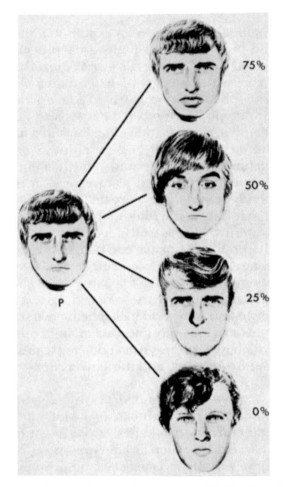

9.14 Prototype face and exemplar faces incorporating 75, 50, 25, and 0 percent of the prototype, used in Solso and McCarthy (1981).

zation of art for two reasons. First, it is useful in understanding the classification of art periods and of individual artists' styles. The process of forming these cognitive categories follows the same rules as the formation of pseudomemories. From experiences with single examples of say, baroque art, we form a general impression of this style, so that upon seeing a painting for the first time that embraces the important features of this period, we immediately "recognize" it as a member of the baroque period. Theoretically, it would be possible to create a prototype painting of a period (or of an artist) that would include the salient features of the category (much as the prototype face contained salient features of the exemplar faces). Although I know of no experiment that has done this, it is probable that most observers would recognize the prototype as representing a specific period or artist (which is not to say that they would actually accept it as an original).

Second, it is likely that our impression of a given painting follows the same procedure as prototype formation mentioned above. Recall the discussion of eye movements in chapter 6, and how the process of viewing a painting is accomplished through a series of eye movements and fixations. During each fixation, information is perceived and passed on to the brain for further processing and associations. The final impression is a composite of these many impressions, much as the formation of a prototypical memory is accomplished through perception of features that are recombined in memory.

Verbal Labels and Visual Perception

Art is not viewed in an intellectual vacuum but in context. One of the most important semantic contextual cues is a label or title. Earlier we saw how Kandinsky gave a clue about the content of his abstract painting through the use of a title, *Cossacks*. Although Kandinsky was interested in creating a type of visual music devoid of verbal labels, his title is nevertheless an important interpretative clue about the painting's meaning. Less helpful are labels by some artists of the "minimal" school, such as Malevich's *Black Square* (a painting of a black square), Loewensberg's cryptic *No. 50* (a pattern of horizontal and vertical black lines on a white field), or the unhelpful Kline's *Untitled Painting* (bold slashes of black and blue).

The attachment of a verbal label influences not only what we remember but also how long the object is remembered. Perhaps it is this fact that has inhibited many modern artists from giving meaningful labels to their art. They choose not to bias the viewer.

Cognitive psychologists have also presented convincing evidence of the importance of pictures in text comprehension. One such experiment was done by Bransford and Johnson (1972), based on the following story:

> If the balloons popped, the sound would not be able to carry since everything would be too far away from the correct floor. A closed window would also prevent the sound from carrying

since most buildings tend to be well insulated. Since the whole operation depends on a steady flow of electricity, a break in the middle of the wire would also cause problems. Of course the fellow could shout, but the human voice is not loud enough to carry that far. An additional problem would be no accompaniment to the message. It is clear that the best situation would involve less distance. Then there would be fewer potential problems. With face-to-face contact, the least number of things could go wrong. (Bransford and Johnson 1972, p. 11)

This passage is opaque. From the text alone you may have no idea what is being described, but if you saw the picture in figure 9.15 the cloud would be lifted and the meaning of the paragraph and the picture would become perfectly clear. In the actual experiment several conditions were presented; some people saw the relevant picture before reading the passage, some after,

9.15 Context and memory: appropriate context (left) and inappropriate context (right). From Bransford and Johnson (1972).

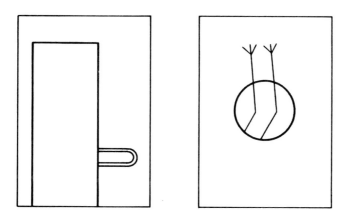

9.16 Droodles: a midget playing a trombone in a telephone booth (left); an early bird who caught a very strong worm (right). From Bower, Karlin, and Dueck (1975).

and some saw inappropriate pictures. Only when the appropriate picture was shown before reading the passage was the memory for the passage enhanced. Additional experiments by Bransford have shown that context is an important factor in the understanding of pictures.

An even more direct demonstration of the role of verbal labels in picture comprehension was done by Bower, Karlin, and Dueck (1975), who used simple line drawings, called droodles several years ago by the cartoonist Roger Price. Look at the two figures in figure 9.16. The droodles are mostly meaningless unless we give them verbal labels. With a label, the previously enigmatic drawing suddenly "comes together" and makes sense. We "get it." Bower, Karlin, and Dueck tested the hypothesis that a major factor in how well a person remembers a picture is whether or not he or she understands it. In one part of the experiment some people were shown drawings with labels and another group were shown the same drawings without labels; during a subsequent memory task, the label group recalled far more features of the drawings than those who did not have the advantage of the title.

"LEVEL 3" ART

Bower, Karlin, and Dueck's simple experiment brings up a serious theoretical issue regarding the structural properties of art and language. For some time people have conceptualized language as having (at least) two distinct levels.

On the surface is the medium—the oddly shaped little letters on this page, or the sounds of a voice—and below is a "deep structure" that contains the meaning of the message.

Paintings can likewise be interpreted as having a multidimensional notation system. There are, on one hand, the surface characteristics of art: the lines, colors, contrasts, shapes, contours, and other features that make up the physical art objects. Surface characteristics, for example, may be a green expanse, partly in shadow and partly brightly lit, occupied by small white four-legged shapes; or a somewhat glossy black cylindrical object that sits atop what appears to be a human head (male). Then, at the next deeper level, there is the semantic interpretation of these features: part of a pastoral scene; a stovepipe hat. Here features are combined into meaningful objects. From these objects general categories are formed that allow inferences about the art to be drawn.

There is yet a third level in this scheme of artistic expression (applicable to art, music, literature, and science), which is the most important of all (although all levels are essential and interactive). I call this level simply "Level 3." Here both the featural and semantic interpretations of an object, sound, or idea are grasped, and much more. Level 3 appreciation goes well beyond the elementary perception of features and what they mean. In some instances, Level 3 interpretation of art may be only tangentially related to featural and semantic perception. It even goes beyond what a painting infers. Kandinsky's *Cossacks* is comprised of lines, colors, contrasts, and so on; features. We all see them. At another level, we understand that some of these lines represent cossacks who are engaged in battle; meaning. Most of us "understand" what this painting means. Level 3 comprehension is as much a feeling as a cognition; it is the Tao of the painting and yet, like the Tao (as Lao Tsu wrote), "the Tao that is the true Tao is the Tao that cannot be told." It is, at the same time, a painting's most direct meaning and its most vague. It is being "at one" with the art; it is commingling a painting with universal properties of the mind; it is seeing one's primal mind in a painting.

May the Force be with you.

—Obi-Wan Kenobi

It cannot be explained, but when attained cannot be confused. It is the intense wisdom of art; its captivating beauty; its penetrating philosophy. It is what makes direct contact with the biological archetypes of the old-brained creatures we all are. It is the primeval cord that binds us together and runs through all humanity. It is the invisible thread that unites me with van Gogh,

Picasso, and Mondrian; and joins you with . . . ? Level 3 experiences may occur in response to all kinds of art, from prehistoric forms to Peter Max, but emerge most frequently in response to any art that stimulates responsive brain structures. It is "as if" the *painting* understood you and was reading your mind. It is a level of cognizance that arouses profound emotions and thoughts, and yet is itself inexplicable. It touches us.

Connections: In Mind and Art

Art, music, literature, and science may all "touch" us at the third level of cognition. Furthermore, this level of awareness may be due to an intricate web of connections activated in the brain. The idea that "one idea leads to another" or that things in this world are "associated" with each other—earth and sea, the moon and sun, Mimi and Alfredo—has been the cornerstone of mental chemistry since (at least) the philosophy of Aristotle during the fourth century B.C. "Associationism," as the school of thought was called during the last century, was a principal theory of the mind during psychology's long philosophic phase and formed the basis for modern learning theories (as espoused by Pavlov, Skinner, Underwood, Kausler, Bower, John Anderson, and countless others). The idea that complex mental operations are based on simple connections is intuitively appealing. Today that kernel idea of associationism has been expanded greatly and modified. One element that has been added is the attention to the connecting "node" in associated elements. Thus, Mimi and Alfredo are not associated in some nebulous way, but are associated through a propositional statement in which basic elements are connected by a node, such as "Mimi loved Alfredo" or "Alfredo hid Mimi's key" or "Mimi touched Alfredo." (I think she "touched" him at the third level.) These structures are sometimes called "propositional networks" and, in their more complex form, consist of richly interconnected informational structures capable of expressing very complex ideas.

One basic assumption of neoassociationism is that the nodes in a network of memory associations have a level of activation that spreads among other nodes. When the level of activation reaches a high enough value, that portion of the network becomes conscious. In the case of Kandinsky's *Cossacks,* when thinking about the red patches in the context of the title we become conscious of the relation between these two elements, and, through the activation of other propositional networks, the relation of both of them to the larger meaning of the painting.

The idea that knowledge is not stored in a single brain cell but is distributed through tens of thousands has enjoyed exceptional interest among cognitive psychologists identified with neural network models, or PDP (parallel distributing processing) or simply "connectionism" (see the discussion in chapter 2). Our knowledge of Rockwell's *Thanksgiving,* for example, is represented as a pattern of neural activation distributed over numerous interconnected cells. Various bits of information may be stored in the same network so that they represent a prototype or schema. Schemes, such as a "college office schema" or a "Renoir schema" (see chapter 5), or an "Americana schema" (this chapter), although not explicitly stored entities, may be constructed from a knowledge base of bits and pieces of similarly stored information. When we look at Rockwell's *Thanksgiving,* the sights activate units and further activation spreads throughout the network. Initially, we "see" only surface things: contours and shapes, a checkered tablecloth, a spherical pumpkin, and so on. The brain sees richer things in this picture and consequently fills in the missing details. It does so through the activation of "hidden units," bits and pieces of knowledge that constitute a schema. From this schema a multitude of inferences are made about these people, their conversation, their lives. The painting alone does not tell us such things as that these people are related, that they are pleased to be with each other, that they are Americans, that somewhere there is a turkey, that they live in a house that has windows and doors, that they have a dog and go to church. Each of these inferences is activated by a schema. In addition, our Thanksgiving schema tells us something of the probability of these inferences. For example, the Thanksgiving schema may indicate that, in the absence of conflicting information, a particular statement is true: that the man and woman in the picture are mother and son. Such a strong inference might be called a "default" inference, appropriately named for a computer program that, in the absence of an explicit command, becomes the mode of operation. Other inferences may be less probable, such as the inference that the people own a dog. Each factor could (theoretically) be assigned a probability value. Our brain tells us those things through the activation of memory units that are fragments of a larger picture.

The Hidden Units of Art

A basic tenet of neural network models is that information can be conceptualized as having units and connections between units. The connections between units can be modified: they can grow stronger or weaker so that the output is appropriate to the input. Between the input and output of a system there are mediating "hidden units." These hidden units are fundamental in the model, as they enable a neural network to form representations of the outer world (see Rumelhart and McClelland 1986). Can connectionism help us understand the deeper cognitive aspects of art?

One way to conceptualize informational units and their associations (using the example of Rockwell's *Thanksgiving*) is shown in figure 9.17. Here the input stimuli are the woman, the man, the pumpkin, and so on; we infer that they are related, that somewhere, not too far away, there is a turkey, and so on. This is a relatively simple "neural" network model, in which each feature is associated to each inference. The strength or probability of the connection between the input stimuli and the output (in this case the inference) is designated by the width of the associative line. Here, the sight of a pumpkin may be associated with a turkey, the service ribbons might lead to the inference that the man knows how to shoot a gun, and so on. We can see that it requires an awful mess of haywire to tinker together this many associations.

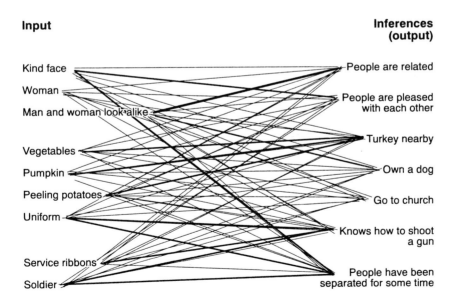

9.17 Associations between input features and inferences, based on Rockwell's *Thanksgiving*.

Another way of representing this picture is shown in figure 9.18, in which three hidden units are placed between the input stimuli and the output inferences. These hidden units are variously activated, partly depending on the features attended to and partly on the development of the strength of the unit. Thus, the inference that there are a turkey and dog someplace nearby and that the people go to church is activated by the "Thanksgiving" unit, which in turn is activated by the surface features of food, potatoes, and pumpkin.

Note that the number of connections in a multiple-layer net is fewer than in a single-layer net. Also note that the hidden units in this scheme are collective impressions (a type of schema) of the surface features. The representations formed in hidden units give the system tremendous power that enables it to handle complex forms of computation. In addition, hidden units help explain the ability of humans to represent high-level concepts such as the meaning of a work of art. They may even help us to understand Level 3 perception.

In the above example, only a few of the connections between the units are shown. In actuality, the number of associations is far greater than could

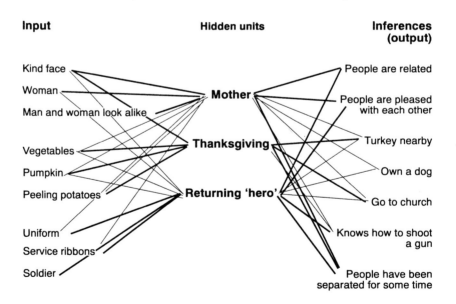

9.18 Hidden units, input, and inferences in Rockwell's *Thanksgiving*. **Strength shown by width of the connecting line.**

be shown in a single figure. Also, the growth of hidden units is, seemingly, controlled by initiatory and excitatory connections whose functions can be described mathematically.

Neural Nets and Art

The concept of a neural network, capable of powerful generalizations and inferences, was introduced in chapter 2 in our discussion of the brain and vision. Recall that the neural network approach to cognition and perception adopts a brain metaphor of information processing in which inferences (to art, for example) are drawn upon a huge number of neurons activated by massive parallel processing. In previous applications, in which the PDP model learns visual material, the stimuli have been composed of rather simple geometric forms, such as how the system learns to discriminate between a T and a U. Here we extend this general concept (developed by Rumelhart and McClelland 1986, Rumelhart, Hinton, and Williams 1986, and others) to include the analysis of complex two-dimensional art.

In order to form the associations between a painting (Rockwell's *Thanksgiving,* for example) and the inferences about that painting, it is postulated that three layers are involved. The first is that of input stimuli, or in this case the features of this painting (e.g., the faces, clothing, furniture, and foodstuffs). These percepts are associated with output reactions or inferences (e.g., that the people are related, that a turkey is nearby, that they own a dog, and that the people have been separated for some time). The validity of these unseen inferences is variable; some are more likely than others. The third component is the hidden units, which are modifiable connections that mediate between input and output components. As previously described, these units can be thematically organized (e.g., the Mom, Thanksgiving, or returning hero schemata). A diagram of the model is shown in figure 9.19, in which only four features of the painting are shown as input units, connected in a network of presently inactive nodes to output inferences. Of course, we do not operate in such an unsystematic way, in which sensations originating from a picture are indiscriminately associated with impressions. (If we did, we would be as likely to infer that "Mom" knows how to shoot a gun as that she goes to church. While all inferences are possible, the former inference is less likely than the latter one.)

The reason some inferences are more plausible than others is because certain connections have been learned and others inhibited or not learned.

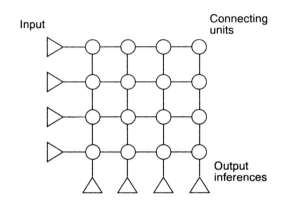

9.19 A processing module showing inputs, associations, and outputs.

The training of a neural network (in which it learns connections between input and output components) is shown in figure 9.20, in which the cross-hatched nodes indicate a connection between a given input unit and output unit. These connections are "neurally inspired": to show the actual neural circuitry is impossible, but this simplified model is meant to resemble the architecture and processing of cortical neurons.

In the network represented in figure 9.20, we see that the first input object is a pumpkin and the other the hands of the woman peeling potatoes— both features of a Thanksgiving schema. For this neural net we can represent the input stimuli of pumpkin and hands as a 1010 pattern, in which the first and third units are switched on. These input units impinge on connecting units that connect in turn to the output, which in this case is the inference that there is a turkey lurking nearby and that the people go to church; a 1100 pattern.

The strength of the connection is determined by previous experience and learning. The ability of a network to form and modify connections is governed by the *delta rule,* a simple but elegant learning heuristic developed by McClelland and Rumelhart (1986) based on an original suggestion by Hebb (1949). The basic idea is that if two cells fire at the same time the strength of the connection between them increases. Thus, the strength of connections may be adjusted through contiguous actions, which can take place in a self-activated recursive circuit that is lawfully described by the delta rule.[5] The growth of connections can be weighted negatively as well as

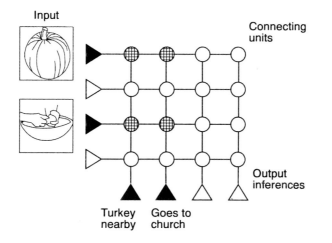

9.20   The training of a neural network.

positively, so that the outputs of "turkey nearby" and "goes to church" are more likely than "knows how to shoot a gun" and "owns a dog."

Another step in this process of forming inferences is the formation of connections between other features of the work and output illations on a partially trained network. In this case suppose the "Thanksgiving" connection is in place (see figure 9.20). Then focus on the faces of the two people as input stimuli (see figure 9.21), which can be noted as a 0101 pattern, associated with the output responses "the people are related" and they are "pleased with each other," a 0011 pattern in our example. Once this new pattern is learned, when the faces are perceived the output "related" and "pleased" is given. Note that, even though existing units are in place that lead to different conclusions (e.g., the connection between pumpkin and turkey), they are inactive because the input units are not active. In the interpretation of art, whether realistic or abstract, the strength of the connections may be strong or weak. Some input cues may be more reliably associated with output inferences; in a sense, some cues may be more diagnostic than others. A pumpkin may predict a turkey more reliably than potatoes may. The model is equally applicable to art that contains no pumpkins and potatoes, although the consistency of inferences is more widely influenced by individual patterns of activation.

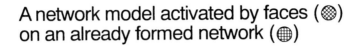

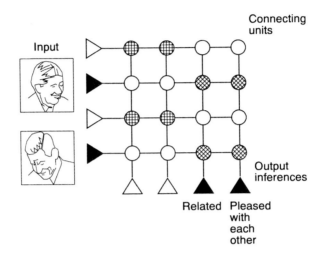

9.21 Forming associations on a partially trained network.

CONNECTIONISM AND MONDRIAN

As we have just seen, cognitive scientists have been searching for neural units that are the basic building blocks of cognition and the processing of information. Years ago, the Dutch painter Piet Mondrian searched for fundamental visual elements that were the basic components of art. In an autobiographical essay Mondrian recognizes the influence of Picasso and Léger (see figure 9.3) on his work and his philosophy of art. His work is characterized by his credo of "always farther," as he continually sought more and more basic forms. Mondrian, whose block compositions of fundamental colors

All true art arises intuitively from the universal.

—Piet Mondrian

have influenced several generations of artists, not to mention popular and advertising media, aspired to create an art that reflected the objective laws of the universe. In modern cognitive terms, Mondrian looked for deeper semantic representations that could reveal the immutable realities of humanity, rather than the "surface" characteristics that seemed to come and go with the changing world. His pursuit of "always farther" caused him to search for the indivisible forms of art. He saw his work as a combination of ethics, morality, nature, geometry, and balance. By finding the essential qualities of these things and representing them visually, it may be possible to explain the principles that govern society, ethics, and humankind.

We can catch a glimpse of Mondrian's stylistic development in the three views of a tree, each more abstract than the previous, shown in figure 9.22. These are but a sample of the entire series he drew. In the top painting the artist has given a somewhat stylized picture of a tree. We see and understand both its surface and deep structures with little difficulty. The middle tree is a much more abstract version of the same subject. The lines that represent branches also form patterns that are interesting. Finally, in the lower tree Mondrian shows an abstraction of a tree using only the essential elements. It is as if he wants to show the pure essence of "treeness." To the naive viewer, the surface meaning is obscure—he or she doesn't know what the picture means—yet to others Mondrian has captured a view of the basic structures and connections of this object. In this abstract view of a tree, the artist has invented a type of visual vocabulary in which symbols are given meaning and organized by means of an optical grammar that unifies the painting.

Having experimented with this new vocabulary and grammar of painting, Mondrian proceeded to search for even more fundamental universal elements. He wrote that "these universal means of expression were discovered in modern painting by a logical and gradual progress toward ever more abstract form and color. Once the solution was discovered, there followed the exact representation of relations alone, that is to say, of the essential and fundamental element in any plastic emotion of the beautiful" (Whitford 1987, p. 15). One example of the abstraction he achieved is shown in figure 9.23. In this composition the artist used the basic colors, red, yellow, and blue, and white, separated by black lines. When we view this painting we scan its parts, mentally weighing its elements and looking for balance and a connection between them. We soon see that the painting is not a haphazard assortment of bordered rectangles but a carefully crafted composition in which some features recede and others advance.

The strength of this painting is in its balance of forms. The larger, red and blue rectangles in the upper left are equalized by the smaller yellows in the lower right; the white panel at bottom left is delicately balanced with other forms and so on. Our eye and mind engage in an interesting fugue in which one part is played off against another. Our reaction to this painting is

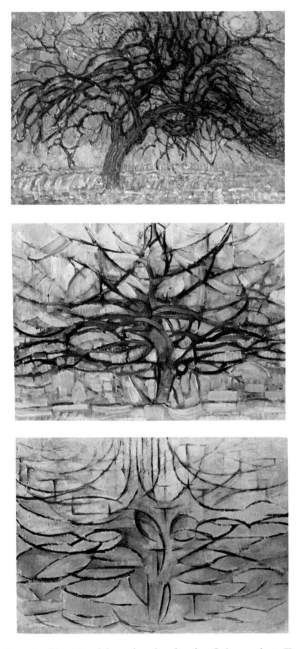

9.22 Three paintings by Piet Mondrian, showing levels of abstraction. Top to bottom: *The Red Tree* (1908), *The Gray Tree* (1912), *Flowering Apple Tree* (c. 1912).

9.23 Piet Mondrian, Tableau II (1921–1925).

the result of both facilitating factors and inhibiting factors. Note that the composition is divided by clear horizontal and vertical lines, to become known as Mondrian's signature. Each line intersects with other lines, or makes a simple connection with other lines. These lines separate the square and rectangular features from each other but also serve another function. They suggest the interaction between units of the painting. As with the analysis of

Thanksgiving, it would be possible to hypothesize the input, output, and hidden units, and I would suggest that you try this exercise. (I would be interested to see some of the results.) It may be that the colors red, white, and blue constellate around a patriotic theme, which might lead some to infer Mondrian was painting Old Glory. (The negative weight associated with yellow remains problematic in this interpretation.) Others may infer a cityscape, aroused by the grid design reminiscent of streets and crossings. From this schema, one may further associate the painting with noise and the honking of horns. Indeed, the model is applicable to all the art contained in this book and more. It is a universal model that can be applied to all forms of stimulation.

It should be apparent that the inferences drawn from this painting have far less generality than those drawn from the Rockwell painting, for which the schemes and inferences are widely shared and our past learning has established definite nodes from which inferences are drawn. In effect, the viewer has greater freedom in interpreting Mondrian's *Tableau II* because the input stimuli are less familiar (and hence coalesce less canonically) than those in the Rockwell (where schematics abound). Also, it is likely that the hidden units here are poorly associated with the input stimuli (for most viewers). These effects may be exactly what Mondrian aimed for: to have the viewer search for connections. It is why some people call this art cerebral.

To me, these many components of Mondrian's work resemble modern theories of parallel distributing processing or connectionism, in which basic elements of cognition are sought (always farther), the interaction between (neural) units is governed by inhibitory or excitatory rules, and basic units of information interact. There is even a remarkable similarity between some of Mondrian's paintings and pictures of cortical neurons (compare his trees with figures 2.4 and 9.19). Even his later works, based on rectangular figures of differing colors, resemble modern, computer-aided brain imaging techniques (see figure 2.7). These similarities do not suggest that Mondrian foresaw the current theories and techniques of mental processing—he did not—but do suggest that in his search for basic elements of artistic expression, he used a vocabulary and grammar that embodied many theoretical aspects of neurally inspired models of the mind such as connectionism.

Both scientists and artists dream of elegant paradigms of the universe that are meaningful to the human mind. The "inner" world of the mind and the "outer" world of science and art are conjoined through the physical and philosophic manifestations of the human mind's relentless search for truth and beauty. Science and art are products of the mind; they are of the mind and yet they *are* also the mind. On the surface, we "appreciate" art, literature, music, ideas, and science; at the core, we see our own mind unveiled in this wonderful stuff. The common denominator that unites all is the mind. Scientific and artistic explorations are the most intimate inquiries into the structure and operations of the mind. Art is more than paint smeared on a canvas; it is a glass in which the human mind is reflected. Art bestows upon eyes the vision to see inward. Mondrian, like many artists and scientists, sought out basic realities of the universe. At a sufficient level of abstraction, his answers and the answers of science to universal questions are the same. ▪

Notes

1 The Big Window: Science and Vision

1. Some experimental work has been done using a prosthesis for the blind that stimulates the visual cortex directly, producing sensations that resemble vision but without light.

2. This is particularly true outside the fovea. At the fovea, where the photoreceptive cells are densely squeezed together, the cones are so compressed that they appear more rod-shaped than cone-shaped.

2 The Brain and Vision

1. I am ignoring the philosophic question of whether art (as well as nature, science, truth, and so on) exists outside of human experience of it. Although such questions as "Does a tree that falls in the forest make any noise if not heard by a human?" or "Can things not experienced by the mind be 'art'?" may be laudable topics for philosophers and graduate seminars, they are outside the ken of this book. It may be that spontaneous art exists in the natural structure of the universe and that creatures, such as us, discover it occasionally. But then, it seems to me that to understand "natural art," as well as created art, would require a brain. The question of the *existence* of art is not addressed here; only that of the *experience* of art. This book's focus is the essential details of the psychology of art as experienced by humans with brains. On the other hand, I hope that we might also find more general cognitive principles that govern visual experiences, including the viewing of art.

2. Here "man," "his," and "he" are used as generic pronouns.

3 Figure and Form Perception

1. By coincidence, as I was writing this section, the local classical music station played the piano version of *Pictures at an Exhibition*. It seems that as I look at the Kandinsky painting and hear the Mussorgsky music, the visual rendition is very much in tune with the music, especially the gratings. The opening and closing passages, for example, are a series of broad, loud chords with dramatic pauses; musical gratings. And some of the intermediate passages are light, melodic, almost whimsical; see the middle portion of figure 3.5 for a visualization of these attributes.

2. It has been demonstrated that vertical and horizontal stimuli are initially registered in different parts of the visual cortex in animals. It is possible that fundamentally different initial processing is involved in the coding of these two types of gratings, which may be related to higher-order interpretations.

3. In 1956, Hartline, Wagner, and Ratliff had conducted significant research on the eye of the horseshoe crab (*Limulus*) in which lateral inhibition effects were noted.

4 Visual Cognition

1. Wertheimer was of Czech background. Wertheimer, Koffka, and Köhler all contributed to the founding of Gestalt psychology. They suffered under Nazi repression, and the journal they founded, *Psychologische Forschung* (Psychological Research), was banned. In 1938 all three emigrated to the United States, where they continued to write in the field of perception.

5 Context, Cognition, and Art

1. There is much more to Duchamp's *L.H.O.O.Q.* than meets the eye. The art critic Robert Hughes comments that the artist "combines with the schoolboy graffito of the moustache and goatee; but then a further level of anxiety reveals itself, since giving male attributes to the most famous and highly fetishized female portrait ever painted is also a subtler joke on Leonardo's own homosexuality (then a forbidden subject) and on Duchamp's own interest in the confusion of sexual roles" (Hughes 1980, p. 66).

6 The Eyes Have It: Eye Movements and the Perception of Art

1. See Chi, Glaser, and Farr's excellent collection *The Nature of Expertise* (1988) for further examples.

2. Many creative artists, of course, violate this principle precisely for the shock value of the violation, and some would argue that the main *purpose* of art is to disturb the viewer to make some visual, social, political, moral, or psychological point. See the discussion of visual dissonance in chapter 5.

3. With only a bit of imagination we could imagine a verbal balloon over her head that would announce (in a Mae West type of intonation), "Nice flowers, big fellow. Whadda ya have in mind?"

4. Data reported by Molnar. Data do not total 100 percent because other regions were sampled.

7 A Truly Marvelous Feast: Visual Perspective

1. A similar phenomenon can be observed if you try to touch the ends of each index finger. Try it. Now, close one eye and try it. Why is this difficult? What other cues do you use to do this successfully?

2. Try this little demonstration. Select an object for viewing. Hold up your index fingers, with one closer to your eye than the other. Close one eye. Align the object, your distant finger, your near finger, and your eye. Now, move your head to the right (or left). It appears that both fingers move, but the closer one moves farther and faster while the distant object does not appear to move at all.

3. These simulations, called "virtual reality" systems, are particularly effective in training pilots, astronauts, and the like. Even though this technology represents a significant improvement in recreating the world as it actually is, it is far from convincing. As a subject in one of these contraptions, I can say that the experience resembled "reality," but not for a moment was I convinced that what I saw *was* "reality." Perhaps the next generation of virtual reality programs will come even closer to the real thing and spin off a new art form. It is predictable that they will find a market in arcade and home computer games. (If they become flawless, a person could, theoretically, have all the benefits of, say, an ocean voyage, a dogfight, or a hunting trip without leaving home.) Developments in this exciting new field bear watching.

4. Indeed, we often find fun in creatures visually confused. Take the cartoon world, in which a recurrent theme comes when a sympathetic character (e.g., the Roadrunner) is pursued by a "villain" (e.g., Wile E. Coyote). The pursued quickly paints a black "tunnel" on a mountainside. The pursuer, running like a flying speedball, perceives the black "tunnel" to have depth and is flattened like a pancake. The theme sometimes gets even more ridiculous when the pursuer actually enters the tunnel only to find he is in a train tunnel and a speeding locomotive is bearing down on him. "Yikes! How could that happen!" The stuff of Saturday morning in America.

5. Figure 7.18B has the ends of the Y's closed. Our brain organizes these closed structures (the Y's) as complete two-dimensional forms. We now "see" Y's, not features that are part of another whole structure. Conversely, in 7.18A the lines making up the sides of the box are open, which invites us to continue with our sight until we find connecting lines. These lines are seen as a gestalt, part of a larger configuration. In this case, the most stable configuration is a cube.

8 Perspective and the History of Art

1. One artist invented a hat with an extra long bill upon which he hung a wire grid. Through this contraption he saw the world and used the grid to reconstruct what he saw on a canvas. Such ingenious devices may interest the neophyte artist and can easily be made with odds and ends lying around the house. (Note: not to be worn on first dates, job interviews, or when visiting an ornery proctologist.)

2. For a detailed analysis of the perspective in *The Last Supper* see Wright (1983, pp. 94–99).

3. Art historians may apply a finer taxonomy to artists of this period, which would include symbolism, Nabis, neoimpressionism, pointillism, fauvism, and expressionism, among others.

9 Connections: Canonic Representations, Memory, and the Cognition of Art

1. It may come as a surprise to many that Rockwell greatly admired Picasso. I have been unable to determine if the respect was reciprocal.

2. For some people "art *is* the only true reality." This topic is an honorable theme for philosophic deliberation but, alas, would take us too far afield if considered here.

3. The Picasso museum in Paris contains a wonderful collection of African masks juxtaposed with similar Picasso paintings (see figure 9.13).

4. You can experience the phenomenon of pseudomemory at the Exploritorium in San Francisco, as the face experiment is part of the permanent display on memory at that science pavilion.

5. The basic delta rule for learning connections in a computer simulation is defined mathematically as

$$\Delta w_{ji} = n(T_{pi} - O_{pi})I_{pi},$$

where on any given trial the neural network generates an output pattern designated O_p in response to the input pattern I_p. The difference, or delta (Δ), between the actual output, which initially may be random, and the "desired" output ("correct" inference) is determined by subtracting vector O_p from the target output designated as T_p of a training pattern. The delta rule stipulates that the posttrial weight of a connection (designated w_{ji}) between an input unit (U_i) and an output unit (O_j) is a function of the activation of the input unit (I_{pi}) and the delta ($T_{pi} - O_{pi}$) associated with the output units.

In the rule, the amount of learning is proportional to the *difference* (hence Δ) between the actual activation achieved and the inference activation. Further details are found in Rumelhart and McClelland (1986).

References

Allman, W. F. (1989). *Apprentices of wonder: Inside the neural network revolution*. New York: Bantam.

Anderson, J. R., and Reiser, B. J. (1978). Schema-directed processes in language comprehension. In A. Lesgold, J. Pellegrino, S. Fokkima, and R. Glaser (Eds.), *Cognitive psychology and instruction*. New York: Plenum.

Anderson, R. C., and Pichert, J. W. (1978). Recall of previously unrecallable information following a shift in perspective. *Journal of Verbal Learning and Verbal Behavior, 17,* 1–12.

Arnheim, R. (1974). *Art and visual perception*. Berkeley: University of California Press.

Beck, J. 1966. Effect of orientation and of shape similarity on perceptual grouping. *Perception and Psychophysics 1,* 300–302.

Berlyne, D. E. (1971). *Aesthetics and psychobiology*. New York: Appleton-Century-Crofts.

Bersson, R. (1991) *Worlds of art*. Mountain View, CA: Mayfield.

Biederman, I., Glass, A. L., and Stacy, E. W. (1973). Searching for objects in real world scenes. *Journal of Experimental Psychology, 97,* 22–27.

Bower, G. H., Karlin, M. B., and Dueck, A. (1975). Comprehension and memory for pictures. *Memory and Cognition, 3,* 216–220.

Bransford, J. D., and Johnson, M. K. (1972). Contextual prerequisites for understanding: Some investigations of comprehension and recall. *Journal of Verbal Learning and Verbal Behavior, 11,* 717–726.

Brewer, W. F., and Treyens, J. C. (1981). Role of schemata in memory for places. *Cognitive Psychology, 13,* 193–209.

Chi, M. T. H., Glaser, R., and Farr, M. J. (Eds.). (1988). *The nature of expertise.* Hillsdale, NJ: Erlbaum.

Coren, L. A., Porac, C., and Ward, L. M. (1978). *Sensation and perception.* New York: Academic Press.

Cornsweet, T. M. (1970). *Visual perception.* New York: Academic Press.

De Grandis, L. (1986). *Theory and use of color.* Englewood Cliffs, NJ: Prentice-Hall.

Dowling, J. E., and Boycott, B. B. (1966). Organization of the primate retina: Electron microscopy. *Proceedings of the Royal Society* (London), Series B, *166,* 80–111.

Ferrier, J.-L. (1988). *Art of our century.* New York: Prentice Hall Press.

Fisher, R. (1966). Space-time coordinates of excited and tranquilized states. In I. Jakab (Ed.), *Psychiatry and art. Vol. 1.* Basel: Karger.

Galton, F. (1853). *The narrative of an explorer in tropical Africa.* London: J. Murray.

Gibson, J. J. (1950). *The perception of the visual world.* Boston: Houghton Mifflin.

Gibson, J. J. (1979). *The ecological approach to visual perception.* Boston: Houghton Mifflin.

Gleitman, H. (1981). *Psychology.* New York: W. W. Norton.

Gombrich, E. H. (1963). *Art and illusion.* Princeton, NJ: Princeton University Press.

Gombrich, E. H. (1982). *The image and the eye.* Oxford: Phaidon.

Gregory, R. L. (1978). *Eye and brain: The psychology of seeing.* New York: McGraw-Hill.

Gregory, R. L. (1987). *The Oxford companion to the mind.* Oxford: Oxford University Press.

Gregory, R. L., and Gombrich, E. H. (Eds.). (1973). *Illusion in nature and art.* New York: Charles Scribner's Sons.

Harris, L. J. (1978). Sex differences in spatial ability: Possible environmental, genetic, and neurological factors. In M. Kinsbourne (Ed.), *Asymmetrical functions of the brain*. Cambridge, UK: Cambridge University Press.

Hartline, H. K., Wagner, H. G., and Ratliff, F. (1956). Inhibition in the eye of *Limulus*. *Journal of General Physiology, 39*, 651–673.

Hebb, D. O. (1949). *The organization of behavior*. New York: Wiley.

Hofstadter, A., and Kuhns, R. (1976). *Philosophies of art and beauty*. Chicago: University of Chicago Press.

Holland, D., and Quinn, N. (Eds.). (1987). *Cultural models in language and thought*. New York: Cambridge University Press.

Hubel, D. H. (1963). The visual cortex of the brain. *Scientific American*, Nov., 54–62.

Hubel, D. H., and Wiesel, T. N. (1963). Receptive fields of cells in the striate cortex of very young, visually inexperienced kittens. *Journal of Neurophysiology, 26*, 994–1002.

Hubel, D. H., and Wiesel, T. N. (1965). Receptive fields of single neurons in two nonstriated visual areas (18 and 19) of the cat. *Journal of Neurophysiology, 28*, 229–289.

Hubel, D. H., and Wiesel, T. N. (1979). Brain mechanisms and vision. *Scientific American, 242*, 150–162.

Hughes, R. (1980). *The shock of the new*. New York: Knopf.

James, T. G. H. (1985). *Egyptian painting*. London: British Museum Publications.

James, W. (1890). *The principles of psychology*. New York: Holt.

Kandinsky, W. (1969). *Du spirituel dans l'art et dans la peinture en particulier*. Paris: Denoel-Gonthier.

Kaufman, L., and Richards, W. (1969). Spontaneous fixation tendencies for visual forms. *Perception and Psychophysics, 5*, 85–88.

Kinston, J. (1989). *Arts and artist*. London: Bloomsbury Books.

Koestler, A. (1983). The act of creation. Quoted in K. Hanks and J. Parry, *Wake up your creative genius*. Los Altos, CA: William Koffmann.

Kubovy, M. (1986). *The psychology of perspective and Renaissance art.* Cambridge, UK: Cambridge University Press.

Kuffler, S. W., and Nicholls, J. G. (1976). *From neuron to brain.* Sunderland, MA: Sinauer Associates.

Kundel, H. L., Nodine, C. F., Thickman, D. I., Carmody, D., and Toto, L. (1985). Nodule detection with and without a chest image. *Investigative Radiology, 20,* 94–99.

Lassen, N. A., Ingvar, D. H., and Skinhøj, E. (1978). Brain function and blood flow. *Scientific American, 239,* 62–71.

Levy, J., Trevarthen, C., and Sperry, R. W. (1972). Perception of bilateral chimeric figures following hemispheric deconnexion. *Brain, 95,* 61–78.

Lewis, H. P. (1966). *Child art: The beginnings of self-affirmation.* Emoryville, CA: Diablo Press.

Locher, P. J., and Nodine, C. F. (1987). Symmetry catches the eye. In J. K. O'Regan and A. Levy-Schoen (Eds.), *Eye Movements: From Physiology to Cognition.* North-Holland: Elsevier Science Publishers.

Loran, E. (1943). *Cézanne's composition.* Berkeley: University of California Press.

McClelland, J. L., and Rumelhart, D. E. (1988). *Explorations in parallel distributed processing.* Cambridge, MA: Bradford.

Mach, E. (1984). *Contributions to the analysis of sensations.* Trans. C. M. Williams. Chicago: Open Court.

Malins, F. (1980). *Understanding paintings: Elements of composition.* Englewood Cliffs, NJ: Prentice-Hall.

Marr, D. (1982). *Vision.* San Francisco: Freeman.

Matlin, M. W. (1988). *Sensation and perception.* Needham Heights, MA: Allyn and Bacon.

Molnar, F. (1974). *Perception visuelle de l'unité.* Thesis, University of Nanterre.

Molnar, F. (1981). About the role of visual exploration in aesthetics. In H. Day (Ed.), *Advances in intrinsic motivation and aesthetics.* New York: Plenum Press.

Mondrian, P. (1957). Quoted in M. Seuphor, *Piet Mondrian: Life and work*. New York: Abrams.

Nodine, C. F., Carmody, D. P., and Kundel, H. L. (1978). Searching for NINA. In J. W. Senders, D. F. Fisher, and R. A. Monty (Eds.), *Eye movements and the higher psychological functions*. Hillsdale, NJ: Erlbaum.

Nodine, C. F., and Kundel, H. L. (1987). Perception and display in diagnostic imaging. *RadioGraphs, 7*, 1241–1250.

Nodine, C. F., Locher, P. J., and Krupinski, E. A. (1993). The role of formal art training on perception and aesthetic judgement of art compositions. *Leonardo, 26*, 219–227.

Norton, D., and Stark, L. (1971). Eye movements and visual perception. *Scientific American, 224*, 34–43.

Palmer, S. E. (1975). The effects of contextual scenes on the identification of objects. *Memory & Cognition, 3*, 519–526.

Palmer, S. E., Rosch, E., and Chase, P. (1981). Canonical perspective and the perception of objects. In J. Long and A. Baddeley (Eds.), *Attention and performance IX*. Hillsdale, NJ: Erlbaum.

Pedretti, C. (1973). *Leonardo*. London: Thames & Hudson.

Piper, D. (1991) *The illustrated history of art*. New York: Crescent Books.

Plato (1941). *The Republic*. Trans. F. M. Cornford. Oxford: Oxford.

Porter, T., and Goodman, S. (1988). *Designer primer*. New York: Charles Scribner's Sons.

Ramachandran, V. S. (1988). Perceiving shape from shading. *Scientific American, 259*, 76–83.

Rumelhart, D. E., Hinton, G. E., and Williams, R. J. (1986). Learning internal representations by error propagation. In D. E. Rumelhart, J. L. McClelland, and the PDP research groups (Eds.), *Parallel distributed processing: Explorations in the microstructure of cognition. Vol. 1*. Cambridge, MA: Bradford.

Rumelhart, D. E., McClelland, J. L., and the PDP research group (Eds.). (1986). *Parallel distributed processing: Explorations in the microstructure of cognition. Vol. 1*. Cambridge, MA: Bradford.

Salapatek, P. (1975). Pattern perception in early infancy. In L. B. Cohen and P. Salapatek (Eds.), *Infant perception: From sensation to cognition. Vol. 1.* New York: Academic Press.

Shepard, R. N. (1987). Evolution of a mesh between principles of the mind and regularities of the world. In John Dupré (Ed.), *The latest on the best: Essays on evolution and optimality.* Cambridge, MA: Bradford.

Shepard, R. N. (1990). *Mind sights.* San Francisco: Freeman.

Sinclair, S. (1985). *How animals see.* London: Croom Helm.

Solso, R. L. (1991). *Cognitive psychology.* Needham Heights, MA: Allyn and Bacon.

Solso, R. L., and McCarthy, J. (1981). Prototype formation for faces: A case of pseudomemory. *British Journal of Psychology, 72,* 499–503.

Sporre, D. (1989). *A history of the arts.* London: Bloomsbury Books.

Stark, L., and Ellis, S. R. (1981). Scanpaths revisited: Cognitive models direct active looking. In D. F. Fisher, R. A. Monty, and J. Senders (Eds.), *Eye movements: Cognition and visual perception.* Hillsdale, NJ: Lawrence Erlbaum Associates.

Tulving, E. (1989a). Remembering and knowing the past. *American Scientist, 77,* 361–367.

Tulving, E. (1989b). Memory: Performance, knowledge, and experience. *European Journal of Cognitive Psychology, 1,* 3–36.

Vitz, P. C., and Glimcher, A. B. (1984). *Modern art and modern science.* New York: Praeger.

Werblin, F. W., and Dowling, J. E. (1969). Organization of the retina of the mudpuppy, *Necturus maculosus.* II: Intracellular recording. *Journal of Neurophysiology, 32,* 339–355.

Whitford, F. (1987). *Understanding abstract art.* New York: E. P. Dutton.

Wood, M., Cole, B., and Gealt, A. (1989). *Art and the western world.* New York: Simon and Schuster.

Wright, L. (1983). *Perspective in perspective.* London: Routledge & Kegan Paul.

Yarbus, A. L. (1967). *Eye movements and vision.* Trans. L. A. Riggs. New York: Plenum Press.

Illustration Credits

Figure 1.1: The Art Institute of Chicago. Robert A. Waller Fund, 1910.2. Photograph © 1993 The Art Institute of Chicago. All rights reserved.

Figure 1.2: The Museum of Modern Art, New York. Acquired through the Lillie P. Bliss Collection.

Figure 1.3: The Art Institute of Chicago. Friends of American Art Collection, 1942.51. Photograph © 1993 The Art Institute of Chicago. All rights reserved.

Figure 1.10: Reproduced by permission of Weidenfeld and Nicolson Ltd.

Figure 1.11: Reproduced by permission of Cambridge University Press.

Figure 1.13: Reproduced by permission of the Royal Society, London, and B. B. Boycott.

Figure 2.1: Clark Nelson/Parke-Bernet, 1965.

Figure 2.2 (painting): Reproduced by permission of the Tate Gallery, London.

Figure 2.6: Reproduced by permission of The American Physiological Society.

Figure 2.7: Reproduced by permission of Niels A. Lassen.

Figure 2.9 top: Tate Gallery, London/Art Resource, New York. Reproduced courtesy Roy Lichtenstein. © Roy Lichtenstein.

Figure 2.9 bottom: Österreichische Galerie, Vienna; reproduced by permission of Erich Lessing/Art Resource, New York.

Figure 2.10 (painting): The Art Institute of Chicago.

Figure 5.2: © 1989 Computer Creations Corporation. All rights reserved. This image may not be further reproduced without express written authorization.

Figure 5.4: Giraudon/Art Resource, New York.

Figure 5.5: Städelsches Kunstinstitut, Frankfurt am Main. Photograph by Ursula Edelmann.

Figure 5.6: Statens Konstmuseer, Stockholm.

Figure 5.9: Reproduced by permission of Psychonomic Society, Inc., and Stephen E. Palmer.

Figure 5.10: Reproduced by permission of Irv Biederman.

Figure 5.11: By permission of the Kröller-Müller Stichting, Otterlo, Netherlands.

Figure 5.12: Reproduced by permission of Academic Press.

Figure 5.13, part 1: Werner Forman/Art Resource, New York.

Figure 5.13, part 2: Antwerp Cathedral.

Figure 5.13, part 3: Musée d'Orsay, Paris.

Figure 5.13, part 4: Art Resource, New York.

Figure 5.14: © 1994 C. Herscovici/ARS, New York.

Figure 5.15: © 1994 ARS, New York/ADAGP, Paris.

Unnumbered figure on page 129: Reproduced by permission of Lawrence Stark.

Figure 6.1: The Museum of Modern Art, New York.

Figure 6.3: Reproduced by permission of Academic Press.

Figure 6.4: Reproduced by permission of Plenum Publishing Corporation.

Figure 6.5: Reproduced by permission of Plenum Publishing Corporation.

Figure 6.6: The Art Institute of Chicago. Gift of Georgia O'Keeffe, 1947.712 © 1994 The Georgia O'Keeffe Foundation/ARS, New York. Photograph © 1993 The Art Institute of Chicago. All rights reserved.

Figure 6.7: Reproduced by permission of Lawrence Stark.

Figure 6.8: Reproduced by permission of Calvin F. Nodine and the Radiological Society of North America. Cartoon reproduced from *The World of Hirschfeld* (New York: H. N. Abrams, Inc., 1970), p. 104, by permission of Albert Hirschfeld.

Figure 6.9: Reproduced by permission of Calvin F. Nodine and the MIT Press.

Figure 6.10: Reproduced by permission of Calvin F. Nodine and the MIT Press.

Figure 6.11: Reproduced by permission of Plenum Publishing Corporation.

Figure 6.12: Reproduced by permission of Plenum Publishing Corporation.

Figure 6.13: Reproduced by permission of Plenum Publishing Corporation.

Figure 6.14: Reproduced by permission of Plenum Publishing Corporation.

Figure 7.1: Foto Marburg/Art Resource, New York.

Figure 7.9: Reproduced by permission of George V. Kelvin Science Graphics.

Figure 7.11: Reproduced by permission of the U.S. Department of Energy.

Figure 7.20: Reproduced by permission of Roger N. Shepard.

Figure 7.21: Reproduced by permission of Roger N. Shepard.

Figure 7.22: Reproduced from Malins, *Understanding Paintings,* by permission of Phaidon Press Limited.

Figure 7.23: Reproduced from Malins, *Understanding Paintings,* by permission of Phaidon Press Limited.

Figure 7.27: Pinacoteca di Brera, Milan; by permission of the Soprintendenza per i Beni Artistici e Storici. (Reproduced from Malins, *Understanding Paintings,* by permission of Phaidon Press Limited.)

Figure 8.4: Art Resource, New York.

Figure 8.5: British Museum, London.

Figure 8.8: Reproduced by permission of Princeton University Press.

Figure 8.9: Reproduced from G. M. A. Richter, *Perspective in Greek and Roman Art,* by permission of Phaidon Press.

Figure 8.10: Reproduced by permission of Princeton University Press.

Figure 8.11: Reproduced by permission of Princeton University Press.

Figure 8.12: Tokyo National Museum.

Figure 8.13: Reproduced from Malins, *Understanding Paintings,* by permission of Phaidon Press Limited.

Figure 8.14: Reproduced by courtesy of the Trustees, The National Gallery, London.

Figure 8.18: Foto Marburg/Art Resource, New York.

Figure 8.20: Alinari/Art Resource, New York.

Figure 8.22: Reproduced by permission of the University of Michigan, University Library.

Figure 8.23 (painting): Giraudon/Art Resource, New York.

Figure 8.24 (diagram): Reproduced by permission of the University of California Press. © 1943, 1971 Erle Loran.

Figure 8.25 (painting): Giraudon/Art Resource, New York.

Figure 8.26: Tate Gallery, London/Art Resource, New York. © 1994 ARS, New York/SPADEM, Paris.

Figure 8.27: © 1960 M. C. Escher Foundation, Baarn, Holland. All rights reserved.

Figure 8.28: Courtesy Roy Lichtenstein. © Roy Lichtenstein.

Figure 8.29: Collection of Robert L. Solso.

Figure 9.1: Reproduced by permission of the Norman Rockwell Family Trust. © 1945, 1961 the Norman Rockwell Family Trust.

Figure 9.2: Giraudon/Art Resource, New York. © 1994 C. Herscovici/ARS, New York.

Figure 9.3 top: © 1994 ARS, New York/SPADEM, Paris.

Figure 9.3 bottom: Tate Gallery, London/Art Resource, New York. © 1994 ARS, New York/ADAGP, Paris.

Figure 9.8: Reproduced by permission of Diablo Press.

Figure 9.9: Reproduced by permission of the International Association for the Study of Attention and Performance and Stephen E. Palmer.

Figure 9.10: The Museum of Modern Art, New York. Purchase.

Figure 9.11: The Museum of Modern Art, New York. Acquired through the Lillie P. Bliss Bequest. © 1994 ARS, New York/SPADEM, Paris.

Figure 9.15: Reproduced by permission of Academic Press.

Figure 9.16: Reproduced by permission of Psychonomic Society, Inc., and Gordon H. Bower.

Figure 9.22 (all three paintings): Haags Gemeentemuseum, The Hague.

Figure 9.23: Giraudon/Art Resource, New York.

Index

Page numbers in italics indicate illustrations.